LOVE, PEACE, and SOUL

Behind the Scenes of America's Favorite Dance Show
Soul Train: Classic Moments

ERICKA BLOUNT DANOIS

Backbeat
Books

An Imprint of Hal Leonard Corporation

Published in 2013 by Backbeat Books
An Imprint of Hal Leonard Corporation
7777 West Bluemound Road
Milwaukee, WI 53213

Trade Book Division Editorial Offices
33 Plymouth St., Montclair, NJ 07042

Book design by UB Communications

Printed in the United States of America

Library of Congress Cataloging-in-Publication Data is available upon request.

ISBN 978-1-4803-4101-2

www.backbeatbooks.com

LOVE,
PEACE,
and SOUL

CONTENTS

Contents

FOREWORD

ove! Peace! and *soooooouuuuuul!*" I loved to hear him say that. You could feel it.

With *Soul Train* we saw ourselves looking good and feeling good. And what enhanced it so much was its creator. Don Cornelius was a class act. He dressed classy. He was articulate. As African Americans we saw a strong black man with dignity and character and integrity. From a cultural standpoint, it's impossible to measure the show's impact and influence. It affected us. We could express ourselves freely. It made us feel proud about ourselves.

Like Don, I got my start in radio. I'd start off my radio show, "This is your six foot four bundle of joy, 212 pounds of Mrs. Bell's baby boy, soft as medicated cotton, rich as double X cream, tender as a mother's love, the women's pet, the men's threat, and the playboy's pride and joy, the baby boy! Al Bell!" Don put the rhyming style of black radio deejays on television.

As a kid I worked for a white gentleman. He raised pedigreed bulldogs and I'd have to clean up after them. He may have paid me ten cents a week. He would walk around and say: "Niggers can't do nothing but sing and dance." But I saw Don Cornelius take that and let us see it as an art form. To sit and watch and see those young people come and create—it was so artistic. I can't dance, I can't do the two-step—but he made me feel like I could dance!

He provided the entertainment, but he also doled out information, education, and history weekly. He informed us about historical figures. The cultural impact of the show was profound, revolutionary, and evolutionary at the same time. It was one of the few times that we had the opportunity to see ourselves on television in a manner where it lifted our pride and increased our self-esteem.

Economically, it provided for us at the record labels and gave us a platform that allowed us to expose our music to a larger segment of our population and increase the impact of our music. You probably had more white Americans viewing *Soul Train* than black. For the record labels, it put us in the position where we could get exposure. We didn't have any more than sixty or seventy black radio stations across America. We were limited and hadn't completely come out of the race music era. Chain stores like Woolworth's wouldn't carry our music, or it would be in the back room somewhere. Don exposing the music started increasing the demand. It didn't break down the wall, but it started putting a little crack in it.

It provided the ability for you to see our great artists on television. Before that, exposure was on the small-club circuits. *Soul Train* allowed us to do in one hour what it would take us to do in six months of touring. It increased our sales. It began to influence the pop stations over time to play black music. It made the major labels pay attention and see that soul music had great economic potential. The prevailing opinion then was, "You can't sell black records." Or our songs would get covered by a white artist after getting popular on the black stations. On the local Chicago show, we put on Johnnie Taylor, the Bar-Kays, Carla and Rufus Thomas—all of our artists. I couldn't get support in Memphis, so I used Chicago as my backyard. Chicago was like a suburban Mississippi.

When we signed Richard Pryor to Stax, he recorded four or five different shows, some at the Soul Train Club in San Francisco, and I edited it down to one album. I told him, "I want you to come by and see what I've done. He came in and sat in the studio, and I played it through. We listened. I asked, "What do you think?"

He laughed and said, "They gonna say, 'That nigger's crazy!!'"

When it came time to title the album, several weeks later, it came to me, we are gonna title it "That Nigger's Crazy." Richard performed part of the album when he hosted an episode of *Soul Train*.

The first time that Prince was on *Soul Train* was for the song I marketed called "The Most Beautiful Girl in the World." He had just changed his name to the symbol. Warner Brothers told him that the record was dated and they didn't want to release it. He asked me if I could market it and sent it to me overnight. You heard pure African American Prince. It was a masterpiece.

We went to "I Ain't Never Heard of It" Mississippi, "Does It Exist?" Alabama, and "It Doesn't Have a Name" Louisiana—all of the tertiary markets—and treated them like they were WBLS in New York. Soon the large markets were calling us. The song was a worldwide hit.

We were doing what we were doing out of necessity—we owned black insurance companies, black banks. It was really the equal rights era, not the civil rights era, because we were in pursuit of equal rights. We had realized what we could achieve from a business standpoint and we were supportive of each other.

I was the first black speaker at the NARM convention (National Association of Record Merchandisers). A man named George O'Hare, a merchandise manager at Sears, had let me put my entire Stax catalog in his Sears stores. The subject of my address was "Black Is Beautiful . . . Business." Soon after that, the Harvard Report came out. Black music division infrastructure at the major labels replicated the marketing division at Stax. Things started falling apart. Big business copies, acquires, or destroys.

Through everything, *Soul Train* kept letting us see us as us, and be us as us, and be proud of it. It was a part of our lives. It represented uncompromised authenticity. When you saw us on *Soul Train*, we weren't trying to be anything other than us. When you went to any of the other shows, you were in somebody else's house; when you went to *Soul Train* you went home.

At *Soul Train*, everything is everything. Everything is all right.

—Al Bell, former chairman and owner of Stax Records

PREFACE

When I began to think about writing about *Soul Train*, it was a result of a culmination of many things—a reverence for a childhood spent sitting on my deejay father's lap listening to his hefty record collection with earphones that I had to hold to keep on my tiny ears. It was the first visceral reaction I had to music, crying at the gorgeous sounds of Minnie Riperton's five-octave vocal range. It was spending Sundays mimicking my mother's dance moves as she cleaned the house to the lyrics of Chaka Khan and later the 12-inch club hits she and my father bought from their nights spent at Larry Levan's Garage nightclub in New York. It was spending countless Saturday afternoons in front of our broken-down black-and-white television set (with the hanger in place of an antenna and a pair of pliers used to turn the knob) watching *Soul Train* with my sister. In the '70s, *Soul Train* was "appointment television"—a cultural bonding necessity.

While watching some of the television shows my daughters watch, I wanted to write about the lack of cultural programming on television today. I wrote a tongue-in-cheek "Where are they now?" piece—searching and finding *Soul Train* dancer Cheryl Song (the "long-haired Asian chic," to most fans). But the book took root over a battle about my *Best of Soul Train* DVDs. My colleague, Dr. Todd Steven Burroughs, was salivating at the chance to take them home and watch them uninterrupted over our Thanksgiving break in 2009. My family was expecting me to bring them to our annual get-together. Todd and I compromised by splitting them up. But the tension this created served to turn on the proverbial lightbulb. We couldn't be the only two families desperate for the nostalgia of live performance, eclectic fashion, feverish dancing, and a superbly cool host spanning three decades of the best in music.

We watched *Soul Train* through the '70s, where regional dances and the golden years of soul, disco, and funk music were given a national platform. We watched as the alternately sexualized and conservative culture of the '80s brought back boy bands, New Jack Swing, and a new culture dubbed hip-hop. And through the '90s and the 2000's, when the show struggled to maintain an identity while it mixed all of these genres together, resulting in a sometimes disjointed but still entertaining product.

From my perch in front of the television set, I couldn't see the struggles behind the scenes or that the iconic Soul Train Scramble Board was fixed was something that was born out of necessity. Cornelius told journalist Steven Ivory: "One time when the dancers couldn't figure out the mystery name on the [Soul Train] Board, white viewers all across the country called into TV stations, saying things like, 'See, these dumb monkeys can't even spell. Take this shit off the air!'"

Not long after I got a publishing contract, Don Cornelius committed suicide. There couldn't be a more macabre ending to a life filled with bringing enjoyment to the masses on his Saturday show along with the various award shows. Notoriously private, many of his secrets died along with him. In writing the book, I was forced to interview around him—those people who were close to him, people who worked on the show, the artists, the dancers, the people who could re-create the scenes that my daughters will never get to experience first-hand. For them, they will never bang the side of the television set to make the picture clear or wait up until two in the morning for a showing on WNEW-TV New York, when in the early '80s the show—without warning—was suddenly switched from the noon showing to a two in the morning time slot. But they could experience it from the eyes of those people who were there.

There were many people who helped and were as devoted to this project as I was. I want to thank author, lawyer, and filmmaker Jam Donaldson for getting me started and introducing me to the right people—our love for books as children provided the foundation. Thanks to my mother, Linda Blount Berry, my father, Walter

Blount, and my sister, Elissa Blount Moorhead, for providing the home where reading, music, television, and culture were a priority. Thank you to my agents, John Rudolph, Jane Dystel, and Miriam Goderich of Dystel and Goderich Agency for believing in me and hanging in there on our sometimes bumpy rides. Thank you to my editors Mike Edison and Bernadette Malavarca and publisher John Cerullo. Thanks to my research assistant and a brilliant writer and friend, Kirsten West Savali. And my transcriber Stephen Gilberg—you're much stronger than I am; transcribing is my own personal hell. Thanks to Tim Sampson for always being there in a pinch, and for our countless hours dissecting *Mad Men*. Thanks to Todd Steven Burroughs for reading all of my early drafts and persevering along the *Soul Train* ride from the beginning and all the bumps along the way. Thanks to Jonathan Martin and Llewellyn Berry for taking a first read at the unedited manuscript and giving their uncensored opinion. Thank you to Laurence Panton, who made sure I did not succumb to my procrastinating ways. And thanks to my manager, Enrico Mowatt, for his innovative ideas, good meals, and many of my Chicago introductions. Thanks to Ali Danois, April Silver, Drake Holiday, and Daphne Dufresne for their relentless efforts for getting my Kickstarter underway when I needed to do last-minute interviews in Los Angeles. Thank you to all of my Kickstarter donors and to Pierre Bennu for his wonderful videography.

Thank you to Bowlegged Lou and Michael Gonzales for giving me contacts in the music industry to interview. Same for Jay King, Rebecca Proudfoot, Derrick Mays, Perry Jones, Gary Harris, Howard Hewett, Zoro, Liane Mori, my second mother, Phyllis Kelly of Larrymore Kelly & Associates, Theresa Moore at T-Time Productions, Lathan Hodge, Jolyn Matsumuro, Karen E. Lee, Monica Alexander, Beth Yenni-Soloway, Beverly Paige, Bill Adler, Dan Charnas, Russell Simmons, Adair Curtis, Derek Fleming, Stephanie Grimes-Washington, Keith Washington, and Kangol from UTFO. Thanks to Nick Puzo of Soultrainfans.com and Questlove for their obsessive commitment to the details of the show and letting me in on a massive collection of episodes. Thank you to my L.A. friends for housing me, getting me contacts and everything

I needed—Melissa Haizlip, J. Kevin Swain, Scot Brown, Chuck Johnson, Marcus Guillory, Virgil Roberts, Dr. Todd Boyd, Derek Fleming, Liane Mori, P. Frank Williams, Alex Tucker, Dr. Darnell Hunt at UCLA, Louie Ski Carr, Cheryl Song, Deniese Payne, Sheila Marmon, Peter and Milton Allen, Kevin John Goff, Shabba Doo, Larry Dunn, David Lombard, and O'Bryan Burnette II.

Thanks to Dyana R. Williams for everything, always. Thanks to Christopher P. Lehman in helping me with research. Thanks for Aida Chapman-Ayala for being so patient with my incessant questioning and for all of your help with research and our wonderful conversations. Thanks to my Chicago friends: Jake Austen, Breahon Jones, Jiba Anderson, Marshall Thompson, Bobby Hutton, Clint Ghent, George O'Hare, Vickie Wilson and Terry Glover at *Ebony* magazine, Jamilah Lemieux and Kierna Mayo at Ebony.com, Ivy Jackson, and Don Jackson. Thanks to my *Soul Train* folks: Michelle Tennant-Timmons, Tony Cornelius, Kim Porter Fluellen, Kenard Gibbs, and Stephen McMillian and Joe Walker from Soultrain.com. Thanks to the investigators: Jon Leiberman and Detective Dan Myers. Thanks to my Columbia colleagues: Sam Freedman, Lisa Spinelli, Wayne Dawkins, and Dan Charnas and mentors like Bob Kaiser, Kristin Hunter-Lattany, Donald Bogle, and Herman Beavers. Thanks to Rachel Noerdlinger for helping with a great interview with Al Sharpton. Thanks to Kemba Dunham for getting it started by helping me find Cheryl Song.

Thank you to my daughters, Maia Danois, who helped me navigate technology—editing on a PDF—and Laila Danois, who helped me organize my interview tapes and the episode listings. And thanks to both of them for watching countless hours of *Soul Train* episodes and for tolerating my dancing.

For those that remember putting pennies on the record player needle, recording songs off the radio, record stores, shag carpet, drive-ins, and busy signals, I hope you can wax nostalgic. Music always transports you back to the moments, the memories.

These are the *Soul Train* memories, for those who couldn't be there.

INTRODUCTION

It was early morning on February 1, 2012, an average, 60-degree day in Los Angeles. Detective Dan Myers's phone rang by his bedside. He was already awake. He looked over at the clock. It was five in the morning. This was the time he normally arose to get prepared to go into the office. On the other end of the line his lieutenant, Mark Tappan, told him to report to 12685 Mulholland Drive. "Donald Cornelius is dead from an apparent suicide."

Myers couldn't place the name right away, though he knew it was a famous one. When Myers walked into Cornelius's house, he walked past an original painting of Michael Jackson in the hallway leading to the bedroom and it dawned on him—"Don Cornelius. He's Mr. *Soul Train*."

Labor Day, September 5, 2011, was the first and last time I ever saw Don Cornelius in person. Raised in the Bronzeville neighborhood on the South Side of Chicago, he had come home to be honored for *Soul Train*'s fortieth anniversary. He was welcomed at the Expo 72 Gallery on E. Randolph Street, which featured an exhibition of rare photos and vintage footage of his show. And to top it off, the Windy City was honoring him with a street sign emblazoned with his name and the *Soul Train* logo. "This is the biggest thing that ever happened to me," he gushed.

The day before Labor Day, the steely, still-smooth "train" operator was impeccably turned out in all black leather jacket and pants and alligator shoes, serving as a panelist at a screening of the VH1 documentary, *The Hippest Trip in America*. He was in rare form—sometimes he was so blunt that audience members would visibly squirm. Sometimes the whole room would fall silent, unnerved by his inappropriate honesty. "You used to be thinner!" he interrupted his childhood friend, panel moderator WBEZ's Richard Steele, as he spoke to the audience. "You're still smooth, though—just smooth and *round*." Sometimes he was blunt and funny. When Steele goaded him about losing a game of basketball to Marvin Gaye on an episode of *Soul Train*, he retorted from the panel: "It was a lot of trick camera work... nigga!" When it came time for the question and answer session and someone from the audience provided more statement than question, he quipped with, "Brother, you got a teleprompter back here? That was the longest fucking question I ever heard!" And when a docent talked about her travel tours and queried him about some of his former addresses in Chicago in hopes of showing tourists his old residences, he looked at his ex-wife and mother of his children, Delores, who sat in the audience, and asked her, "Delores, is that somebody we owe some money to?" The crowd laughed. Some people looked uncomfortable. Straight answers weren't part of his personality. I was immediately impressed.

The Don Cornelius I had grown up watching was laid-back, the latest slang bobbing in the waves of his profoundly bass announcer's voice, always showing respect to the artists who appeared on *Soul Train*, asking thoughtful questions, giving a conversational, in-your-living-room style to his interviews. This Cornelius was irreverent. He was someone who acted like he didn't need to impress anyone—like he had nothing left to lose.

One of his first homes, purchased in 1972 as *Soul Train* started to reach its stride, rested high on the cliffs in Sherman Oaks, California, on the scary, winding, slivers of the single-lane streets of Mulholland Drive. It was a trek to get to, pocketed in exclusiveness and isolation, tucked behind a long driveway leading to the front door.

By the time of his death, he had come full circle, returning to this house after a bitter divorce and a settlement that granted his ex-wife, Viktoria Chapman-Cornelius, a million dollar home and $10,000 per month in spousal support, and support for his adopted daughter (college tuition). Bathed in a masculine 1970's avocado green, the bachelor pad looked untouched for the last forty years, a veritable time capsule. The bathroom's green bidet and spa, with matching green "C" monogrammed hand towels and curtains, gold trimmings, and a big button telephone beside the bidet, told the tale of a once-upon-a-time luxurious living. Green carpeting, black leather-backed chairs, and rows of suits hung in cleaner's bags invoked images of cool-posed pimps holding court. The Lucite grand piano where his artist, R&B crooner O'Bryan, composed "Lady, I Love You" (when Cornelius tried a stint at artist management) was still elegant, sitting alone by the glass entrance to the backyard overlooking the neglected swimming pool.

There was little evidence of *Soul Train* memorabilia inside the house. Just a box prepared to ship with episodes on DVD, a plaque from the National Academy of Recording Arts and Sciences—a National Trustees Award for the creation of the longest-running first-run nationally syndicated program—and two Rolls Royce convertibles in the garage, with ST1 and ST2 (for "Soul Train 1" and "Soul Train 2") engraved on the license plates. There were pictures in frames of his granddaughter, Christina Cornelius, as a baby, now tall and thin with model looks. She enjoyed his playful nature, his corny jokes.

On the night table by his bed, an iPhone was charging next to bottles of antiseizure medicine along with medicine for bladder control and Avodart for his prostate. He had never fully recovered from a congenital malformation in the blood vessels of his brain—and a brain aneurysm he had fifteen years ago.

In 1983, Cornelius had life-threatening surgery that lasted twenty-one hours. He didn't want anyone to see him after the surgery—his hair was cut, he was weak and immobile. They stopped production of the show from January 1, 1983, until April 30, but six months after the surgery he insisted on returning to work.

Music videos and music-oriented programming on cable stations like MTV and BET had given rise to new, unexpected competition. Television budgets were tightening and sponsors were drying up. Cornelius's son, Anthony, and other executives suggested they make some cuts. Don's reply: "Stop right there. Do you know how many people we employ? How many livelihoods we affect? We're gonna do it one way or another." And the train kept rolling.

—

Don Cornelius had made a way out of no-way in the television industry. Like Oprah and Tyler Perry would do after him, he opted for syndication when major networks weren't interested. He paved the way for BET's Bob Johnson to purchase his own network by understanding that black people would tune in to see their images on television, and wound up creating a multi-billion-dollar empire. *Soul Train*, born from the template of black radio, the language and entrepreneurial spirit of black deejays who brokered time and courted sponsors, paved the way for Radio One's, and later TV One's, Cathy Hughes. It opened the doors for anyone who sought to own anything in the wide, unwieldy, and unwelcoming canvas of the media world. At the time there were no outlets of its kind that presented black music as a whole. Where Flip Wilson opened the door with his variety show *The Flip Wilson Show*, Cornelius kicked the door down. And then he bought the door.

His success set the stage for dance shows like *So You Think You Can Dance* and variety shows like the Wayans's *In Living Color*. Cornelius created a show that made formerly no-name artists go Platinum. It gave a young activist named Jesse Jackson a spotlight when he gave a weekly update on the progress of Operation Breadbasket on the Chicago show. It provided a place to host beauty pageants with Hal Jackson's Talented Teens and award scholarships to students. It was one of the first unapologetically black shows—behind the camera and in front of it.

LOVE,
PEACE,
and SOUL

1

FAKE IT TILL YOU MAKE IT

We'll be on the moon with the few who'll last, when we leave
the earth with a big, bad blast!
                                        —radio disc jockey Jocko Henderson

On the South Side of Chicago, amidst the empty buildings on the black side of town in an area nicknamed "The Valley," Donald Cortez Cornelius's mind was always turning. After he returned home from Korea in 1956, where he'd served in the Air Force as an aviator crash crewman, he'd been restless and often frustrated with the string of dead-end jobs he'd been forced to take on to make money for his young family. He had married his high school sweetheart, a fair-skinned beauty, Delores Harrison, and they had two sons soon after—Anthony in 1958 and Raymond in 1959.

Always a sharp dresser, Cornelius wore suits daily in high school, often tailor-made with money saved from his part-time job at the post office—$75 Brooks Brothers three-button roll suits with Florsheim wingtips on his feet and Fedora hats hanging on his head. A talented artist, he studied cartooning at DuSable High School, a school that had turned out the best and the brightest in the black music world, including Nat King Cole, Dinah Washington, and saxophonists Clifford Jordan and Gene Ammons.

Cornelius didn't have money for college, so for over ten years, he'd sold tires, used cars, and insurance. He'd even driven cabs. But in his heart, he longed to be part of the music scene.

As a kid, Cornelius had been a mainstay on the basement party circuit. "Blue light" basement parties or "quarter parties" (made infamous by the raucous party in the 1975 cult classic movie *Cooley High*) were distant Northern cousins of the juke joint culture of the South and children of the "rent parties" that began in the 1920s. Teenagers would hang out on the weekends in the basement of someone's house—usually one of the girls— and play 45 rpm records and dance. A girl in Cornelius's neighborhood, June Young, who lived on St. Lawrence Avenue, would host quarter parties every Friday and Saturday night.

These "quarter parties" (where teenagers were charged a quarter for admission) or "waistline parties" (where female partygoers were charged according to their waist size) were working-class black America's answer to sock hops. They were the premier weekend hangout spots in every inner-city to show off the latest fashions and dances and to mingle with the opposite sex, especially for teens not yet old enough to hit the nightclub circuit. The kids came dressed to sweat. The slow songs required the two-step, and if you were lucky—grinding. The lights were off or a blue light set the mood. Parents stayed out of the way, but usually were within earshot upstairs.

High school dances were popular, happened every other week, started at seven-thirty in the evening and ended at eleven, and cost fifty cents to get in. When the high school clubs ended, fraternity houses like the Sigma House or the Tuskegee Club on Fiftieth and South Parkway would have parties that lasted until one in the morning and didn't require identification for teens.

When Cornelius got older he could be seen in Chicago nightclubs doing dances like the Monkey, the Shimmy, the Strut, the Madison, and the Grind. Sometimes the kids would show off their moves in what they called a "soul train" line, where two parallel lines of dancers would form and a couple or a single dancer would parade down through the middle, showing off steps they had practiced in front of their mirrors before the party. It wasn't just fun and games—kids could earn enough money winning dance contests at local clubs like Perv's House to pay their rent for the month.

But those days were long in the past for Cornelius. By 1966, he had joined the Chicago Police Department and taken a job as a beat cop.

One day he made a traffic stop and gave the driver the routine spiel, ordering him to hand over his license and registration. The offender turned out to be Roy Wood, who was the news director of WVON. As Wood listened, he was taken by Cornelius's deep, rumbling, seductive baritone. While he lamented getting a ticket, Wood couldn't help but ask Cornelius, "Have you ever thought about getting into radio?"

On the spot, Wood invited Cornelius to come to WVON to discuss a possible job situation. The station was owned by the Chess brothers, Leonard and Phil, who owned Chess Records on 2120 South Michigan Avenue. The record label was home to the best blues and soul artists in the nation, and artists like Etta James, Muddy Waters, the Dells, Chuck Berry, Bo Diddley, Howlin' Wolf, and Fontella Bass helped to put the label on the map. The Chess brothers bought the radio station for $1 million in 1962 so that WVON could get its records first, fresh from the pressing plants. Within a year they grossed three times that amount in sales.

At the time, WVON was considered the capital of black radio in the nation and was the hottest station in Chicago, with its twenty-four-hour black-oriented programming and well-known personalities like Herb Kent, "The Cool Gent," who played classic 1950s R&B and soul records from seven thirty in the evening to eleven on his "dusty oldies" show. He endeared himself to the community with his ultracool talking and rhyming style.

Other popular deejays were Pervis Spann, "The Blues Man," who played blues starting at midnight and hung up on male callers because "Why would I be up late at night talking to men when a soft, sexy voice was more appealing?"; "Your Boy" Sid McCoy, whose deep and resonant voice created opportunities for him outside of radio later on as an actor on *Mod Squad*, *Sanford and Son*, *Room 222*, and *The Cosby Show*; and Bill Crain, "The Butterball," who introduced Motown records to Chicago and had his signature line, "Never be rude to a young dude."

3

Berry Gordy gave WVON records before any other station in the country. Tom Joyner, better known as the Fly Jock, worked briefly at WVON, earning his nickname by moonlighting between WGCI-FM and KKDA in Dallas, clocking seven million hours of frequent-flier miles.

All of these disc jockeys learned their style from "The Godfather," Al Benson, who deejayed for WGES in Chicago and hooked thousands of listeners with his creative approach to the King's English and his thick Mississippi Delta accent. He wore bright suits—reds, oranges, and greens—and rode in a chauffeur-driven white Cadillac. He spoke directly to black working-class audiences, using street vernacular: "If you've got plenty of geets [money] on you, go right in the store," he would tell listeners without explaining the meaning of slang terms. He would often mispronounce words and sometimes talk with a mouthful of food. He assured naysayers, "My people know what I mean." His fan base answered his loyalty and authenticity in dollars. He earned a whopping $400,000 a year in the 1950s.

WVON, which actually broadcasted out of Cicero, Illinois, outrated all the other stations in Chicago, even with a weak 1,000-watt signal. At all different times of the day, you could hear the sounds of WVON drifting out of the windows—the only cool breeze that city residents with no air-conditioning in the summertime could get. All of the disc jockeys were well known in the community and were pivotal to the civil rights movement, donating money to groups like Operation Breadbasket, the Urban League, the NAACP, and the Student Nonviolent Coordinating Committee. Disc jockey E. Rodney Jones, known at WVON as the "Madd Lad" and as a musician with a golden ear, found Reverend Jesse Jackson when Jackson was known as the "country preacher," and Jones became instrumental in Jackson's rise to prominence in Chicago.

Jackson, born to a sixteen-year-old mother in the poorest section of Greenville, South Carolina, became a student activist in college at North Carolina A&T. He began his lifelong devotion to activism when he led a group to support four students attempting to desegregate Woolworth's in Greensboro, North Carolina. He was one of thousands of black college students who attempted to desegregate public accommodations in the South.

Jackson easily stepped into a leadership role during voter registration drives in Selma, Alabama, in 1965, ingratiating himself to Dr. Martin L. King Jr. and his Southern Christian Leadership Conference (SCLC). King sent him to Chicago to establish a frontline office for Operation Breadbasket—an organization designed to provide economic opportunities for blacks, including pressuring local white-owned stores to hire them. E. Rodney Jones gave Jackson a platform by broadcasting Operation Breadbasket's mass meetings every Saturday morning on the radio.

Every Friday night, WVON disc jockey Wesley South, who interviewed Martin Luther King Jr. consistently and other major players of the civil rights movement, eventually provided Jackson a platform on his show to discuss community issues of the week. With these weekly broadcasts, Jackson was on his way to becoming a civil rights leader in his own right.

In addition to having their day jobs, E. Rodney Jones and Pervis Spann owned the Burning Spear nightclub on Fifty-Fifth and State Street. Jones and Spann also staged high school record hops, featuring both local artists and big names like Aretha Franklin and the Jackson Five. They brought some of these soul acts—like Little Stevie Wonder, who recorded his live version of "Fingertips" here—to places like the Regal Theater at Forty-Seventh and the now-called King Street (then called South Parkway). It was next to the Savoy Ballroom.

Eventually Cornelius would follow in their footsteps when he partnered with disc jockey Joe Cobb, whose signature line on the radio was "I'm having more fun than a one-legged man in a football-kicking contest!" Together, they did local promotion for artists at high school auditoriums around town. Because they couldn't charge the kids much, Cornelius and Cobb had to take local artists like the Chi-Lites, Jerry Butler, and Tyrone Davis around to several high schools in a single day in order to generate enough money to turn a profit. They'd pack up, move to one school, pack up and move to another, like a caravan or a train—a soul train.

When Cornelius first came to WVON, he met with General Manager Lucky Cordell. Despite Cornelius's commanding presence, Cordell found him affable and easy to get along with. Though not as outgoing as the other deejays, he still seemed like a perfect fit for the station, what with his self-possessed confidence and his arresting, sexy, booming voice that could surge across the studio.

At first, Wood—the traffic ticket cop who Cornelius later found out was the news director at WVON, a former disc jockey turned newsman as he referred to himself—hired Cornelius to read the news. Cornelius was thrilled with the job, knowing the reputation the station had around town. To him, it was the first job he'd ever had that didn't *feel* like a job. Despite turning thirty in 1967, he felt like he was just getting started in his career. And he hoped that getting his foot in the door would lead to his real dream—one that he had secretly harbored since he was a kid, never telling anyone because he thought it was so far-fetched— to be a deejay.

Though he had the voice, Cornelius had no experience in broadcasting. Before he began at the radio station, he was working during the day as an agent at the Golden State Mutual Life Company with Joseph Hutchinson, who was well known around town for playing the guitar with his daughter's group, the Hutchinson Sunbeams—later recrowned the Emotions by Stax Records. Cornelius made $250 a week as an agent, but money was always still tight at home. He thought long and hard about making a good impression at his new job and decided to spend $400 to take a broadcasting course at the Columbia Broadcasting School on N. LaSalle Street so he would be ready when he showed up for work at WVON in a few weeks.

On the first day of the course, his instructor told the class that none of them were likely to get a job in radio. "And if you did, if you were good enough, it would mean starting out in some little town." Cornelius was undeterred, though it was a test of wills to stay afloat in school with little money and two young sons and a wife. But the course turned out to be a fantastic investment. In a few short weeks, he learned the technical side of show business, boosted his confidence, and came prepared for his new job.

When he first showed up to work at WVON's ramshackle office at 3350 S. Kedzie Avenue on the Southwest side of town, Cornelius ended up doing a number of things for the station— answering the telephone for the station's talk show host, Wesley South, or pinch-hitting for sick deejays—but his main job was reading the news and working as a reporter covering the height of the civil rights movement. He was paid $100 per week. During the winter he drove his Oldsmobile with no heat in subzero weather to the station. Still, he felt like he was close to where he wanted to be.

It was a heady time to be a reporter and reading the news at the station. The years leading up to 1970 were a gumbo convergence of the counterculture movement, the black power movement, and the antiwar movement. On the Chicago streets, gangs like the Vice Lords, the Black Stone Rangers, and the Disciples had grown more emboldened as widespread disillusionment filled the pockets of the city's most poverty-stricken areas.

On April 4, 1968, all of the WVON deejays took to the airwaves when riots erupted—deejays like Pervis Spann spoke with measured tones into the microphone, telling people, "Violence is not the way." The WVON "Good Guys" stayed on the air talking for twenty-four hours nonstop, telling people to just "cool out and stop destroying your own property." The disc jockeys even took to the streets and talked to gang leaders. Social activism was the norm at the station—the deejays created tapes to send to soldiers to Vietnam to soothe them in battle and gave a platform to burgeoning leaders of the civil rights movement.

Part of the reason a door had opened for Cornelius in media had stemmed from the fallout of the riots in 1967, and following Martin Luther King's assassination, the National Advisory Commission on Civil Disorders (better known as the Kerner Commission) was established by Lyndon B. Johnson to determine the cause of the upheaval. In the report, the media were criticized for sensationalizing the riots, for not examining their causes, and for not reporting on them from an insider's view because of a lack of black representation. The report's findings: "Our nation is moving toward two societies: one black, one white—separate and unequal." The doors slowly began to open.

Cornelius was there to cover the movement and its aftermath as a news reporter. But his first passion, music, was always in the back of his mind. And he saw firsthand how more and more black musicians were taking control of their careers. Trumpeter Phil Cohran, an astronomer and astrologer, founded and operated the Artistic Heritage Ensemble out of the Afro Arts Community Center on Oakwood and Drexel Boulevards, near Thirty-Fifth Street. The center offered free concerts, and classes in Swahili, Hebrew, Arabic, dance, and art. Oscar Brown Jr., Syl Johnson, and other well-known local musicians would come to play.

And then there was Curtis Mayfield. Following in the footsteps of one of Chicago's most famous soul crooners, Sam Cooke, who had created his own record label, SAR, Mayfield created the Curtom music publishing and record company, signing groups like the Five Stairsteps, Donny Hathaway, the Staple Singers, and eventually Jerry Butler. In 1970, he launched his solo career with his eponymous first album, *Curtis*.

Don Cornelius couldn't ignore his real passion for much longer. He was most comfortable when he sat in an absent deejay's seat behind the microphone, electrifying listeners by introducing them to the new names and sounds of soul music. Most nights he would hang out at the jazz clubs along Sixty-Third and Cottage Grove—Chicago's answer to New York's Fifty-Second Street.

Meanwhile, Roy Wood began moonlighting as a sports anchor at the local UHF television station, WCIU-TV, Channel 26. WCIU was a leader in truly diverse ethnic programming, with shows aimed at Spanish viewers, Asians, and blacks; talk shows in Polish, Greek, and Lithuanian; and even a polka show. WCIU also hosted two dance shows aimed at little kids: *Kiddie-A-Go-Go*, which featured preteens and sometimes even toddlers frolicking to the latest popular songs, and *Red, Hot and Blue*, hosted by black deejay Big Bill Hill.

Wood invited Cornelius to join him at the television station, and soon Don landed a job as a sports anchor. His first on-camera appearance was on the show *A Black's View of the News*, where he coanchored with Wood and Olympic great Jesse Owens.

As Wood and Cornelius became more visible around the city, Leonard Chess demanded that they both choose between their careers at the radio station or the television station. While Wood stayed at WVON, Cornelius left to work full-time in television, armed with the knowledge that the owners at WCIU-TV were welcoming to his creative ventures, and a bold idea he had for a brand-new show.

====

While Cornelius was planning his next move in the world of black Chicago, George O'Hare Jr., a tall, expressive, Irish Catholic man with a gentle spirit and a buoyant smile, was working as a volunteer with Jesse Jackson's Operation PUSH, while serving as a manager at Sears, Roebuck and Company. He called himself the luckiest person in the world—his friends just called him a nigger lover. But every time they said it, a feeling would travel through his chest, an excitement ready to burst, a feeling that their words were tinged with jealousy.

O'Hare had been raised to hate Negroes by his father, George O'Hare Sr., who owned the Tivoli Tap Room, a bar near the Tivoli Theater on Sixty-Third Street in the Woodlawn neighborhood on the South Side of Chicago. Right outside the bar, his father's beautiful black Doberman pinscher kept watch over the patrons. In appropriately racist fashion, George Sr. named the dog Stepin' Fetchit for his imposing black figure.

After graduating from Austin High School on the West Side, O'Hare Jr. took his first job as a salesman at Sears, Roebuck selling encyclopedias, vacuum cleaners, and sewing machines, before becoming the division manager. At the time, Sears, Roebuck was completely disinterested in black employees or even black customers. Whenever a black person applied for employment or credit, O'Hare was instructed to mark an X in the upper left hand corner of their applications. These would be passed along to upper management who quickly deposited their applications into their "circular files," namely the trash cans.

O'Hare was surprised when his boss, Gordon M. Metcalf, called him into his immaculate office one day and asked him, "How do you like your job?"

"I like it very much," O'Hare started, searching for the right answers. "I like the people. I like the job."

"We'd like you to join the Junior Chamber of Commerce," Metcalf intoned. "These are men that change the world."

Eager to keep his job, O'Hare acquiesced, although reluctantly. In those days before he began volunteering with Operation Breadbasket, he wasn't the type of person to join any organization—particularly one that had politically left leanings. He had been raised that black people were uneducated and inferior. At his job when O'Hare asked about advertising vacuum cleaners to blacks, executives were shocked that they cleaned their houses.

After O'Hare's second week of volunteering with the Junior Chamber of Commerce, Metcalf asked him if he would come see Dr. Martin Luther King Jr. speak at the Theological Seminary near the University of Chicago.

"Hell, no," O'Hare responded flatly. "He's a Communist. He's a troublemaker."

But his boss was insistent, so O'Hare took his own car and followed Metcalf to the seminary. Yet as soon as Dr. King began to speak, O'Hare was spellbound, lost in a zone on Dr. King's every word. Afterward, O'Hare spent the thirty-mile drive home in Chicago traffic mulling over what he'd seen and heard. It took him an hour to get home, and all the while, as he sat staring into the dashboard, he asked himself over and over, "Why do I hate him?" Even though O'Hare was raised to be racist, King's message made perfect sense.

He went to see King speak several times, mesmerized by his intonation, his articulation of the struggles of the working class, his beautiful mastery of the King's English. King would introduce O'Hare to a young preacher, Rev. Jesse Jackson, who would in turn convince him to volunteer with Operation Breadbasket.

The more time O'Hare spent volunteering and working with local activists like Jackson and Dick Gregory, the less he understood his own racist upbringing. O'Hare would eventually become best friends with comedian and outspoken activist Dick Gregory, watching his rise on the comedy circuit beginning at Hugh Hefner's first Playboy Club in Chicago. Later, O'Hare would march with Dr. King and become an outspoken critic of racism. In an ironic twist, O'Hare eventually became the legal guardian to Lincoln Perry (stage name Stepin' Fetchit), and revealed to Lincoln just before O'Hare's death how his father thought so little of blacks that he named his dog Stepin' Fetchit, too.

One day that year, O'Hare got the assignment to pick up Dr. King and bring him to the radio station WVON to be interviewed on air by Wesley South, who hosted the late night talk show *Hot Line*. At the time, Dr. King was living in a run-down building in Chicago to demonstrate the city's poverty. When King visited Cicero, where the station was broadcast, he was shaking—and said that he had never seen the level of hate that he experienced in Chicago. O'Hare, who normally went home on the Stevenson Expressway, made a stop off of California Avenue to take King to WVON on Kedzie Avenue as they both sat quietly in the car. O'Hare wasn't really aware of the magnitude of Dr. King's appeal to the community until he got to the station and thousands of admirers were there waiting for him outside the doors of WVON. Traffic had ground to a halt on Kedzie Avenue as listeners flocked to the station to catch a glimpse of the charismatic preacher.

Inside the station, Don Cornelius sat on a milk crate, having finished reading the news. Every so often he looked up and couldn't help but stare at O'Hare. *What was this white guy doing with Dr. King?*

So Cornelius asked George, "Are you Dr. King's lawyer?"

"No," said O'Hare.

"His manager?" asked Cornelius.

"No, I'm not. I'm just a volunteer," O'Hare answered, amused. "I volunteer with the preachers with the civil rights movement."

"Well, where do you work?" Cornelius asked.

"I'm a manager at Sears, Roebuck," O'Hare answered. "An advertising manager."

Now, Cornelius was intrigued. Here was a white man who was comfortable in both black and white circles. Plus, he was the manager of the most prestigious retail store in the country, with his fingers in the pot of millions of dollars in advertising.

"You want to go out for drinks?" Cornelius asked.

They met that night for the first round at two in the morning at Flukie's Lounge on South Cottage Grove Avenue.

"I'm thinking about doing a black version of *American Bandstand*," Cornelius told O'Hare as they sat at the bar in the back of the tavern.

"It will never work," O'Hare shot him down. "Look at what happened with Nat King Cole." Cornelius knew that Cole, one of America's most beloved talents, wasn't able to keep his variety show on the air because sponsors in the South refused to support a black host. *The Nat King Cole Show* shut down after just a year on the air. Cole infamously stated that "Madison Avenue was afraid of the dark."

But Cornelius had seen deejays get their own sponsors to keep their shows afloat at WVON, many of them knocking down a 30 percent commission by brokering ad time. He thought he would take the same idea to television. And O'Hare was impressed with Cornelius's burning desire to create a show in a time period when it seemed impossible for a black person to do so.

When Flukie's closed, they found another bar open on Seventy-Ninth Street. They drank straight through until five in the morning, and then O'Hare had a meeting at Sears a few hours later at nine. At this point, he was only halfway convinced, and mostly because of Cornelius's persistence. O'Hare thought about pitching the idea, but in the back of his mind, he feared that his reputation would go down the drain if it were a failure.

But Cornelius wasn't finished. One day soon after that, he came to O'Hare's office unannounced, stepped calmly over to his cubicle, and sat down next to him. O'Hare had his back to Cornelius, the phone cradled to his ear as he spoke on the telephone.

Cornelius leaned over and whispered in his ear, "Soul Train."

O'Hare put the phone down, turned around, and called out to his secretary, "Hold all my calls."

———

Buoyed by O'Hare's interest in the project, Cornelius scrounged up the nerve to approach station owners Howard Shapiro and Bill O'Connor. Cornelius pitched it as a "black *American Bandstand.*" It would take months of meetings with Shapiro to convince him that the show would fit in with their other shows aimed at multicultural audiences. Eventually Shapiro acquiesced, answering, "Sure, we'll try that, too."

At the same time that Cornelius was pitching his boss on the show, O'Hare approached his supervisor Gordon Metcalf. O'Hare was surprised by the response—Metcalf thought any show that had music that people wanted to listen to might get over on an audience, no matter who or what race the host was.

O'Hare was already paying $70,000 per year on advertising for appliances for Sears. But when Metcalf heard the title, he was reluctant.

"What's a soul train?" he asked.

"I really don't know," O'Hare answered. "That's the title."

"Well, what's it gonna be about?"

"Dancing," O'Hare really didn't know all of the details. He was just trying to get the deal done to get Don off of his back. He could see how passionate Cornelius was to be successful.

His boss finally agreed to advertise 45 rpm records.

O'Hare went to Channel 26 to finish the deal. One executive pulled him to the side, telling him, "We can do this together, George. We don't need Don Cornelius."

"I don't think you understand. This is not a business thing for me; this is something I believe in," O'Hare told him.

Metcalf's decision to fund the show seemed like a bold move for racial progress, but there was a strong financial incentive driving the decision. Metcalf was among a small group of advertisers looking toward the future of Sears, Roebuck, and courting the black market seemed like smart business. It was just that like most other advertisers, Metcalf hadn't known how to reach them—until now.

With Sears's commitment, Cornelius convinced management at WCIU to let him use the station's cramped studio for the set in the attic of the Board of Trade building—then the city's tallest building. At a time when color television was the hippest thing in town, the show was filmed live in black-and-white. The dressing room was literally a closet. The floor was black with a green spot in the middle where the artists stood in close proximity to the dancers in a ten-by-ten-foot space without air-conditioning. The one window-unit air conditioner would freeze with ice and shut down. Once, one of the cameras—in the style of the Nixon-Kennedy debate cameras—caught on fire. This was still 1950s-style television. Even in the winter it was so hot in the cramped space that they would try to run the broken air conditioner. The dancers would sweat, and the smell was unbearable. In order to get to the back of the set, there was a door in the audio room to pass through. The turntable was right next to the door. As people would walk through the door, the record would skip as the live show was on air.

Cornelius got the idea to call the show "Soul Train" from his traveling to and from high school record hops. He reached out to his list of contacts from WVON and from the artists he'd been promoting in high school auditoriums. Joseph Hutchinson, the father of the Emotions singers, was the first person he contacted, then Jerry Butler, and the Chi-Lites. He booked all of them for the first show.

He approached his buddy, WVON deejay Joe Cobb, about doing promotions for the program while in the studio at the radio station. Cornelius was holding the copy for promotion of the show and he asked Cobb to read it. "Channel 26, will be airing the *Sooooooooouuuul Traiiiiin!*" Cobb sung into the microphone. He was just joking, but Cornelius told him, "I like that. Do that again for me." The name stuck, as did the bombastic approach to stretching it out.

He also reached out to his colleague at WVON, Don Jackson, the first black advertising sales manager at the station, as well as the youngest, to help him develop the show. Cornelius told Jackson that the show would have the hippest dancers from around town and first-class acts from the Chicago music scene.

"Man, there's no way in hell a show called 'Soul Train' will ever make it. Thank you, but no thank you," Jackson said with an affable smile.

Meanwhile, Cornelius still had to get a show together. The first thing he needed to do was to find dancers—but not just any dancers. He needed the kind that would keep the attention of an audience used to seeing the latest dances at the clubs around town.

At first, he simply advertised for dancers in the black newspaper, the *Chicago Defender*. But it would take a chance meeting with a childhood friend to get the personnel that would make a name for the show.

A diminutive teenaged smooth talker named Clint Ghent danced nightly at Southside clubs. When he went to college on a basketball scholarship, he caught the attention of a dance professor at Central State University in Ohio. Every time he passed her classroom after basketball practice, the sounds of soul music drew him in and he'd dance in the hallway outside of her class. She noticed his talent and helped to enroll him in a six-month program at Juilliard. Ghent returned to Chicago with a certificate in choreography from the program and would eventually choreograph for the Emotions, the Chi-Lites, the Whispers, and the Jackson Five before they signed with Motown.

One night after coming back to Chicago from the program at Juilliard and deciding to drop out of Central State, Ghent went to dance at the Guys and Gals club on Sixty-Ninth Street and ran into Don Cornelius. Don was always checking out the dancers in the clubs and on the streets—he wanted to capture the same uninhibited, boisterous joy they exhibited dancing there and translate it to the show.

"Clint, baby, I want to see you before you leave," Don said.

"What's going on?" Ghent asked, leaning against the door leading out of the club.

"Hey, man, I'm putting together a dance show. I need the best dancers. Can you get them together?"

Ghent got right on it. The dancers he found turned out to be the baddest dancers from clubs around town, performing the latest crazes like the Monkey, the Funky Broadway, and the Bop. The idea was to capture the real-life energy of a smoky, hole-in-the-wall club—a place where people came to dance until the sun rises...and sets again.

———

On August 17, 1970, *Soul Train*, the local Chicago version, premiered on a set the size of a small dining room. One camera was manned by a cockeyed cameraman who was physically unable to use the viewfinder. He had to move around to catch different angles of the artists and dancers. Only one camera had a zoom lens. Filmed live, there was no opportunity for mistakes. The dancers were paid only a lunch of Kentucky Fried Chicken and grape soda, it being standard practice at the time for dancers on dance and variety shows not to get paid.

The show opened up with a clip of a real train coming down the tracks. Then it cut to Don Cornelius, who wore a low-cut tank top, accented by chains and leather. His hair was done in an Afro that he parted neatly on the left-hand side. He talked to the audience in the rhyming style he had learned from working at WVON, using lines like "We'll be dealing some good feeling for the next sixty minutes."

For the rest of the show, the dancers angled for airtime, throwing out wild dance moves that would hopefully keep the camera trained on them for a minute. Jerry Butler came on and sang "For Your Precious Love." The Emotions sang a few of their tunes that didn't chart, including "I Can't Stand No More Heartaches" and "So I Can Love You," but the songs were well known locally from the sisters singing them at the Regal Theater, where they had won many talent shows, and at the Mount Mariah Baptist Church, where their father served as a pastor. But it was the dancers who stole the show, with their cool, laid-back gliding and strutting.

The show went off smoothly, remarkably without any glitches. At the end, Cornelius signed off with what would become his signature line: "And you can bet your last money, it's all gonna be a stone gas, honey! I'm Don Cornelius, and in parting, we wish you love, peace, and soul!"

—

Despite the show running flawlessly, after the first episode aired O'Hare was skeptical. The size of the set, the cheap quality of the programming and equipment, and the minimum visibility of a UHF station all signaled disaster. There was no way a station like this could garner any kind of popularity. He'd put his neck on the line with Metcalf, and now he worried that his boss was going to think he was a failure.

"It's not gonna work," O'Hare told Cornelius gently. "You're not gonna keep this show. Let's go have a drink."

But Cornelius was insistent that O'Hare just be patient, that the show would strike a chord, particularly with teenagers.

Two days after *Soul Train* had been on the air, Cornelius walked down the streets on the South Side with O'Hare. They were heading to a bar for a drink. As they talked, they walked into a bar on Sixty-Third and Cottage Grove. Heads turned as they sized up Cornelius. Then several people at the bar called out in unison: "Soooooouuuuuuuul Traaaaain!"

O'Hare's eyes grew wide as he turned toward his friend.

Cornelius eased out a confident smile, thinking, "This is going to be bigger than I ever imagined."

2

HOLLYWOOD SWINGING

Bending bottles, maneuvering schemes, false expressions,
washed-up dreams/Everybody makes believe in Hollywood,
Hollywood

—Chaka Khan

Dick Clark, as meek and clean-cut as he seemed, had always been a fast talker. Chicago's *Soul Train* was gaining ground fast and was quickly becoming the talk of the industry. Clark, host of the national ABC show, *American Bandstand*, dreamed up dollar signs and came to Chicago to have lunch with Cornelius. They ate at Johnny's Steakhouse on the corner of Van Buren and Wells. No matter how many different ways Clark asked to buy the show, Cornelius refused.

Cornelius became good friends with a man named Tom E. Kuhn, who worked for the ad agency Allen, Anderson, Niefeld and Paley. Kuhn was the advertising account executive for Johnson Products.

Kuhn—tall, blonde, blue-eyed, and handsome—was as smooth and cool as Cornelius. He saw potential in the low-budget black-and-white version of the show and felt that if it were in color it could really make a splash in the marketplace. With the success of the show locally, Cornelius was working to create a pilot to sell the show to a national market. Kuhn introduced George E. Johnson (an entrepreneur who had grown up picking cotton and beans when living with relatives in Richton,

Mississippi) to watch the show and eventually to make an investment in the pilot.

Johnson had grown up in Chicago admiring the black entrepreneurs and professionals between Rhodes Avenue and Cottage Grove Avenue on Thirty-Fourth Street. But the entrepreneur he was most impressed with was one he would end up working for—a man named S. B. Fuller, who Johnson believed was taking people off of welfare and making them independent. Fuller started his company, Fuller Products, with twenty-five dollars—a refund he received from the insurance on his car.

Fuller bought soap with the money from the insurance, handmade the labels, and started selling his soap. Johnson became the head production chemist for Fuller. Johnson followed this model and with a loan for $250, which he was turned down for initially from the bank when he said he wanted to start a business (he went to another bank and told them he needed the loan to take his wife on a vacation, and they granted it to him). His first product was called Ultra Wave Hair Culture, a hair relaxer for men, and by 1960 the company had taken over a three-story building. Johnson eventually became one of the largest black-owned manufacturers of hair and facial cosmetics in the world.

When Reverend Martin Luther King Jr. came to Chicago with Reverend James Bevel for the Southern Christian Leadership Conference (SCLC) in 1966 for their northern campaign to draw attention to slums, he visited the offices of Johnson Products. When King got to the top of the steps, he looked around as Johnson recalled, and said, "Now, this is black power."

On January 14, 1971, Johnson Products became the first black-owned company to appear on the American Stock Exchange.

A perfectionist, Johnson agreed to sign on to invest in *Soul Train* at the urging of Kuhn, only if the production quality was top-notch. Cornelius would emulate his insistence on perfection.

But he almost backed out when he met Cornelius in person. "He was quite a wild dresser," Johnson said. "He had on high-heel green boots and loud clothes. But he was right for the show." By 1971, the time was now for Cornelius to take the show national. He traveled back and forth to California to find a national distributor with a pilot featuring performances by the Dells, the Staple Singers, Tyrone Davis, and the Chi-Lites taped at the CBS building in Chicago with the help of his friend Carl Davis, who was working for Columbia Records at the time. By mid-1971, he found a distributor, Tribune Entertainment, who took notice when Cornelius secured the star power of Gladys Knight for the first show, and began production of the show. Meanwhile, the local Chicago version continued production until 1976. Early on Cornelius would make the commute back and forth to oversee both shows, but eventually handed over the reins of the Chicago show to the staff and hosting duties to Clint Ghent.

Johnson had invested money for the pilot and bartered a deal with Cornelius in which Johnson would own 50 percent of the show. They contacted Metromedia Studios in Los Angeles in hopes of gaining entrance for production. On Saturdays their stages were closed, but Cornelius convinced Metromedia to let them use their stages at a reduced price. They taped four shows on a Saturday to keep the costs down, which were over one hundred thousand dollars per day of taping.

The show aired six minutes of commercials. Cornelius owned three and Johnson owned three. Johnson used one and half minutes and sold the rest to the syndicator, while Cornelius sold his three minutes and earned money for his salary. This was standard fare for local network affiliates who aired syndicated programming during "fringe time"—following network news, immediately after prime time scheduled programming, or late night or Saturday mornings and afternoons. First-run syndicated programs like *Wheel of Fortune* or daytime talk shows were sold directly to local markets. First-run shows were sold in either cash or barter deals. Barter deals were more often consummated for new, untested, or older programs—where the syndicator offered a program to a local television station in exchange for a split of the advertising revenue. This was a familiar process for Cornelius— this was the same way radio deejays brokered airtime at WVON.

Six years later, Johnson gave him half of his stock in return for commercial placement. In exchange, Cornelius was required to keep commercials for Johnson Products on for ten years without compensation. By 1975, Johnson Products' profits—in large part generated from *Soul Train* advertising—reached $35 million.

===

Don Cornelius walks with measured steps onto the set. A commanding presence at six foot five inches, he stops, turns toward the camera, and lifts his microphone toward his mouth. Behind him stands a plywood replica of the head of a passenger train decorated with neon lights and pastel colors—vibrant blues, raspberries, and yellows frame the background. The colors accent Cornelius's own outfit: a sky-blue, double-breasted nylon trench coat with a blue butterfly-collared oxford shirt and a blue-and-green tie. He's wearing a sparkling pinky ring and patterned, lizard-skinned, knee-high platform boots. His Afro is neat, almost perfect. For the national debut of the show, his tinted glasses hide the satisfaction in his eyes.

The cameramen stir around him. The dancers stand poised in their psychedelic coloring—violet butterfly collars, red and black leather, green dashikis—ready to vie for on-camera close-up opportunities.

During the opening sequence, an elementary cartoon of a red, yellow, and blue freight train with "Soul Train" written in white lettering on its side grooves around the hills along a countryside. The train wiggles back and forth to the beat of King Curtis's "Hot Potatoes," released on Bobby Robinson's Enjoy label. As the train dances, Sid McCoy, Cornelius's buddy and former radio deejay for WVON radio in Chicago, gives the introduction. His voice is smooth; his words tumble along like a well-oiled diesel as he announces, "*Soul Train*—The hippest trip in America. Sixty nonstop minutes across the tracks of your mind into the exciting world of soul!"

The camera flashes to Gladys Knight on the dance floor, moving with the Soul Train Dancers; then the girl group, the Honey Cone; soul crooner Bobby Hutton; and finally, special guest star Eddie Kendricks (who just recently embarked on a solo career from the Temptations), as Sid McCoy announces them as the featured guests.

The camera pans to a close-up of Cornelius, standing on a podium, reading from a cue card, talking in a rhyming style in what will become his national trademark—a deep, sonorous baritone: "Stay tuned for the Honey Cone. They will be sho' nuff rocking 'em back, and that ain't no fiction baby—that's a natural fact!"

This was black radio on television. And Cornelius was ready. He had been practicing introducing artists like Marvin Gaye in front of his mirror since back in his Chicago years.

The Honey Cone was one the sexiest, hottest girl groups in the country when, in the spring of 1971, their song "Want Ads" became a No. 1 hit on the *Billboard* charts and the R&B singles chart. It was their first single off of their *Soulful Tapestry* album. On *Soul Train*, Edna Wright led the group with her gold-colored curly hair and nose-scrunching smile, and mesmerized the audience with her scratchy wail, moving the dancers as she roared: "Wanted. Young man, single and free!" Shelly Clark wore a low-slung black dress, with her long hair in a ponytail, while Carolyn Willis was dressed conservatively like a schoolteacher. All of the guests, including the Honey Cone, walked around singing, dancing, and mingling with the dancers.

This national debut of *Soul Train* illustrated that there was a void that Cornelius was able to fill with undiluted black-generated content—something he would find that both black and white audiences would tune in to watch. Despite the fact that television was a conservative medium and the beloved Nat King Cole was unable to get sponsorship with a culturally conservative show, Cornelius was steadily gaining new sponsors. And he had hired black people behind the scenes, too. When James Brown came onboard to perform, he was floored by the quality of the program—the production quality and the set design—and kept asking Cornelius, "Who's behind you on this?" implying that without a white benefactor the program couldn't have been created with this level of perfection.

There was a new generation—black, white, young, and hip—that was ready for this kind of show. No one knew then that on television—the nation's most powerful medium—the show would become a cultural phenomenon, charting a new course for music and bringing regional dances and black youth culture to a national stage.

On the national debut the spotlight was heavy on the extroverted style of the dancers. Cornelius understood the magnetism of the dancers and recognized early on that they would be the stars, and that the success of the show rested heavily on their arresting styling—at least until he could court big-name artists.

After the Honey Cone performed their first act, the deejay played a recording of "Love Machine," by the Politicians, and the camera proceeded to give all of its attention to the dancers, spending the entire song wandering around to discover fresh-faced, skinny teenagers in overalls and matching tops-and-shorts sets. Every few moments it quickly flashed from one camera shot to the next, giving the television audience the feeling of a nightclub with flashing strobe lights.

On the set the dancers wiggled on platforms that looked like the exits at railroad stations. There were railroad tracks painted on the floor, and a makeshift cave that represented a train tunnel that the dancers moved through, following the painted train tracks that spilled out of it. Signs for railroad stations for cities like Cleveland and Detroit were posted on the back wall representing the seven cities that syndicators sponsored.

On the first episode of *Soul Train*, Don Cornelius introduced the creamy falsetto of Eddie Kendricks, who had recently left the Temptations after David Ruffin had been replaced by Dennis Edwards. Kendricks left the group by walking off the stage one night after at a gig at the Copa in New York, and never came back.

When Dennis Edwards joined the Temptations, they moved away from love songs and went psychedelic. Kendricks, however, wanted to sing ballads, model, act, and be an all-around entertainer. When Ruffin joined the group, Kendricks wasn't singing as many leads. Kendricks felt stifled by the group, and wanted to go solo. Ruffin was on drugs and couldn't be counted on to show up to gigs. When he was finally fired, Kendricks threatened to leave. Kendricks left at the same time baritone singer and choreographer Paul Williams was kicked out for drinking.

He would follow with a successful solo career. When he appeared on *Soul Train*, he had just recorded his first solo album, entitled *All By Myself*, on Motown's imprint label, Tamla. The album featured the song "This Used to Be the Home of Johnnie Mae," sung in his natural tenor.

"Here's the man who gained fame by being the lead singer of one of the world's most popular groups, the Temptations. *Soul Train*, welcome Mr. Eddie Kendricks!" Cornelius announced to the Soul Train Gang.

Kendricks sang the ballad "I Did It All for You" as the teenagers slow danced, two-stepping in unison, as the women's hands rested on the men's shoulders—many of them looking uncomfortable in front of the camera.

But the group that would catapult the show toward enviable success would feature a young twenty-seven-year-old Gladys Knight and her cousins and brother, the Pips. As Cornelius's arm flashes toward the stage, with a self-assured look, he cracks a slight smile and announces to the television audience, "Let's put our hands together for four beautiful people who represent a mighty mountain of soul—the very gifted and talented Gladys Knight dancing, singing, swinging Pips!"

The camera pans into the dancing Pips and fades out to a close-up of Gladys's face, hair in a ponytail in a sunny yellow dress and knee-high laced-up sandals. She struggles to move her mouth in time to lip-sync as they sing, "Get aboard the friendship train, everybody shake a hand, shake a hand," As she sings, she walks through the audience shaking the hands of the Soul Train Dancers: "It looks like mankind is on the eve of destruction. Oh, yes it is! People, let me tell you now. We've got to learn to live with each other."

Three more segments were devoted to the dancers—one where Cornelius showcased two teenagers from the crowd to demonstrate various regional dances. The couple, Jan Robinson and Rodney Mullins, from Chicago, performed dances like the

Breakdown and the Popeye—popular dances from their hometown. In the final dance component of the show, Cornelius held a freestyle dance contest between all of the Soul Train Dancers, explaining that the judges would be critiquing based on enthusiasm and how well the couples danced as a team. The winners would be eligible to compete the next spring in the finals for $10,000 in college scholarships, he said, as they grooved to Simtec and Wiley's "Getting Over the Hump."

R&B crooner Bobby Hutton, dressed in a suit with a purple bow tie and ruffled purple shirt, was the last performer after Kendricks, the Honey Cone, and Gladys Knight and the Pips finished one more set. Hutton sang "You're My Only Reason" as couples slow danced.

Cornelius closed out the show with what would become his iconic signature sign-off: "You can bet your last money it's all gonna be a stone gas, honey!" And he finished with, "Always in parting, we wish you love," as he paused and kissed his hand, saying " Peace," as he put his two fingers in a peace sign, "and souuuuuuuuull!" as he balled his fist in the black power salute toward the crowd.

In between the psychedelic dance numbers, there were Afro Sheen and Ultra Sheen commercials created by Johnson Products, celebrating a new consciousness blossoming in the black community. Chemically treated conks and processes and straightening combs were no longer popular as black people tried to figure out a new identity to accompany a burgeoning black power movement. Black college students were fighting to learn black history at historically black colleges. Pan Africanism had become popular in the '60s with the independence of African nations, and was linking people of color around the globe to a common story.

These new commercials reflected the new Afrocentric sentiment. The tag line, *Watu Wazuri*, was sung in Kiswahili and translated to *Beautiful people use Afro Sheen*. It was sung by Donny Hathaway and his wife Eulaulah Hathaway, with music from the Chicago ensemble the Pharoahs (the group was the precursor to Earth, Wind and Fire, featuring Louis Satterfield, Don

Myrick, and Ben Israel). It was the boldest black advertising ever seen on television, and it brought a new black identity into the homes of all of America.

These unapologetic commercials were the brainchildren of Emmet McBain, a hip ad man who worked for Vince Cullers and Associates, the first black-owned full-service advertising agency. He later cofounded Burrell-McBain advertising with Tom Burrell, another black advertiser. The ads in Swahili resonated with the community so much that radio stations were calling to have the ads replayed. Afro Sheen shot to number one in the marketplace. Cullers became the first black advertising agency with national account billing.

There were other, lighter fare commercials, including one where a brother blows a bugle after admiring a woman's ass as she walks down the street before they get into a discussion on how she got her Afro to look so fabulous. In another commercial, the ghost of Frederick Douglass appears and admonishes a young man for going out into the world with his "hair looking like that." He tells him, "I've been watching the progress of our people, and I'm quite familiar with the natural. I am also aware that it is worn as an expression of pride and dignity." The young man quickly gets his Afro sparkling with Afro Sheen as the ghost disappears, presumably satisfied that he has done his duty to rid the world of unkempt naturals.

Over the years the commercials that aired on *Soul Train* followed the changes in the culture of black Americans. By the '80s, when perms, s-curls, and jheri curls became the latest fashion, Johnson Products reverted back to airing commercials for products that catered to relaxed and chemically treated hair. Always keeping an eye on the bottom line, the company was careful to showcase the broad breadth of the black hair-care experience and keep its fingers on the pulse of changes in fashion and culture.

The partnership between *Soul Train* and Johnson Products would mark the first time that a black advertiser sponsored a nationally syndicated show. Johnson Products saw its sales soar and became the first black business to trade on the American

Stock Exchange. *Soul Train* was able to continue its programming with a level of autonomy that would not have been possible if it had had to rely on a national sponsor that had to cater to Southern affiliates.

——

By scoring this disparate and reputable group of artists to perform on the first show—from superstars like Gladys Knight and Eddie Kendricks to budding local talent like Bobby Hutton—Cornelius was able to garner the attention of record companies, who realized that he could promote not only their top-tier artists but also fledgling ones who they were trying to break. The phone wouldn't stop ringing. By the second week, the show was topped only by the 1971 World Series in ratings.

But what really catapulted the show was the fact that Cornelius was filling a void. There simply was no other show showcasing the full scope of black music on television at a time when hits were flowing effortlessly.

His Chicago connections continued to save him during his first years of production. When he sold car insurance before working at WVON, he worked in the same building where the girl group the Emotions appeared on the gospel show *Jubilee Showcase* every Sunday. He became good friends with Joe Hutchinson, the girls' father and manager, and both Joe and Don became good friends with Joe Jackson, father and manager of the Jackson Five. Most of the Jacksons Five's early shows were in Chicago, about thirty minutes from Gary, Indiana, where they lived, and all of these groups would perform numerous times on *Soul Train* in the first few years of the show.

The behind-the-camera talent was plucked from the darlings of Hollywood's black elite. Mark Warren was hired as a freelancer on contract for the first four episodes, just a few months after he became the first black director to win an Emmy for his work on the popular counterculture comedy show *Rowan and Martin's Laugh-In*, where *Saturday Night Live* creator and producer Lorne Michaels also got his start as a writer.

Warren had lots of experience with the visual effects of the day—quick zoom-ins, camera transitions, fade-outs, Dutch angles, superimposing images—all directly from working on *Laugh-In*, which contributed to making the look of *Soul Train* snappy and hip.

Because *Soul Train* was a freelance gig, Warren didn't have anything to lose if it didn't take off, but having his name attached to the show was a big advantage for Cornelius, and garnered industry credibility for the show right away.

After Warren's last episode of his contract with *Soul Train*, he went on to direct the sequel to *Cotton Comes to Harlem*, a blaxploitation film called *Come Back, Charleston Blue*, starring Godfrey Cambridge and produced by Samuel Goldwyn Jr.

Laugh-In producer and director George Schlatter had introduced Warren to a young animator named Leo Sullivan. Sullivan was contracted for the first four episodes of *Soul Train* animating the train in the opening sequence. Young and energetic, Sullivan would moonlight on many jobs. He was one of the Magnificent Seven (the seven animators had nicknamed themselves) who had worked on animating the Fat Albert kids for Bill Cosby's popular cartoon that aired on November 12, 1969. While he was developing the Cosby characters for *Fat Albert and the Cosby Kids*, he was also working another freelance job at night. It wasn't just the nature of the business that inspired his work ethic—for the first time after the civil rights movement more opportunities were opening up for minorities in the industry, and he and other talent were taking the opportunities. Sullivan had received his first opportunity to work in animation with Bob Clampett, who created Tweety Bird and Sylvester the Cat.

Incidentally, Schlatter had hired Warren to work on a pilot called *Turn-On*, which aired on ABC and would become one of the most infamous flops in television history—one station even stopped the airing of the first show midway through the program because of what it considered the show's risqué content. Later, when ABC received a pilot called *All in the Family* about a loudmouthed bigot, the network was squeamish after being burned by *Turn-On* and passed on it. CBS began airing *All in the Family* that year.

—

Despite the doors beginning to open for blacks in media and television, by the early 1970s, advertisers, especially in the South, were still unconvinced that audiences would tune in to watch a black host, let alone dancers with the kind of explosive energy and psychedelic styling seen on *Soul Train*. Plus, Cornelius didn't have national name recognition.

Cornelius was friends with Ellis B. Haizlip, at the time the only other black host of a nationally broadcast black-oriented affairs and music program. Haizlip's show on public broadcasting station WNET in New York entitled *Soul!* was inspired as a black version of *The Tonight Show*. But it was much hipper, hosted by Haizlip—who dressed in the colorful clothing of the artists, musicians, intellectuals, athletes, and poets he invited to join him on the show—from an earthy set that could have doubled as his living room. Stan Lathan, who would later direct various shows, including *Hill Street Blues* and *Sanford and Son*, directed the series.

Haizlip, a theatrical producer, had an eye for spotting talent on the brink of stardom. In 1972, he devoted a full show to showcasing the performing talents of Nick Ashford and Valerie Simpson, who were known as behind-the-scenes songwriters, not the dynamic singing duo that they would become. Artists who weren't considered mainstream enough to be on *The Tonight Show Starring Johnny Carson* or *The Ed Sullivan Show*—Joe Tex, Amiri Baraka, Ron O'Neal—were given a platform to perform and to discuss their work and their views on social issues.

It was a much headier answer to showcasing entertainment than *Soul Train*. It featured poet Nikki Giovanni interviewing James Baldwin, Haizlip questioning Louis Farrakhan about homophobia in the Nation of Islam; a half-hour-long set of Earth, Wind and Fire playing live; and a roundtable discussion with Sidney Poitier, Harry Belafonte, and Haizlip discussing the fate of blacks in Hollywood. By 1973, Haizlip sensed that the end was drawing near for the show. There were rumblings that shows in some markets weren't being aired or were being aired late at night, when no one could see them. Funders were asking if he could "integrate" the show. Haizlip's response? "We're integrating the *network*."

Cornelius had many of the same obstacles to overcome. His laid-back demeanor gave no hint to the extent of the barriers he had had to overcome to get to this point. For the first ten weeks of production of the Chicago *Soul Train* show, he had gone without a salary as the host, producer, and salesperson. All three of the major networks had turned him down for the national show. Convincing syndicators of the value and potential of *Soul Train* was still an uphill battle. Cornelius spent his own money to travel to pitch the show in person to local station managers around the country, and out of the twenty-five markets that he visited, only nine picked up the show. And even then, some of them stuck *Soul Train* on Saturday mornings, right after cartoons, which for many of the advertisers was their worst time slot. Some affiliates had the show running on Friday evenings, others as late as two o'clock on Saturday mornings. Some of the syndicators, he found, weren't airing the show when they promised they would. But at least he was able to pick up syndication in two Southern states—Texas and Georgia.

Cornelius realized the advantages of catering to kids and teens. He and his sponsors knew, like Dick Clark before them, that teens from the soon-to-be-populous baby boomer generation had buying power, and were particularly susceptible to advertisers. In a few markets *Soul Train* aired right after a new Motown production on ABC—*The Jackson 5ive* cartoon series. The animated version of the singing group had begun airing just a month before *Soul Train's* national debut, but already it had hooked in younger viewers.

The powerbrokers in Hollywood smirked at the idea of a black host and a dance show. "When they smirked I smiled," Cornelius later said, "I knew what the viewer reaction would be."

But no matter how much money changed hands, the secret to the show's success would come to be from an unpaid group of teenagers. It was the dancers that caught the audience's attention, with their platform heels, their loud-colored bell-bottoms, dashikis, intricate hairstyles, and patterned shirts. Their braids swirled, and their Afros bounced in time to their wild dancing—all high-leg kicks, splits, and gymnastics.

When viewers tuned in every week to watch their eclectic fashion, dancing acrobatics, and shapely girl-next-door beauty, they saw a little bit of themselves.

3

BOOGIE NIGHTS, HALTER TOPS, AND HOT PANTS

Dancing is the loftiest, the most moving, the most beautiful of the arts, because it is no mere translation or abstraction from life; it is life itself.

—Havelock Ellis

The one thing that can solve most of our problems is dancing.

—James Brown

Ain't I'm clean?" he asked. Then he smiled a devilish grin. Rufus Thomas opened his hot-pink cape and revealed a matching shirt, shorts, and blazer, before the camera panned down to his white go-go boots to the delight of the 112,000-person crowd at the L.A. Coliseum. Thomas was performing for the live show and the 1972 seminal musical documentary *Wattstax*.

"Breakdown chill'ren/break on down!" Thomas instructed the crowd as he performed the song of the same name. The camera panned to a woman in a short red dress demonstrating the Breakdown—moving vigorously, the camera moving right up to her crotch. Then the camera panned to Leo "Fluky Luke" Williamson and Greg "Campbellock Jr." Pope—two Soul Train Dancers commissioned to dance at the taping by one of the directors, Larry Shaw. They were locking and slapping hands, applejack hats perched at a rakish tilt on their heads. The camera turned to Fred Berry, another Soul Train Dancer, winding his chunky midsection in slow motion like he was making love to the air.

Thomas had begun his career in vaudeville and as part of the Rabbit Foot Minstrels—skilled in comedic timing and performing skits; he understood very well how to work a crowd. Al Bell, the president of Stax Records, Thomas's label, would travel to cities around the nation and witness the new dances kids were doing. In Chicago, Bell saw kids doing a dance they called the Push and Pull. He got on the phone and dialed up Thomas and described the dance to him. When Bell came back to Memphis, he and Thomas recorded the song "Do the Push and Pull," and went back to Chicago to begin to market it. They followed the same marketing format, finding dances around the country for much of Thomas's repertoire, including "Do the Funky Chicken," "Funky Robot," "The Funky Bird," and "Do the Double Bump."

Bell understood brilliantly that in black cultural circles, the creative dances that people came up with at basement parties were equally as important as the music they danced to—and that on Friday nights dancing was a kind of therapy from the week's stress. It was a colorful and necessary way to begin a new workweek, brush off the indignities of racism, and throw away any class pretensions.

Soul Train brought the basement scene and the club scene to national television. Regional dances were brought to a national stage. Audiences—black and white—were suddenly able to learn new dances on Saturday morning to take to the club Saturday night. The Soul Train Dancers—everyday people who audiences could relate to—also taught television audiences the latest fashions and the hippest hairdos. The dancers were the definition of cool as audiences sat watching the broad-collared shirts, wide belts and bell-bottoms, bobbing heads, and legs and arms moving in rhythmic patterns across their television screens.

Most of the dancers on the show came from modest backgrounds. The Soul Train Dancers weren't schooled in studios or dance companies. Cornelius would lord over them without acknowledging them and rarely spoke to them, which just made them work that much harder. For the dancers, coming to the set was like a pilgrimage—a refuge from the stress of their daily lives. And it wasn't easy getting onboard. Initially, auditions were held at Denker Recreation Center by the center's director Pamela Brown, but eventually so many dancers began to show up that the best way to gain entry was by knowing someone on the show. Dancing on *Soul Train* became one of the most coveted ways for dancers to aspire toward excellence and, later, stardom.

=

Don Campbell, a shy, self-contained teenager, sat at the lunch table next to the jukebox at the Los Angeles Trade Technical College sketching furiously. Campbell, five feet eleven with over two hundred pounds of solid muscle, was a commercial art student at the school, but his real passion was expressing himself through visual art, painting, and sketching. His current subject was Sam Williams, who was wearing knickers and suspenders, and was glued to the jukebox, listening to Rufus Thomas and frenetically doing the Funky Chicken. He was putting his foot behind his leg and raising his elbows like a chicken. Williams took Campbell under his wing, working daily to teach him to dance. He started with the Funky Chicken, but Campbell was awkward and stiffened up his joints, locking them, when they were supposed to move fluidly. Williams kept encouraging him. When Campbell locked his arm, Williams told him, "Do that again—I like that." Every time Campbell made a mistake, it seemed that Williams liked it. Williams coined a term for what Campbell was doing: *locking*. Instead of turning his wrists, Campbell flipped them around, locked the joint, and pointed his finger; he would bend his knees slightly and lock them at the joint, jump up, and land on his knees. Williams started calling him "Campbellock." The two of them began making the rounds at local clubs, joining in dance contests.

Williams and Campbell toured the club circuit in Los Angeles—Maverick's Flat on Wednesday and Thursday, the Summit Club and Pier 7 in the Valley every other night. Campbell met two dancers that frequented Maverick's—one nicknamed Jimmy

"Scoo B Doo" Foster and another named Fred "Mr. Penguin" Berry. Berry, a chubby teen who weighed over two hundred pounds, was agile and mesmerizing to watch dance as he glided effortlessly into front handsprings and mimed in slow motion. He would jump off of chairs and do splits. He moved sensually. He was electrifying.

The three of them were thick as thieves. Leo "Fluky Luke" Williamson, the head cheerleader at Crenshaw High School, would join their crew later when Campbell met him at a dance at the school.

They all would go club-hopping daily and were regulars at the Summit on the Hill on Stocker Street and Overhill Drive where musical groups like Bloodstone played regularly and there was a motel next to the club for the after-party with girls they would meet at the club. The most popular club in Los Angeles was the Climax in Beverly Hills, complete with a sauna room, movie theater, swimming pool, and glass dance floor that lit up. Climax stopped serving liquor at two in the morning, but kept the club open and served breakfast.

When *Soul Train* coordinator Pam Brown, a pretty, conservative woman, saw the three of them—Foster, Campbellock, and Berry— she immediately invited them to dance on the show. Brown was working at Denker Recreation Center in West Los Angeles on Thirty-Fifth Place when Cornelius hired her to be a dance coordinator on the show. At the time, *Soul Train* advertisements ran in the *Los Angeles Sentinel* and were running repeatedly on the radio for dance auditions. Brown would hold auditions at local parks, where dancers would form lines and Brown would pick the best ones. Occasionally, Cornelius would accompany her to the Climax (later Osko's of *Thank God It's Friday* fame, where they played horror movies on one floor and patrons could play chess and listen to jazz on another), the Citadel, and Maverick's.

———

Damita Jo Freeman, a young, energetic dancer with a girlish smile, was oblivious to all that was going on around her. Her mother, a schoolteacher, always kept a close eye on her and was so overly protective that potential dates were afraid to even call her. From the time she was five years old, she was watching and picking up moves from dancers on television. By the time she was eight, she was enrolled in classes with the most towering figure in the history of ballet, famed creator of modern ballet and co-founder of the New York City Ballet, George Balanchine. Damita would come straight home from school to be in classes by three thirty. From the time she was little she had almost forgotten she was black, immersed in a white world where her dancing classmates strived for the Stuttgart Ballet. Balanchine told her that she would be heading to the Dance Theater of Harlem. While she loved the graceful beauty of dancers, she resented a man, or anyone, telling her where she was going to go. She told him she would prefer to be a go-go dancer. She was only half joking.

At home, Damita loved to watch dance shows like *Hullabaloo* and *Shindig!*, where the girls would change their hair color every week. She thought it was fascinating. She had always wanted to perform that kind of dancing—go-go dancing—though she also liked ballet. But mostly, she always wanted to be on television.

When Damita graduated from high school, Balanchine landed her a job with conductor and composer Leonard Bernstein at the Joseph Papp Theater performing in his operetta *Candide*. Before she left to go on tour, her friends took her out for a night of dancing at Maverick's Flat.

She thought the club was immaculate—the smell of sweat danced with the patrons. The place was lit with orange and yellow and red lights that would change periodically according to the music. She was mesmerized by the teenagers all around her doing the latest dances—the Penguin, the Breakdown, and the Cha-cha-cha (also called the Texas Hop). No liquor was served at Maverick's, so she drank ice-cold Coca-Cola. There were no live shows like Kool and the Gang or the Delfonics that night; the deejays were spinning records and she started dancing, showing off the dances—the Rock Steady and the Penguin. Dressed in hot pants and go-go boots, with her hair styled in a neat Afro, she would pick up her leg and play an air guitar, mimicking anyone's dance moves that came up to her. Many of the girls on the dance floor, she noticed, were too cool to sweat so the guys would take over the floor. One of the guys was such a good dancer she couldn't stop watching him.

Damita leaned over to her friend, "I gotta tell this guy he dances so good."

"Don't tell him that—his head is already big," a friend of the dancer overheard her.

"I don't care," Damita told him and yelled out, "Hey you, on the floor—!"

"Hey—yeah?" he shouted back.

"You dance real good!"

He nodded and kept dancing. It wasn't until the next night that she would get the opportunity to dance with him at the club, Climax, on South La Cienega. As soon as he saw her, he grabbed her. She froze for a minute before she relaxed and started doing the Penguin, then the Rock Steady. Meanwhile, her new partner, Don "Campbellock" Campbell, was locking and dropping down into splits. Damita started imitating him and kicking her leg up high, pointing and letting it rest in the air like a ballerina to the thumping bass.

Then the other guys surrounded her, dancers that went by the nicknames of "Lil' Joe" who, at around five foot five, was flamboyant and quick-witted, and protective of anyone he called a friend; Perry "Get Down" Brown, who often wore jumpsuits he sewed; and Jimmy "Scoo B Doo" Foster, a handsome lady's man, with thick sideburns. When the song ended, they all fell into each other laughing. They made plans to go to the next club. But before they left, Pam Brown, who was there scouting for dancers, approached Damita and asked her about coming on *Soul Train*. Pam added that if Damita had any friends who wanted to come, they were welcome, too.

Fifteen-year-old Adolfo "Shabba Doo" Quinones—shy, daydreaming, and studious—sat in front of the television set all day in the

Cabrini-Green Projects where his family lived, watching the dance shows *American Bandstand*, *Shindig!*, and the local Chicago dance show, *Red Hot and Blues*, on his family's black-and-white television—a set so old it cast a blue hue. He and his younger thirteen-year-old sister, Fawn, were of mixed heritage, Puerto Rican and black, but they still belted out the words to James Brown's "Say It Loud (I'm Black and I'm Proud)" with conviction as they watched him perform on their television set. The songs from these shows would take hold of Adolfo as he would dance, and he would sing loudly, feeling the only sense of liberation he could find as his family crumbled around him.

In the next year his family's life changed drastically. His father had settled into a life as a career criminal; his mother was a slave to heroin, accepting crumpled wads of money from old men to feed her habit. They would find their furniture on the street after an eviction, seven siblings in all—while Adolfo would find a new family with South Side Chicago gangs like the Disciples, the Latin Kings, and the Black Stone Rangers.

In spite of the chaos of his life, he and Fawn would make their weekly run to waistline parties in Gary, Indiana; clubs in Chicago; or to Art's Skating Rink, across the Dan Ryan Freeway on the I-90 from Chicago in Harvey, Illinois. They would clear the skating rink floor as people pulled in around them to watch their dance routines.

Red Hot and Blues, a local show on WCIU, was on every black teen's radar on Chicago's South Side. The show featured dancers from the neighborhood with a wide range of ages—anywhere from five to fourteen— and was hosted by popular deejay Big Bill Hill from WPOA-FM. It was sponsored by local businesses, and aired almost exclusively R&B music. For a black Chicago teen dreaming of dancing on television, this show was as close as it could get—until another local show, *Soul Train*, began airing on the station.

When Adolfo and Fawn heard about the new local show *Soul Train*, they would skip school at Waller High School on the South Side daily. Fawn's long hair, unruly and puffed out, made an entrance before she did. They both wore bright, colorful satin shirts and stood in a line that stretched around the corner from the Chicago Board of Trade on 141 West Jackson Boulevard. They would show everyone on the ten-by-ten-foot set how to draw a crowd with dances like the Bop, the Mother Popcorn, the Football, The Early Flynn, James Cagney, the Breakdown, the Drop, and the Uncle Willie.

Soul Train and the local teenage dancers were so popular around Chicago that they were becoming instant celebrities. One day, on the way home from his girlfriend's house in Cabrini-Green, regular dancer Crescendo Ward tensed as he saw a group of gang members following him.

"Either I'm going to get beat up or robbed," he said to himself.

As they walked up to him, they asked, "Where you from?"

"West Side."

"West Side?! You about to get your ass whooped!" They surrounded him.

"What you got?! What you got?" one gang member asked as they all started going through his pockets. Silence lifted the wind as it whistled in the city air. Then one of them stopped and looked him up and down.

"*Whooooa, whoooooa, whoa.* That's that dancing motherfucka! I know him. That guy can dance! Cut a move!"

Ward did a James Brown split and came up smooth.

"That's him! That's him!"

They gave him his money back and gave him some extra money in case he needed to take a cab. "It's dangerous in this neighborhood!" they warned, laughing.

By the spring of 1972, Adolfo had turned sixteen and his mother was tired of trying to keep up with him and his siblings on Chicago's streets. Before the school year ended, she packed up their 1964 blue Oldsmobile and drove the family to a new life with their cousins in Placentia, California.

Adolfo found himself floundering in California the way he had in Chicago. That summer he took a job at a drive-in to please and impress his mother. He cleaned up garbage daily in the oppressive sun. One day, he went to grab a garbage bag and instead just slumped down on the wall and leaned his back against it, asking himself, "Is this really what I'm supposed to be doing?"

Every weekend Adolfo and Fawn continued dancing in Los Angeles clubs like Maverick's Flat on Crenshaw Boulevard, where acts like Rufus featuring Chaka Khan were cutting their teeth. They referred to Crenshaw Boulevard as the black Sunset Boulevard—Richard Pryor would perform there a half a dozen times within a month. Adolfo, his sister, and friends would sit in the back of Maverick's Flat, smoking cigarettes, talking shit, miles away from being star-struck, ignoring acts like Rufus and Chaka Khan who performed regularly because they had seen them so many times.

One night Fawn snuck into Adolfo's room and whispered to him. She heard that the Black Student Union at California State University Fullerton was holding a dance contest.

"How are we gonna get there?" Adolpho asked. His eyes were still closed.

"I stole mom's keys."

The college was fifteen minutes away from where they lived. That night, they snuck out the window. Neither of them had a license, so they took turns white knuckling the wheel, driving their mother's Oldsmobile at five miles per hour until they got to the school over an hour later.

When they got to the contest, Adolfo—wearing bell-bottoms, platform shoes, and a long-sleeve body-fitting, three-button open-neck shirt—and Fawn—in hot pants and a halter top, with her hair in two Native American–style braids—came ready to take the crown. But they ended up coming in second place to a dancer named Greg Pope, who had come to be called "Campbellock Jr." They recognized him from appearing on Los Angeles's new national version of *Soul Train*.

They both watched the new national version of the show and were anxious to get on it. It didn't matter that they had appeared on the Chicago version of the show; they would be starting from scratch in Los Angeles.

The move from Chicago to Los Angeles had transformed the show, from Kansas to Oz. The change from black-and-white to color, from the Windy City to the glam of Hollywood, came with a bombastic attitude, colorful shirts, stripes and polka dots, and an uninhibited freedom. The show had traveled miles away from the cool two-stepping bop in Chicago to the wild, acrobatic, high-kicking splits of a whole new world.

Adolfo and Fawn found a friend in Campbellock Jr. when they asked him how they could get on this slick new version of *Soul Train*. Campbellock Jr. was taken with Fawn, fair-skinned with long, thick, black curly hair and a shape that would make Marilyn Monroe envious. In order to get in good with Fawn, he took Adolfo under his wing, teaching him a dance he called "locking" that he had learned on the Chicago *Soul Train* show from watching Don "Campbellock" Campbell. He performed it so well and even looked a little bit like Campbellock that the other dancers started calling him Campbellock Jr. Adolpho got a new nickname, too—"Shabba Doo"—from a riff from one of the tunes by the funk group Bloodstone.

Campbellock Jr. promised to teach Shabba Doo some of his dance moves, and took him to his apartment on Thirty-Ninth and Budlong. His roommate was Jimmy "Scoo B Doo" Foster, who also danced on the show. Greg "Campbellock Jr." Pope sat on the corner of his bed, barking orders at Shabba Doo as he danced in front of the mirror by Campbellock's dresser, in a three-by-five-foot space.

"Jump in the air...Now point!" Campbellock Jr. screeched. Shabba Doo continued all day and throughout the night, with only the sound of Campbellock Jr.'s insistent voice to guide him and the smell of sweat and a mixture of tuna fish and Rice-A-Roni that Campbellock Jr. ate out of a saucepan with a soupspoon. It would take the whole summer for Shabba Doo to perfect the dance and for them to get the choreography down pat.

One night at the Citadel, Don Campbell met a young, pretty white woman who looked out of place on the dance floor. She was dressed like a gypsy, with a scarf tied on her head, big earrings, and baggy pants. She was watching Campbell intently, confounded as she watched him locking. Her name was Antonia Christina Basilotta, but everyone just called her Toni Basil. She had been dancing professionally since she was a child and was already fully immersed in the professional world of choreography. She had worked as an assistant choreographer and as a dancer on the music variety show *Shindig!*, an assistant choreographer on the concert film *T.A.M.I. Show* with James Brown, and an assistant choreographer on the movie *American Graffiti*. Basil was good friends with a dancer from *Soul Train* named Lamont Peterson. Peterson lived in South Central and Basil lived about an hour away in Topanga Canyon, but they would meet up once a month to go clubbing. Basil looked to Peterson to help her find out about the street dance scene. Peterson was known around town for the dances he performed, including the runaway, the bump, and posing and voguing. He told her one day about a dancer he'd seen at the Citadel who had created an incredible new dance. They went to the Citadel that night, and Basil witnessed Don Campbellock as he flew in the door, dazzled the crowd, and flew back out. She imagined him as the Rudolf Nureyev of the streets. He would fly in the air as sweet and beautiful as Dr. J from half court, then jump down to his knees and back up to his feet. She had to meet him.

Basil traveled to clubs regularly looking to find him before she happened upon him at the Citadel again. She went up to him and asked him directly if he could show her a few moves. Before long they grew close and she would pick Campbell up daily in her tiny car and take him to clubs. At the time, she was living with actor Dean Stockwell, as she and Campbell became fast friends and eventually lovers even as she continued to live with the actor. Eventually, people started waiting for them to show up to the club.

Basil eventually decided to make a film of Campbell and try to shop his talents. She took it to Dick Clark's Moffit Lee Productions. About six months later, the choreographer for Roberta Flack's ABC television special, *The First Time Ever*, which aired on June 19, 1973, called her.

"That guy...you brought us the film of—is there more of them [dancers]?"

Executives from Moffitt Lee initially wanted to use the Alvin Ailey dancers but had a union problem with them. They told Basil if she could get a group of dancers together that weren't in the union, they could perform on one show.

——

By the time the first national dance contest premiered on *Soul Train* in 1973, dancers that were fan favorites included "Lil' Joe," Darnell Williams, who had come from London at eighteen years old to the States to be an actor; Tyrone "the Bone" Proctor, who snuck onto the *Soul Train* set by hiding in the trunk of his car to get past security; Sharon Hill, with high cheekbones, blackberry skin, jeweled and beaded cornrows, was one of the sexiest dancers; Patricia Davis, better known as Madame Butterfly, the most popular dancer on the show; Veronica Abercrombie; Thelma Davis; and Damita Jo Freeman, who would later choreograph for stars like Cher, Lionel Richie, and Whitney Houston. A tightly knit crew was formed with Jimmy "Scoo B Doo," a show-off and showstopper; Adolfo "Shabba Doo" Quinones; Fred "Mr. Penguin" Berry; Bill "Slim the Robot" Williams; Fawn Quinones; Greg Campbellock Jr., and Leo "Fluky Luke" Williams.

Pam Brown was the den mother for all the dancers, walking around the set collecting chewing gum from them and making sure their clothes were appropriate. Cornelius was particular about the dancers not wearing revealing clothing that showed off their butt, hips, and breasts.

The judges for the first dance contest (solely between the dancers on *Soul Train*) included O. J. Simpson, a halfback for the Buffalo Bills; Abbey Lincoln, vocalist and movie actress; Quincy Jones, musician and music mogul; Olympic track star Rafer Johnson; and *Ebony* Fashion Fair model Claudia Tate.

Tom E. Kuhn, now *Soul Train*'s executive producer, had followed Cornelius from Chicago. Sitting on the sidelines, Kuhn looked like the blue-eyed version of Ron O'Neal's character,

Priest, from the movie, *Super Fly*. Kuhn recognized the star appeal of Damita Jo and Don Campbellock and leaned over to Cornelius, telling him sagely, "These two are going to make us some money."

Damita Jo and partner Don Campbellock won the dance contest and received a certificate from James Brown.

Before the grand finale of the National Dance Contest, where fifty-two regional winners competed at the Whiskey a Go Go nightclub in West Hollywood in August 1975, there were local contests where dancers competed, often on local dance shows. One of those dancers was a standout football player at Jackson State University who went by the nickname "Sweetness" because everywhere he stepped he had sweet dance moves, on the gridiron and on the club floor.

Walter "Sweetness" Payton learned "locking" from watching dancers like Don Campbellock and Scoo B Doo on television in Tennessee. So inspired, he ended up auditioning for a local dance show, *24Karat Black Gold*, where local black teenagers showed off local dance moves. After exhausting practices on the football field, he would make his way onto the dance set. Payton, a flashy dresser, wore jeans with wide legs, a cutoff shirt and platform heels and danced with the grace of a ballerina—but he and his partner, Mary Jones, lost to a Louisiana couple.

Payton wasn't the only athlete that had the chance to dance on the show. Members of the Los Angeles Lakers would appear in April 1983 featuring Michael Cooper, Dwight Jones, Norm Nixon, and Magic Johnson dancing with the Soul Train Gang to Earth, Wind and Fire's "Fall In Love With Me."

During the National Contest, dancers competed for a 1975 Chevrolet car and runners-up received $2,000 scholarships or the cash equivalent, sponsored by Johnson Products, 7 Up, and local radio stations around the country.

Cornelius had cribbed the idea from *American Bandstand*. Two Soul Train Dancers, Sharon Hill and Tyrone Proctor, had defected to *Bandstand* a year before to dance on Clark's contest and each won a Mazda. When Proctor, who was couch surfing, couldn't afford to pay the $343.23 in taxes it would cost to claim the car, he went to the only person he knew who would have the cash—Cornelius. Though Clark was Cornelius's nemesis and Cornelius had yelled at dancers who were defecting at lunchtime to dance on *Bandstand*—he promptly wrote Proctor a check for $343.23.

—

Members of the original Soul Train Gang, as these popular dancers would come to be called, were in such high demand that they began a traveling tour, opening for artists like the Whispers for $600 per person per week. They were featured on the cover of *Right On!* magazine—black America's answer to teen magazine *Tiger Beat*—and received truckloads of fan mail. Editor Flo Jenkins told Damita Jo that she would need a station wagon to haul all of the mail. Lil' Joe Chism had a weekly column in *Right On!* to keep fans abreast of the happenings with the dancers. Patricia Davis had a column in *Rock and Soul* magazine. Once, one of Sharon Hill's fans wrote in to her to propose marriage:

I think you're fine Sharon. I'd like to marry you. I'm eleven years old, I'm 5'2" tall and weigh 110 lbs.

Hill responded:

Hey David, thanks for wanting to marry me, but you're a little young right now. When you get to be 21, I'll think about it.

It wasn't just the teenaged fans that were enamored with the dancers—the artists that came on the show knew many of them by name. Fred Astaire boasted in a *60 Minutes* interview that he tuned in to *Soul Train* to see the "kids" and their innovative dance moves. Michael Jackson invited the dancers to his home to teach him how to do the robot (and later the moonwalk). With their latest teenage fashions and creative hairstyles, they represented aspiration for every working-class black teenager who tuned in. For the first time, black inner-city teenagers could see each other—at their most joyous and relaxed—live and direct on television to be seen around the country. It sent a powerful, life-affirming message—that there was life outside of the recurring role on the six o'clock news of crime, pain, and poverty—there was simple, organic fun. They could express themselves and it didn't cost any money—they just needed a rhythm track.

Whenever James Brown came on the show, he would eat the boxed KFC fried chicken lunch with the dancers, and he knew many of them by name. There were some marriages consummated: Wallace "Scotty" Scott from the Whispers married a dancer; Mark Wood, a musician from the band Lakeside married dancer Sharon Hill. And there were many affairs: Marvin Gaye's line, "When I first saw you, looking good on the Soul Train Line" in his song "After the Dance" from his *I Want You* album, was infamously inspired by a real one-night stand with a Soul Train Dancer.

Soon offers for bigger gigs started coming in from everywhere. The spotlight and the celebrity fostered competition, and sometimes things would get ugly. Dancers would vie for on-camera close-up opportunities, sometimes pushing each other out of the way, to ham it up for the cameras. Pat Davis, easily a fan favorite for her creative dance moves, natural doe-eyed beauty, and unique 1940s-style outfits and Billie Holiday–style flowers and butterflies in her hair, was a target for jealousy. One day a dancer stole her butterfly and continued to poke her. Davis turned around and punched her, knocking both of them off of the bleachers—and commenced to kicking the other dancer's ass.

Cornelius's laid-back response when he heard about the brawl was, "So, who won the fight?"

Cornelius would make it down the Soul Train Line—where two lines of dancers would form and couples would come down the middle dancing. Cornelius would dance down the line only one time in the history of the show. The Soul Train Line was the highlight of the show and gave the dancers their chance to shine. Every week would become a tug-of-war with the dancers, who would argue about who would go down the line first. It was important, not just to spotlight their dance moves, but—because there were tapings done of two separate shows in one weekend—if you were first, second, or third on the line, you were guaranteed to make the cut and could potentially be on the line for the next four weeks. There was pushing and shoving and sometimes fights getting to be the first to go down the line. It was the opportunity for prime time.

Singer Mary Wells from the Supremes said she really wanted to join the Soul Train Line and Cornelius took her up on it.

"You don't have to dance with anybody—you gonna dance with me," he told Wells, reverting to an even deeper baritone.

Then, one of the dancers yelled out, "Dance with Don!"

"Dance with Don?" Wells asked. "Can I dance with you?" Wells turned to Cornelius.

"Oh, *yeeeeeeah*," he says with anticipation. "But not on television."

"It's a date," Wells said, laughing nervously.

"Yeah, sure you could dance with me. You think I could come down that Soul Train Line?" Don asks the Soul Train Gang.

"*Yeaaaaah*," they answer.

The first time he comes down the line with Wells, strutting like he was back at a Chicago basement party, Wells is smiling in her bright yellow dress as she keeps up with him, and the Soul Train Dancers scream in delight. The second time he comes down he gets a little more daring—to the thrill of the Soul Train Dancers, who rarely got to see that side of him. He tries a jump, landing in a James Brown split, but falls down on his knee and quickly gets off the line. It would be the first and last time he would ever come down the line. But not the last time he would let a pretty female artist lure him out of character.

Other dancers, like Damita Jo, got their opportunities to be onstage with the artists. Her first was with Joe Tex, as he groaned the sublimely salacious tune "I Gotcha." He pulled her up onstage—just her and Joe Tex, without a backup band. Damita Jo wore a baby doll minidress and she shook her shoulders and posed as he sang.

Don Cornelius didn't allow the dancers to mingle with the artists and didn't appreciate any production surprises. He was livid when he saw Damita onstage. He mouthed for her to get down off of the stage. Joe Tex kept singing and Damita didn't know what to do. Cornelius pointed at her and pointed off the stage. She kept dancing. When she came off the stage, Cornelius told her to never get onstage again, while right-hand man, Tom Kuhn, gave her a congratulatory pat on the back.

In the mid-'60s, Joe Tex and James Brown had been embroiled in a bitter feud—one that ended up in gunfire. Tex accused Brown of stealing his microphone kicking tricks. Then Brown covered Tex's single, "Baby You're Right." They released the single around the same time, but Brown had the bigger hit. Then Brown stole Tex's girlfriend, Bea Ford. Tex responded with the song "You Keep Her," then added insult to injury when opening for Brown at a concert—he came on stage with a raggedy cape with holes in it, fell to the floor and screamed, "Please, please, please—get me OUT OF THIS CAPE!" Later that night Brown found Tex at a nightclub, walked in with a shotgun, and started exchanging gunfire with someone across the room as Tex ducked out of the club. They eventually patched things up, but it was no wonder that the next time Damita Jo ended up on the *Soul Train* stage, it was with James Brown.

Brown asked during a break in taping, "Damita Jo, dance with me?" The song he told her would be a new song, entitled "Super Bad."

"Haven't heard of it," she said.

"No one has," he told her.

As the JB's began playing, the horns were humming and Brown gave Damita the look to come and join him. She jumped onstage and kicked one leg high in the air—letting it hang, before launching into a swiveling hip robot. She continued one-legged acrobatics, wearing a kimono, short shorts and knee-high boots, to an approving smile from the "the hardest-working man in show business." Dutch camera angles added to the party atmosphere. After that taping, Brown invited Damita Jo and several other dancers to go with him on tour down to Augusta, Georgia. Damita could only stay for two days of the tour because she was auditioning for the part of the girlfriend of Lawrence Hilton-Jacobs's character, Freddie "Boom Boom" Washington, on a new TV show *Welcome Back, Kotter*. While they were in Augusta, Brown mentioned to her that he would talk to Cornelius about the next show.

"Why?" she asked.

"I paid him to get the dancers to dance with me," Brown said.

"He didn't give us any money," Damita told him. "He's not our manager."

Brown picked up the phone to dial Cornelius. He thought Cornelius was going to pay the dancers directly. He was livid. Damita walked out of the room. After Brown argued with Cornelius, the dancers still went home empty-handed.

———

Soul Train tapings occurred once a month on a weekend, and as many as twelve acts would be booked in one weekend. They would begin at ten in the morning and sometimes would go well into the next morning—sometimes as late as two or three—in part because of the relaxed, familial atmosphere and partly because the staff was still green. Cornelius was often late to arrive on the set, and held up the process. Once Damita Jo's mother called the police because it was four in the morning and her daughter, still a teenager at seventeen, hadn't arrived home.

Soul Train was like a clubhouse for the dancers. They would sit on the bleachers between tapings, read fan mail, eat their KFC lunchboxes and drink their Shasta grape soda, talk, listen to music and dance, and flirt with each other. After the taping they would go to Maverick's, and then eat breakfast at a soul food restaurant on Crenshaw Boulevard.

Sharon Hill came to the show after meeting Pat Davis in a restroom at a skating rink and Davis took to her, promising to get her on the show. Davis found Tyrone Proctor practicing behind the bleachers when she brought Hill on the show, and partnered the two of them together. Proctor and Hill would become regulars on *Soul Train* and *Bandstand*. Some dancers made a living by forming together and touring with artists. Hill and Proctor, along with dancers Connie Blaquino, Pat Davis, Scoo B Doo, Gary Keys, and Don Campbell toured with the Whispers and were paid $600 apiece per week. Damita Jo put together a group called Something Special, featuring herself and dancers Eddie Champion, Scoo B Doo, Pat Davis, and Wanda Fuller, and they opened for singer Tom Jones. Neither of these two groups lasted for more than a few months, however, because as dancers were called for more lucrative billings the groups disbanded.

The protocol of not paying dancers was not unlike other dance shows, but many Soul Train Dancers would gripe about it later. After all, these dancers weren't just teen heartthrobs; they were adored and admired by fans and artists around the world. When people tuned in to the show, they didn't just tune in to see their favorite performers—they tuned in to see their favorite dancers come down the Soul Train Line.

Cornelius and some of the dancers recognized that in lieu of pay, dancers were afforded the opportunity to meet some of the most prolific talent in the music industry and ask them questions (many as innocuous as "What's your astrological sign?"). But many of these kids came from modest means. Don Campbellock's mother berated him daily about not getting paid for the hours he spent at tapings. Some of them didn't have homes to go to. Since more than one taping happened in a day, they had to bring two outfits—and getting new outfits was a challenge for many. Some of the dancers sewed their own outfits. Many of them used suspenders to make room for them to grow into their outfits.

As *Soul Train* grew and the dancers came to understand their appeal and talent, some of them demanded to be paid $50 per show. Don "Campbellock" Campbell was one of them.

Toni Basil told him more than once that *Soul Train* should be paying him for his talent. One day he took her with him to the show. Cornelius knew her from her television appearances and came over to talk with her. She told Cornelius that the show was getting popular because of Campbell and some of the other dancers.

The next time Campbell came down to dance on *Soul Train*, security personnel wouldn't let him in. That would be the last time he appeared on the show.

When Basil was offered an opportunity from Moffitt Lee to have Campbell appear on the 1973 Roberta Flack special, *The First Time Ever*, she asked Campbell to round up his friends from the clubs and from *Soul Train*. Moffitt Lee insisted on a mixed group, so Basil came onboard, along with suggestions from Campbell. The group included Toni Basil, Fawn Quinones, Leo

"Fluky Luke" Williams, Don "Campbellock" Campbell, Fred "Mr. Penguin" Berry, Greg "Campbellock Jr." Pope, Adolfo "Shabba-Doo" Quinones, and Bill "Slim the Robot" Williams.

They dressed flamboyantly—almost like clowns with tied-up bolero-style shirts, elephant leg bell-bottoms, striped socks, and Scooby Doo platform shoes that were synthetic Ultrasuede, with a tan toe and an instep that was colored green. They wore kneepads eventually, but at first they were taking blows landing on their knees. After they got such a strongly positive response, Basil came up with the idea of forming an official group—the Campbellock Lockers (they eventually whittled the name down to just the Lockers). The members were Greg Campbellock Jr., Bill "Slim the Robot" Williams, Leo "Fluky Luke" Williamson, Adolfo "Shabba Doo" Quinones, and Fred "Mr. Penguin" Berry. Fred Lawrence would become their agent for International Creative Management.

Their first gig was an NBC news spot filmed at the club Summit on the Hill, where their first assignment was to perform a four-minute number on *The Carol Burnett Show*.

That led to the *Tonight Show*, and then they became the first dance troupe to perform on the second episode of a new show out of New York called *Saturday Night Live*. They eventually toured with Frank Sinatra and Dean Martin. And they got top billing. The marquee read at the MGM Grand Hotel: "Dean Martin and The Lockers."

Shabba Doo—the young curly-Afro'ed version of a dancer who Basil hoped would garner an adoration similar to that inspired by a young Michael Jackson—would announce to the crowd, "Hi everyone, we're the Lockers, an improvisational style of dance troupe based upon the improvisational style of the individual!" They were in high demand—on Schlitz Malt Liquor commercials, and performing in the seminal music documentary *Wattstax*.

Other dancers that Campbell taught—Shabba Doo, Fluky Luke, Slim the Robot, Fred Berry, and Greg Campbellock Jr.— left *Soul Train* soon after he did.

Damita Jo began to tour with James Brown and eventually defected to *Bandstand* to choreograph for the show and for the

Don Cornelius worked as a news reporter, announcer, and occasional disc jockey at Chicago's premier black radio station, WVON. He met Dr. Martin Luther King and other leaders as a reporter during the civil rights movement. (Photo by 2001 Tribune Entertainment/Getty Images)

A Chicago dancer showing Don Cornelius a few moves on the local Chicago *Soul Train*. (Courtesy of Clint Ghent)

Left: Stax Records president Al Bell. (Courtesy of Tim Sampson, Stax Museum of American Soul Music)

Bottom: Ron DeBlasio, Richard Pryor, Al Bell, and Deanie Parker. Richard Pryor's landmark album *That Nigger's Crazy* was recorded live at the Soul Train nightclub in San Francisco. On the Stax/Partee label, Al Bell used grassroots marketing, pinning posters up in barber and beauty shops to get the album sold. It went No. 1 on the *Billboard* R&B/Soul album chart. (Courtesy of Tim Sampson, Stax Museum of American Soul Music)

Top: Chicago groups: the Chi-Lites and the Dells on the local Chicago show. (Courtesy of Marshall Thompson)

Right: The Mystics, featuring Terry Brown, Bob Banks, and Gerald Brown. Don Cornelius managed the group, which hailed from Cincinnati. Brown would eventually become a singer in the disco group Shalamar. (Courtesy of Gerald Brown)

Bottom: The Emotions. Sisters Sheila, Wanda, and Pamela Hutchinson began as gospel singers under the direction of their father, Joseph Hutchinson, who was good friends with Don Cornelius. (Courtesy of Tim Sampson, Stax Museum of American Soul Music)

Roebuck "Pops" Staples and his daughters Cleotha, Yvonne, and Mavis performing on the local Chicago *Soul Train*. Pops was good friends with Cornelius before he began the local version of the show. (Courtesy of Clint Ghent)

Tyrone Davis was a frequent performer on the local version of the show. (Courtesy of Clint Ghent)

The Stylistics appearing on the local Chicago *Soul Train*. The set was so small that performers on the local show shared the stage with the dancers. (Courtesy of Clint Ghent)

Ike and Tina Turner performing, circa 1972. (Tribune Entertainment/ Photofest)

Aretha Franklin and Don Cornelius on the December 1979 episode when Aretha was promoting her *La Diva* album. On this episode she sang a duet with Smokey Robinson, the first and last time they performed together. (Courtesy Everett Collection)

The Jackson Five were regularly featured on the national show. Cornelius knew them and their father, Joe Jackson, well from their performances locally in Chicago. (Tribune Entertainment/Photofest)

Top: The Lockers dance group formed on *Soul Train* featuring Don "Campbellock" Campbell, Toni Basil, Fred "Mr. Penguin" Berry, Greg "Campbellock Jr." Pope, Adolfo "Shabba Doo" Quinones, Bill "Slim the Robot" Williams, and Leo "Fluky Luke" Williamson. (Courtesy Everett Collection)

Above: Adolfo "Shabba Doo" Quinones and Fred "Mr. Penguin" Berry, members of the dance troupe the Lockers. (Courtesy of Shabba Doo)

Left: Al Green, Jesse Jackson, Rufus Thomas, and Don Cornelius. (Courtesy of Tim Sampson, Stax Museum of American Soul Music)

The Staple Singers with Flip Wilson. (Courtesy of Tim Sampson, Stax Museum of American Soul Music)

Barry and Glodean White. Cornelius hosted an episode at their two-and-a-half-acre estate. (Getty Images)

American Music Awards. Her first job was choreographing for Diana Ross in Las Vegas. She would later choreograph for Cher, Whitney Houston, and Mick Jagger. She danced with Shirley MacLaine and was the dance captain when she, along with dancers like Rudolf Nureyev, danced for the Queen of England. This was just the beginning of the Soul Train Dancers' impact on world culture—a major coup for ordinary kids who felt unwelcomed amid the glamor of Hollywood. Now everyone around the world could learn dances that had previously been relegated to rec centers, street corners, and basement parties. Suddenly the whole world was watching.

The Lockers continued to be in high demand. A friend of Shabba Doo's heard about a new television series that would be based in the Watts section of Los Angeles. He got called in for an audition to play the part of Cochise—a good-looking, suave ladies' man—for a new show that had been written and produced by Eric Monte. The characters were based on the cult classic *Cooley High*, also written by Monte and based on the Chicago high school of the same name. Fred "Penguin" Berry and a few of the other Lockers followed Shabba Doo to the audition to read for producer Bud Yorkin.

Shabba Doo read a few times and was close to getting the part. When Fred "Penguin" Berry auditioned, he gave a different interpretation of the role. After he finished, the producers gave the requisite "Okay, thank you." Instead of walking out, Penguin just sat there.

"Okay, that's good. Thank you."

"I'm not going anywhere."

"Oh, no, you have to."

Penguin locked his arms around the chair.

"You'll have to drag me out of here," he told them.

They fell out laughing, and promptly switched the role from the suave ladies man to the funny fat guy who producers named Freddy "Rerun" Stubbs.

Berry remained with the Lockers, but as the role took off, eventually he had to quit and focus on his role on the new ABC show they would title *What's Happening!!* The Lockers would have a cameo on the show on the first season, appearing as a group called the Rockets.

Cornelius had to swallow his pride in September of 1976 when he hired the Lockers to come back to perform on *Soul Train*. Announcing them to the television audience, he said, "They were among the best to ever dance on the show, [and] we're extremely proud that they have now created one of the most exciting acts in show business—and they've done it all on their own. Let's have a great welcome, gang, for the Lockers!"

The Lockers came on locking, doing high jumps and landing on their knees, back-handsprings and no-hand flips, splits, and acrobatic leaps over each other, one-legged spins, roboting, and locking in sync in a nearly six-minute nonstop performance.

Cornelius gave a warm individual introduction for each of them. He mentioned to Campbell on the air that the group had come back to rub it in Pam Brown's face, therefore putting the onus on *her* for kicking them off the show.

Because of the union AFTRA (American Federation of Television and Radio Artists), the Lockers weren't allowed to perform on *Soul Train* without payment. This time, they not only got paid $500 per person but also had their own dressing rooms. This victory was bittersweet. A year later the group would break up: Fred Berry would pursue his television career full-time. Basil would come out with the bubblegum pop hit "Hey Mickey" and quit the group for a music career. When Basil left, the group voted for Shabba Doo to be the leader against Campbell's wishes. They eventually all went their separate ways.

But not before they had their chance to be on *Soul Train*. Campbellock, watching the show from home a few weeks after the taping, felt tears filling his eyes. He was a star performer. To him, it was a revelation.

4

BLUE-EYED, BROWN-EYED, AND GREEN-EYED SOUL

When did we overcome? And how come nobody told me?!
—Marla Gibbs as Florence Johnston, George
and Louise's maid on *The Jeffersons*

By the early '70s, Don Cornelius had become a household name. He was romancing the blaxploitation era's premier sex symbol and much-sought-after beauty, Pam Grier. He had become well known and wealthy enough that he had become a target when he went out on the town.

One night in New York City, he made a stop at the Leviticus Discotheque in Midtown Manhattan to check out the various versions of the East Coast Hustle. That night three men decided to rob the club and stole $7,000 in cash from Cornelius and the patrons, before making a quick escape.

Cornelius had parties regularly at his house on Mulholland Drive, with beautiful models, dancers, blow, and blow jobs. After Cornelius and Grier split, he dated an assortment of blondes, while Chuck Johnson, the dance coordinator for *Soul Train*, was often given the assignment of taking Cornelius's main woman, Vicky Avila, out on the town to the discos.

Years before in Chicago, Cornelius told Bobby Womack, his cousin by marriage, that he was going to make it to Los Angeles to pick up all of the white women on the Sunset Strip. He took every opportunity to flirt with female guests on the show. When

Lola Falana came on as a guest to promote her acting appearance in the movie *The Klansman*, starring Richard Burton and O. J. Simpson, Cornelius talked with her briefly about the movie and mentioned that her husband, Feliciano "Butch" Tavares, from the funk group, Tavares, had recently been on the show promoting the group's *Check It Out* album.

"They have the most exciting record in town.... One of the members of the group happens to be Lola's husband," Cornelius told the *Soul Train* Gang. "It's a great group and we'll be looking for some big things from them."

"I think you're gonna get it," Lola answers.

"I'd sure like to," Cornelius says as Lola's face drops and he smoothly segues into, "We're gonna dedicate this next one to Lola—Kool and the Gang's 'I Can't Get Enough of That Funky Stuff.'"

It was a new day, and it seemed suddenly that a black host could be a millionaire, have a successful show that critics saluted, *and* be the king of his castle.

Black hosts like Bob Howard had paved the way for Cornelius. Howard—a pianist, comedian, and an actor on Broadway, radio, and television—hosted his own show when television was still in its infancy in 1948. *The Bob Howard Show* lasted thirteen months. Two years later, the DuMont Network gave classically trained pianist and singer Hazel Scott a chance as a hostess of the *Hazel Scott Show* before she was labeled as a Communist sympathizer and listed in *Red Channels: The Report of Communist Influence in Radio and Television*. Though she fought against the labeling in hearings, four months later her show was cancelled. *The Nat King Cole Show* lasted longer, but went off the air after sixty-four weeks as Cole publicly criticized advertising agencies on Madison Avenue for failing to secure sponsors.

By the mid-'70s blacks began appearing in starring roles on prime-time television, too. Network sitcoms had lead characters that represented a well-mannered, idealized, free, and integrated America—characters like Diahann Carroll in *Julia*, Bill Cosby in *I Spy*, and Denise Nicholas and Lloyd Hanes in *Room 222*. Three shows that would resonate with working-class audiences and follow in the footsteps of *Soul Train* by presenting the lifestyle of the everyman were two Norman Lear productions, both written by one of the few black sitcom writers at the time, Eric Monte. The shows, *What's Happening!!* (based on the coming-of-age film *Cooley High*, which Monte also wrote, starring Broadway actress Mabel King) and *Good Times* (about a tightly knit family growing up in the projects in Chicago, starring Esther Rolle and John Amos) would showcase a grittier version of urban life that hadn't been seen on network television previously.

Though it seemed as if there had been a new explosion of color on television, by 1974 only three out of twenty-one hours of prime-time television showcased black or minority shows, and Southern affiliates were still reticent about securing sponsors for these black hosts. The lack of representation behind the camera told an even less optimistic story.

Cornelius balanced the tightrope of maintaining friendships with the power brokers in Hollywood while openly criticizing them. "There is no such thing as visual control," he told *Billboard* that same year, "Control lies with people behind the scenes, the decision makers, and that's the arena where the industry is totally negligent and blatantly discriminatory. The minute number of blacks—and other minorities—represented as writers, directors, and producers is appalling. And when one considers there is not one prime-time show on any of the networks that is produced by a black man or woman, one is further reminded of the existing discriminatory practices that prevail in this country."

Cornelius was adamant about having blacks behind the scenes on his show and having women of color in positions of power. Aida Chapman, a Puerto Rican woman from Harlem, was a producer on the show and his right-hand woman. Pam Brown, a black woman, was the dance coordinator on the show.

Despite Cornelius's critiques of the industry, as a syndicated show charting its own course, *Soul Train* was on its way to unprecedented success. The first season ended in April of 1972 in syndication at Metromedia studios with a bang and a crowd-shaking performance by Ike and Tina Turner. The train was rolling fast and everybody was welcome aboard.

That same year, *Soul Train* featured its first white artist, Dennis Coffey and the Detroit Band. Guitarist Dennis Coffey had made his mark at Motown, introducing the wah-wah guitar on Temptation recordings such as "Cloud Nine," "Ball of Confusion," and "Psychedelic Shack," and had scored the blaxploitation film *Black Belt Jones*. When he signed to Clarence Avant's Sussex Records, he scored his biggest single, the million-selling instrumental "Scorpio," which peaked at No. 6 on the *Billboard* charts.

Coffey had met Cornelius when Coffey played McCormick Place on Lake Shore Drive in Chicago. When Coffey and his second wife were planning their move to Los Angeles, he bumped into Cornelius at the Hyatt Regency Hotel. After they finished talking, Cornelius surprised Coffey when he sent over a bottle of champagne to celebrate. When "Scorpio" took off, Cornelius called Avant and had Coffey booked for *Soul Train*. He would be the first white artist to perform on the show (on January 8, 1972) and one of the first to perform live, ad-libbing, extending, improvising—which created havoc with the production schedule. After that performance, Cornelius insisted on artists' lip-syncing or singing as closely as possible to how the songs sounded on the album.

When the dancers and would-be dancers found out that Coffey was going to be at the next Saturday taping, hundreds of new teenagers lined up to get a chance to see the show. The stage dance floor was packed.

Coffey was the first, but wouldn't be the last white artist to board the train. Before radio segregation, black teens and white teens were able to enjoy the same hits on radio stations. The Rolling Stones and Bill Withers could play back-to-back on a station. When Canadian-born Gino Vanelli scored a hit with the 1974 tune "People Gotta Move," charting at No. 22 on the *Billboard* Hot 100, he was invited by Cornelius to board the train. This was Vanelli's first television appearance. Impressed with his popularity and ease with the black community, Cornelius told him that he didn't really see him as white, but more like "off-white," he joked. After Vanelli's performance, he garnered a larger black audience and went on tour as the opener for Stevie Wonder.

Soul Train hadn't just become integrated; now show producers no longer had to court talent—increasingly, bigger-name artists were coming to them. It was a cultural phenomenon. They were selling *soul*.

━━

A twenty-something Isaac Hayes was hanging around the Stax Records label daily on E. McLemore Avenue in the heart of black Memphis. He was so poor that he would go hungry for days before he would call Stax Vice President Al Bell to see if he could help him get some food. Bell would soon find out that Hayes was actually a visionary musician who could seemingly effortlessly compose innovative orchestral arrangements in his head, and Bell invited him to write music, and eventually perform and record for the label. Ironically, after his first album, *Presenting Isaac Hayes*, made little noise, it would be a bad business decision that would render Hayes a superstar.

Jim Stewart, the owner of Stax and working-class and honest to the bone, had made a handshake deal with producer Jerry Wexler at Atlantic Records, and had missed the fine print in the contract they eventually signed. Atlantic Records who acted as Stax's distributor would own the masters to all of Stax's artists—including top-selling artists like Sam and Dave and Otis Redding. In 1968 Stax took a major blow—losing its most popular artist, Otis Redding, and members of his band the Bar-Kays in a plane crash, and its entire catalog of artists to a fine-print technicality to Atlantic Records. Stax discontinued its relationship with Atlantic and, having lost all its masters, had to start from scratch.

Bell came up with the idea of flooding the market with new Stax records to reboot its catalog with twenty-eight albums from all of their hottest stars like Isaac Hayes, Johnnie Taylor, and the Staple Singers. He hired Dale Warren and John Allen—arrangers from Motown—and got in the studio with them. At the time, Hayes was wooing women in the nightclubs with a soul version of Glen Campbell's "By the Time I Get to Phoenix," and Bell saw Hayes as the perfect combination of pimp, preacher, and musician. Bell told Allen and Warren that he wanted to use the Detroit Philharmonic on four songs he and Hayes had come up with, including an outrageously titled track, "Hyperbolicsyllabic-sesquedalymistic"—an homage to people who overuse and abuse long, difficult words. Other songs included a nearly nineteen-minute version of "By the Time I Get to Phoenix" with an intro-ductory rap, and a twelve-minute version of Burt Bacharach and Hal David's "Walk On By." It was an artistic mountain that no one expected would have market appeal. The album, *Hot Buttered Soul*, with only four songs, unusual titles, and radical arrangements ended up becoming an overnight sensation. People were robbing record stores to get copies. It sold over a million albums and charted on the jazz, pop, R&B, and easy listening charts in 1969, proving that black albums, as opposed to singles, were marketable. It opened up album cover concepts. It started long raps and spoken word parts and brought horns and strings and classical influences to mix with the funky rhythms. A band-wagon of artists—Marvin Gaye, Parliament-Funkadelic, Curtis Mayfield, Stevie Wonder—were now emboldened to take risks lyrically, delve into concept albums, and experiment musically after the success of Hayes's album.

Hayes piggybacked on his success with *Hot Buttered Soul* by scoring the blaxploitation movie *Shaft*, in 1971. He would win a Grammy Award and an Academy Award for the album. But when he appeared on *Soul Train* in 1973, it was only to be interviewed by Don about the role as Mac "Truck" Turner in the blaxploitaton film *Truck Turner*, starring Hayes and Yaphet Kotto.

Isaac Hayes wasn't performing at the time that he came on for the first time in 1973 (he appeared later on two other episodes). Cornelius introduced him as "Black Moses," a nickname he re-ceived from one of the bodyguards, Dino Woodward, at the Stax label. Hayes released the double album, entitled *Black Moses*, in 1971. It was a follow-up to the soundtrack of *Shaft*, which received an Academy Award for Best Original Song, and Hayes became the first black artist to win an Academy Award in a non-acting category. Hayes's focus was quickly moving into movies and acting.

After the success of Melvin Van Peeble's *Sweet Sweetback's Baadasssss Song* (the first blaxploitation film) in 1971 and its accompanying soundtrack, the floodgates opened for blacks to score films. Curtis Mayfield would score the movie *Super Fly* in 1972 and *Sparkle* in 1976, and Bobby Womack that same year would write the music for *Across 110th Street*. Still, most artists weren't completely happy about the content of the blaxploitation genre. On *Soul Train*, Mayfield had the chance to divulge his ambivalence. He told Cornelius on the show, "Some people think the ghetto is just one particular thing, which means everyone is using and dealing dope, which isn't so—it's really just a small segment of our area." Still, there was no denying the genre's popularity and its marketability. The black man as antihero began to dominate the blaxploitation genre and the sentiment of the times. By the early '70s, there were two prevailing sentiments: black people were free to take what they wanted by any means necessary, and everyone was free to express themselves as wildly and loudly as they pleased.

Black women were making waves with the genre—some, like Pam Grier, with leading roles and female antiheroes. Others, like Irena Cara and Lonette McKee, were able to act in an entire movie centered on the struggles of women in the ghetto and in show business. The Sam O'Steen–directed movie, *Sparkle*, was loosely based on the story of the Supremes. Lonette McKee's character, Sister, was the tragic mulatto—sassy, beautiful and talented, and undone by drugs, unrequited love, and an abusive man.

When McKee appeared on *Soul Train*, wearing a jeans pantsuit with tigers painted on each pant leg, she sang the single "Save It" from her album *Lonette*. A child prodigy, she had written and recorded her first single by the time she was fourteen years old, and written the title song for the film *Quadroon* a year later. But while the dancers moved enthusiastically to her music, most didn't know who she was. When Cornelius interviewed her, she told him she was "up for a movie now called *Sparkle* ... knock on wood." But even *Sparkle* wouldn't launch the career of her underappreciated talent—Irene Cara would become the breakout star from that movie.

The soundtrack for *Sparkle* was written and produced by Curtis Mayfield, recorded at Curtom Studios, and sung by Aretha Franklin. It became a Gold record and returned the Queen of Soul to the top of her Queendom on the heels of two underwhelming albums.

When Aretha came onboard *Soul Train* on April 14, 1973, Cornelius dedicated the entire show to her talents as she sang a medley of her hits including "Master of Eyes," "Oh Me Oh My," and performed live with ad-libs—"Rock Steady" and "Daydreaming." Cornelius announced to the *Soul Train* Gang, "It's the almighty Queen of Soul, with an invitation to all of us and to all of you to rock steady—the fabulous Aretha Franklin!" Aretha came onstage wearing a casual pantsuit and a proud Afro. Behind her was a silver-studded sign that read "ARETHA!" She performed live and the audience felt every *ooooooooh* and *oooooaaah* ad-lib she belted out, as her background singers danced behind her.

In another episode, she and Smokey Robinson, longtime childhood friends from Detroit, sat next to each other at the piano, talking about their youth and improvising as they sang.

Stevie Wonder reminisced about an old friend when he performed on a tribute episode for his friend Minnie Riperton, who died from cancer in 1979. Stevie talked about how she and her husband, Richard, sought him out when they were searching for a record deal. Stevie had already been a fan from her time in the acid, psychedelic soul group Rotary Connection, created by Leonard Chess's son, Marshall, and her first solo underappreciated album produced by Charles Stepney, *Come to My Garden*. Stevie had written the melody for "Perfect Angel" years before he met Minnie, but hadn't found anyone that he felt could express the essence of the song until he met her.

The tune that skyrocketed the album almost didn't happen. Stevie insisted that they include another song on the album, so it would meet the standard length requirement for the industry. Minnie suggested a song that she sung to her daughter Maya nightly. That song, "Loving You," which showcased her five-octave range, with the help of radio play, catapulted the album to Gold.

During Riperton's first appearance on *Soul Train*, her infant daughter Maya Rudolph can be heard in the background, and Minnie tells Cornelius that her daughter wants to sing.

About a month after her first appearance on the show, at the age of 31, Minnie would die from breast cancer. Cornelius decided to devote an entire episode in her honor. The tribute show featured Stevie Wonder playing the piano and singing songs from the *Perfect Angel* album.

Cornelius asked Stevie, who had become close friends with her, what he knew about her in her last days. "I felt more than I knew...for as long as she lived, she lived," Stevie answered.

=

By the mid-'70s musicians like Stevie Wonder, Herbie Hancock, Bob James, and Parliament were experimenting with new technology like the Fender Rhodes piano, Moog synthesizers, and equipment for overdubbing as classic soul and R&B sounds were becoming increasingly funkier. Records like James Brown's "Get Up (I Feel Like Being a) Sex Machine" and Sly and the Family Stone's "Thank You (Falettinme Be Mice Elf Agin)" and artists like Rufus featuring Chaka Khan, LaBelle (formerly Patti LaBelle and the Bluebelles), Edwin Starr's War, and self-contained bands like Earth, Wind and Fire, the Gap Band, Tower of Power, Parliament-Funkadelic, and Con Funk Shun were injecting a new kind of funk into soul music.

Funk had taken over the spirit of black community spaces. It was raw, African inspired, in a groove that was unapologetically black, rhythmic and danceable, with punctuating horns and extended vamps. When James Brown wiped the floor with his soles as he performed the dance the Mashed Potato, there was no questioning the choreographed pantomiming that helped launch the Temptations to stardom was fading fast.

On a 1974 episode of *Soul Train*, the camera closes in on a petite dancer—she's six-year-old Deanna Brown, the daughter of James Brown, and she's shaking her long hair from side to side, dressed in a white bell-bottom pantsuit outfit exactly like her father, doing the robot, moving with the funk to her father's single, "Hell," as he jams beside her on stage. This was the title track from Brown's more artistic, topical album of the same name, with a slow funk that was undeniable—a follow-up to the double album *The Payback*, his landmark funk album (an album that was rejected as a soundtrack for the blaxploitation film *Hell Up in Harlem*, ironically for not being "funky enough").

Cornelius knew the band Rufus and Chaka Khan from Chicago, and was good friends with their drummer, Andre Fischer, so he allowed the group to do three, rather than the requisite two, songs during their first appearance. Cornelius also became close with singer and guitarist Tony Maiden—they would often run into each other at Wolfgang Puck's restaurant Spago, in Beverly Hills.

On the band's first appearance, they brought the Tower of Power horn section with them and played "Dance Wit Me," "Tell Me Something Good," and "Have a Good Time." At the time, the group was still playing small clubs regularly, even when their first major hit, "Tell Me Something Good," came out. Their breakout hit, "Sweet Thing," was an afterthought and took fifteen minutes to write. Every time they had another single, they asked to be booked on *Soul Train*. Cornelius never denied them.

Tower of Power was initially reluctant to come on the show because they didn't want to lip-sync and they felt uneasy because the majority of the band was white. Lead vocalist Lenny Williams, who had been a child preacher with his roots in gospel music, convinced the group to go on.

At the time, they had a number one record, "So Very Hard to Go." They performed that and another popular song, "What Is Hip?". Williams, when getting something to eat in Oakland the next day, was getting stopped by everyone—all coming up to him and saying, "Oh, you're that dude that was on TV!"

When Rick James and the Stone City Band came on to publicize their first album, *Come Get It!*, which ended up selling over a million copies, James's outrageous personality was hard to contain. Cornelius said, "So, you're a funky guy."

"I am. And I appreciate all you fu--nkers going out there and buying my records," he answered.

As the show continued to branch out into different sounds, Cornelius booked acts like the jazz-funk fusion of Herbie Hancock and the Headhunters, Donald Byrd and the Blackbyrds, and the jazz and Afrobeat rhythms of Hugh Masekela. Then, Elton John's manager called. Aida Chapman, producer and executive-in-charge of production, answered the call. Elton would be in town doing the *Sonny and Cher Comedy Hour* and they wanted to know if *Soul Train* would be interested in having him. Chapman said yes without hesitation. The only request management had—and it was a big request—was that Elton needed a Lucite piano. Cornelius and Chapman told personnel to get him what he wanted, so they ended up renting one. While Cornelius may have been exploitative when it came to the talent of the dancers, he spared no cost when he knew he had to spend money. Elton, wearing a brown pinstriped suit and a black derby hat with a feather, sang "Bennie and the Jets," which had topped the pop and R&B charts, from his most popular 1973 double album, *Goodbye Yellow Brick Road*. This was his first single to land on the R&B charts and helped audiences to embrace him during his appearance on *Soul Train*. It was a song that was celebrated in the black community, but criticized by some white stations for sounding too black.

On the show, Elton talked about his beginnings backing Patti LaBelle and Major Lance on piano. Then he sang "Philadelphia Freedom"—a tribute to the Philadelphia International sound and to Billie Jean King, who played for the Philadelphia Freedoms tennis team. After his performance in May of 1975, Elton confided in Chapman that he was much happier with the way that he had been treated at *Soul Train* than on the *Sonny and Cher Comedy Hour*. A few months after Elton John appeared on *Soul Train*, David Bowie's manager called. At first, without consulting Cornelius, Chapman hesitated, concerned about how viewers would receive an openly bisexual artist. Bowie's manager flipped, screaming, "How dare you turn down David Bowie?!" Cornelius was livid when he heard what had happened, and

Chapman called back Bowie's manager and booked the star. The dancers were equally as enthralled with Bowie as they were when the first white artist, Dennis Coffey, came to the show as Bowie sang "Fame," a title given to him by John Lennon, which had climbed to No. 1 on the *Billboard* Hot 100. The track was from the album *Young Americans*, with a guitar riff created by Carlos Alomar, who would later play with Iggy Pop, Mick Jagger, and Paul McCartney. The entire album, and "Fame" in particular, was a tribute to Bowie's newfound obsession with soul music—lush strings and R&B rhythms of the Philadelphia Sound. *Young Americans* was primarily recorded at Sigma Sound Studios in Philadelphia.

More white artists followed, including KC & the Sunshine Band (whose drummer after the show said, "I can't wait to get the fuck out of here," disgusted, Chapman deduced, at being on a black show. Chapman told him flatly, "I can assure you if you are ever booked for the show again, you won't be coming with them."); the Average White Band; the Pet Shop Boys: Captain and Tennille; Village People; Duran Duran; Frankie Valli, who sang the title track from the soundtrack of the movie *Grease*: and Rick Dees, who performed in a leather suit and had a backing band that included Theresa Rhandle, Mikki Howard, and Khandi Alexander.

The Norwegian pop band, A-ha, selected three American shows to perform on: *Soul Train*, *Solid Gold*, and *American Bandstand*. Their album, *Hunting High and Low*, had peaked at No. 1 on the *Billboard* Hot 100 chart. In A-ha's performance on *Soul Train*, Gina Schock, the former drummer for the Go-Go's, was part of their lineup. The video for *Take on Me*, a sketch animation based in part on the '80s cult-classic movie *Altered States*, starring William Hurt (the ending of the video mimics the end of *Altered States*, in which Hurt pounds his fist against the walls), was in heavy rotation on MTV at the time, and the Norwegian group was impossible to ignore in the States.

Though over the years white acts helped to broaden *Soul Train's* appeal and gain the attention of record executives eager to expand their white artists' audiences, it was still the black pop mainstream acts like the teenage sensation and musical phenomenon, the Jackson Five, that initially catapulted the "train" to stardom. The group initially appeared on the show on October 7, 1972, and Cornelius rightfully introduced them as "the world's most popular group of entertainers."

The show featured the Jackson Five, with their perfect Afros and baby-face charm in their colorful handmade pantsuits. By then, the group had four chart toppers—"I Want You Back," "ABC," "The Love You Save," and "I'll Be There"—and had little girls crying all over the world at their concerts.

Michael Jackson was the lead singer and teenage heartthrob, but on *Soul Train* Jermaine Jackson, who had just delivered his first eponymous solo album, would be the spotlighted artist, beginning the show with his single "That's How Love Goes." The group performed on a stage prepared especially for them, with the name "Jermaine" hanging behind them in massive black-gold letters.

When in November of 1973 on their next performance on *Soul Train* the Jackson Five performed "Dancin' Machine," from the *Get It Together* album, the Soul Train Dancers went wild and the show became a raucous concert. The song had not yet been released as a single, but was a popular track on the album. During the bridge, Michael debuted the dance, a flawless version of "the mechanical man," his eyes fixed, magically gliding across the stage with bent elbows that moved stiffly and jerkily. He held the audience hostage, bewildering and dazzling with his dance steps, leaving television audiences with jaws dragging on the floor. The dance was popular among teens, but no one had performed it with this kind of grand perfection. When he glided onstage, he had *become* a mechanical man. After his performance, every black kid in America was doing the dance. Michael had learned the dance from watching Soul Train Dancers perform it on the show.

As the *Soul Train* Gang asked the Jackson Five questions, Tyrone "The Bone" Proctor gave Tito Jackson a birthday card signed by them. After the show, some of the most popular dancers from the show, like Patricia Davis, were invited to the Jackson

Five's dressing room. Many of the dancers became good friends with the family and would go to their house frequently, practice dance moves—teaching each other—and became part of the family—attending the wedding of Jermaine Jackson and Hazel Gordy, and participating in family functions.

By the early '70s, superstars like Stevie Wonder, Barry White, Al Green, Diana Ross as a special guest, James Brown, and Aretha Franklin (both Brown and Franklin were given the entire hour) had appeared on *Soul Train*, ensuring the show's long-term viability. Soul Train was fast gaining an international audience, the show was licensed in Puerto Rico, being copied in Japan and Europe, licensed by the BBC, and bootlegged all around the world.

Cornelius was getting flak for what some perceived as a kind of "reverse discrimination," because the majority of acts and dancers were black. But Cornelius both refuted it and accepted that it was true: "The door has always been open to white acts, but I concede that I have a special loyalty to black acts," he admitted. With the proliferation of talent that Cornelius had, he had to turn some of them down. "This was a real problem for us," he said. "The fact remains for black acts—their only chance for national television exposure is *Soul Train*," he said.

Even with his success against the odds and on his own terms, there was an internal struggle that Cornelius was navigating. The success of 1970s shows like Flip Wilson's variety show and Bill Cosby's *The Original Bill Cosby Show* was owed in part to the fact that they were apolitical. But with the success of shows like *Sanford and Son*, *Good Times*, and *What's Happening!!*, black actors and others who held some power in the industry were beginning to get bold. When *Sanford and Son*, starring comedian Redd Foxx, reached the top ten in ratings, Foxx demanded a higher salary. When John Amos, who starred as James Evans on *Good Times*, protested the increasing stereotypical nature of his television son—J. J. Evans—Lear responded by not renewing

Amos's contract in 1976. His costar Esther Rolle, who starred as Florida Evans, took a stand, telling directors to find someone else to take her role. Part of the appeal of the show for her was to show the struggle of a working-class black family, headed by a father, that managed to stay together despite overwhelming circumstances. By the summer of 1977, Esther Rolle left the series.

Cornelius was a race man, but he understood the tenuous nature of making demands in the old-boy network of Hollywood. In between entertaining audiences, he would slip in political messages through Afro-centric commercials: through the appearances of guests stars like Mayor Tom Bradley, a then seventeen-year-old Al Sharpton (who worked for National Youth Movement Incorporated), Wallace Terry (the author of *Bloods: An Oral History of Black Vietnam Veterans*): by giving a young Reverend Jesse Jackson a daily platform on the show in Chicago, which led to the growth of Operation PUSH: and by having artists like Curtis Mayfield talk about his distaste for the movie he scored, *Super Fly*, because the main character was a dope dealer. There were subtle cultural messages that were sent when Cornelius asked Vonetta McGee about her elaborate cornrows that took ten hours to create, or when he allowed Richard Pryor to host an entire episode.

These political flashes were interspersed with great music and electrifying dancing—a light-fare mix of entertainment and education for the masses that Cornelius was able to slip in without drawing the ire of a diverse viewership.

The fact that the episodes had great production also led to the success of the show—taping at Metromedia studios and getting a high-caliber staff had proved essential in ensuring syndicated sales. There were other rewards—because Cornelius was operating as an independent entity by syndicating, he was able to have free rein without anyone dictating who could not appear on the show.

Every week Cornelius would show up to the set, sometimes drunk after a long night and day of drinking, and he would sit in his chair chain-smoking, off in the corner and oversee the minutiae of production, insisting on perfection at every level.

When Cornelius first aimed for reaching markets, he turned his attention toward twenty-five markets, but the syndicating agency was able to premiere the show in only seven. Many of the stations that flat-out refused or claimed to have no open time slots, despite the money they would be receiving, had no other black-oriented entertainment shows running on their stations. Cornelius's friend, record executive Clarence Avant, tried to get all three networks (he referred to them as "prejudiced birds") to carry the show, but they refused.

Still within eight months of the train's departure, twenty-five syndicated stations were carrying the show. And the competition—shows like *American Bandstand*—were beginning to feel threatened.

American Bandstand, like *Soul Train*, was created with the intention of taking radio to television. The success of deejay Bob Horn's Philadelphia rock radio show, *Bandstand*, got him hired to the popular station WFIL in 1952, where he took the radio show to WFIL's television outlet. Dick Clark would act as a fill-in when Horn took vacations. But that would change when Horn was charged with sleeping with underage dancers and for not paying taxes. Then he was involved in two drunk-driving incidents. The charges concerning the underage dancers were dropped on a technicality, and he resolved the other cases. But his reputation was ruined and he left for Texas, never to return. With a pleasant, perpetually youthful personality, Clark crossed over a picket line of dancers protesting Horn's dismissal, and took over his helm permanently. Clark's disposition would set the standard for the show: clean-cut teens dressed conservatively, and guests were thrilled by Clark's hospitality. By 1967, ABC was so impressed with the show that they gave *Bandstand* a trial run.

Shindig!, a dance show that ended on ABC a year before *Bandstand* began, was not all fresh-faced teenage innocence. The go-go dancing girls spewed sexuality from the safety of their cages as they shimmied without restraint. The dancers weren't the only ones that were allowed uninhibited freedoms—the artists were allowed to play live, improvise, and stretch out as long as they desired. The show was a success, but one of the hosts, Jack Good, reportedly walked off because network affiliates weren't thrilled about the increased number of black acts he was booking. The network canceled the show soon after. *Hullabaloo*, on NBC—a decidedly less energetic copycat version of *Shindig!* with much more conservative dancers—ended seven months later, in August of 1966.

By the start of *Soul Train's* second season, the train was rolling so fast that Dick Clark was threatened as *American Bandstand* began slipping in the ratings. Clark had featured black acts on his show—but most of them were crossover superstars. Cornelius filled a void that Clark and many others in Hollywood were just beginning to realize existed.

Clark had been cautious with *Bandstand* and had been rewarded with success. He used an "if it's not broke, don't fix it" philosophy, until his ratings began to slip. By April of 1973, Clark had had enough. A brand-new show called *Soul Unlimited*—with a black host, black dancers, and black acts—showed up on Saturday afternoon in *Bandstand's* time slot.

"I don't dig black people not liking white people," Clark told *Rolling Stone* reporter Ben Fong-Torres. "I've been seeing too much of that for too long already." Clark was referring to the backlash from this brand-new show named *Soul Unlimited*—a virtual copycat of *Soul Train*.

"I'll be damned if I'm going to sit back and watch Clark come in and take this," Cornelius intoned. Cornelius, Clarence Avant, and activists like Reverend Jesse Jackson spearheaded a protest against the copycat show.

The show was a replica of *Soul Train*, down to the black host. Los Angeles radio disc jockey, Buster Jones, from station KGFJ, was the undeniably less-cool version of Cornelius. There were black dancers wearing the eclectic fashion of the day, and 90 percent of the artists that appeared on the show were black. Soul Train Dancers were excited about a new prospect and some of them would sneak off during lunchtime to dance on the new show. Clark was going for Cornelius's jugular.

Ironically, Cornelius borrowed many of the concepts for *Soul Train* directly from *Bandstand* (for example, the dance contest where dancers competed for a car, and the formatting of the show), so much so that the media often referred to *Soul Train* as a black *American Bandstand*. Cornelius even incorporated his company that housed the *Soul Train* brand as DC Productions—the same initials as Dick Clark's DC Productions.

Cornelius was striving to be as good as or better than *Bandstand*, so when a copycat version of his show appeared on Saturday afternoons, he was outraged. The ramifications were astronomical. *Soul Unlimited* was on a network, and there would be no competing with the kind of sponsorship that would court a network show or the dollars put in for promotion or recruiting talent. Artists on *Soul Train* received scale pay for appearing on the show, no matter what their status in the industry was. Even though *Soul Unlimited* was bland in comparison to *Soul Train's* funky style, it would only be a matter of time before Cornelius would no longer be able to court his big-name artists for such comparatively little pay.

The dig in the back to Cornelius was that *Soul Train* had originally been offered to ABC but had been turned down by the network. When asked about that fact by Fong-Torres, Clark insisted that it was *his* time period and if they wanted to put "a black *Bandstand* on, then I'll do it." As the protesting grew louder, Clark went as far as to add the host's name (Jones) to the credits as an executive producer, even though he operated as just a host. Clark told the reporter, "Don't get into this shit," insisting that no title was important: "It's like tits on a bull," he said. Cornelius laughed at what he perceived was Clark's assumption of his naivety. "I know credits mean everything!"

Many of the stations carrying *Soul Train* were ABC affiliates, and *Soul Train* was consistently out-rating *Bandstand*. By this time *Soul Train's* sponsorship had ballooned to seventy markets, with four million viewers. The first showing of *Soul Unlimited* on March 10, 1973, received twice the ratings as *Bandstand* and cut into *Soul Train's* market, Jackson said.

Jesse Jackson, in *Billboard* magazine, expressed these thoughts to ABC Vice President Martin Pompadur: "*Soul Train's* success has partially been at the expense of Dick Clark's

American Bandstand. Many of the stations carrying *Soul Train* are ABC affiliated...Clark launched a campaign to recruit Soul Train Dancers for *American Bandstand,* selling them on the fact that *Bandstand* was a network show...Clark then began aiming the cameras at the black dancers, whose fashions and steps have been a key factor in *Soul Train's* cult-like success with both blacks and whites."

Then Avant sent a letter reminding ABC that he had pitched the network *Soul Train* many months before and it had turned the show down. Judy Price, a producer for *Soul Unlimited,* felt that Avant's and Jackson's letters were "unfortunate and inhuman," and that *Soul Train* as an all-black show equaled segregation.

But Clark agreed to a meeting with Cornelius and Jackson at the PUSH offices in Chicago. Clark told Fong-Torres, "Don avoided me for three weeks; he was so—in his guts—so riled up, so put upon, the ghetto paranoia put him into this thing about racism."

The agreement was that Clark would ask ABC to drop *Soul Unlimited* and, in return, he and Cornelius would coproduce some black specials for the network. Cornelius told Clark he had no objections to working with him, but that it would look "kinda silly," adding, "I admire him and always have and would love to work with him. But considering what has happened, I don't know. It is a possibility in the future."

By June of 1973, *Soul Unlimited* was cancelled and *Soul Train* roared with increased vigor. It seemed like the struggle was finally over. Or at least it appeared that way for the people watching from the comforts of their homes.

———

By 1974, life was good. Record executives were vying for Cornelius's ear. *Billboard* magazine devoted twenty-five pages for a special spotlight on the show, with personal ads taken out from record labels—from the majors to the mom-and-pop independents—with loving quotes from many of the tastemakers in the industry. In just three years, *Soul Train* and Don Cornelius Productions had become a million dollar industry.

That same year the show changed the theme song to "TSOP (The Sound of Philadelphia)," composed by Gamble and Huff and performed by the studio group MFSB, featuring vocals by the Three Degrees. Gamble and Huff originally wanted to call the song "The Soul Train Theme," but Cornelius, by now extremely protective of the brand, refused. He would regret it when the song became a pop and R&B hit.

The set was revamped, featuring a flashing neon Soul Train sign, neon train tracks, and a newly designed tunnel that dancers shimmied through. *Soul Train* staples—the *Soul Train* Line segment (where couples showed off their moves exclusively for the camera as they moved down two lines of people) and the Soul Train Scramble Board (where dancers have to correctly unscramble the name of a person in black history in less than sixty seconds)—were implemented. The Scramble Board was fixed—the contestants knew the answers ahead of time—because Cornelius was always looking to project black people in a positive light, and he didn't want anyone struggling to spell someone's name. But there were mistakes. In the 1974 episode with Sly and the Family Stone, the clock ran to zero because the dancers were having a hard time spelling the name of the group, Graham Central Station. They spelled "Central" like "S-C-E-N-T." On another episode, producers made the mistake: the answer to the puzzle was "The Kool and the Gang" rather than just "Kool and the Gang." Dancers fell off stages, partners sometimes dropped each other as they attempted acrobatic moves, records skipped, and Cornelius sometimes flubbed his cue cards. But for the majority of the time, with Cornelius's insistence on perfection, the shows went off weekly without hitches. Failure was not an option for him at this point; he knew after Clark's show that there were competitors waiting to move in on him. Audiences were treated to top-notch productions and seamlessly radio-styled shows.

Cornelius hired a new animator, John Koelle, who designed a sophisticated and intricately detailed train that danced with new energy and swung around in midair, nearly blasting through the television screen as it moved along to the music. Tomas E. Kuhn, brought by Cornelius from Chicago to Los Angeles, was promoted to Executive in Charge of Production for the show.

Soul Train was epitomizing the dawning of a new era—black America was free, stylish, and hip—something to be emulated rather than laughed at like the characters on *Amos 'n' Andy*. Within a few years the focus on nonviolent integration had shifted to a new economic and cultural empowerment. The cry for black power had multiple meanings—economic self-sufficiency, a new beauty paradigm, a new cultural freedom and focus on individuality. Because Cornelius owned the show, he was able to present these new images on his own terms.

Top artists were coming faster than Cornelius could book them. He continued to book budding activists and politicians like Reverend Al Sharpton and Jesse Jackson, actors like Fred Williamson, Vonetta McGee and Pam Grier, basketball heroes like Elgin Baylor and Magic Johnson, and comedians as diverse as Richard Pryor, Dick Gregory, Marsha Warfield, and Cheech and Chong. Chuck Berry, James Brown, Jackie Wilson, the Jackson Five, the Supremes, Curtis Mayfield, Stevie Wonder, Barry White and his forty-piece Love Unlimited Orchestra (performing live), the O'Jays, and the Temptations had all made appearances—many of them frequent appearances.

Of all the artists Cornelius met and befriended, it would be Barry White who would become his tightest running buddy. It was easy to see how the two would connect—they both projected a no-nonsense alpha male sensibility with deep baritone voices and a street edge. Cornelius became so close to the family that White's kids referred to him as "Uncle Don." White was one of the first artists to insist that he couldn't lip-sync. It was a costly venture to have White and the Love Unlimited Orchestra perform live, but Cornelius would do anything for him.

The two of them became so close that Cornelius did a special show devoted to White's family at White's two-and-a-half-acre home. There, Cornelius spent an hour-long episode talking with him, spending time with his wife and his children (who were toddlers), and performing. In one segment, White performed the track "Ecstasy" poolside under dim lights, with a waterfall in the background, while Love Unlimited sat under an umbrella singing backup.

But only one artist, Al Green, would transport audiences to the black church. On April 6, 1974, Green gave one of the most electrifying performances *Soul Train* viewers would ever witness.

Green arrived on the set with his arm in a mud-colored sling around his neck—he had broken a bone in his hand at a show in Milwaukee, Wisconsin. Standing on the *Soul Train* stage, lights flickering on and off on the Soul Train sign, he began the song "Jesus Is Waiting," with the Lord's Prayer. The Soul Train Dancers gathered around him on the darkened set, some immobile, some swaying like a congregation. "Our Father, which art in heaven, hallowed be thy name," he started with answers of "YES!" from the crowd. "Give us this day, our daily bread, forgive us debts as we forgive our debtors, deliver us from evil." "Aaameeen!" they answered. "That's why we are a living witness today, to say that Jesus is...Waiting, well, well, well," as he launched into the song, singing live. For seven minutes *Soul Train* was transformed into a storefront church, with waves of "Amen!" and "That's alright!" heads bobbing, swaying, and catching the spirit.

Later, Green caught the spirit again, during the bridge of "Here I am (Come and Take Me)," holding a rose with his good hand and two-stepping across the stage. The organist regaled the audience, before Green lifted his hand to silence the band. This was as undiluted a black religious expression as national television had ever seen. This would be his last performance on *Soul Train*. Six months later, on October 18, Al Green would have a spiritual awakening of the worst kind.

On that October day Green brought home his girlfriend Mary Woodson and a houseguest, Beth Williams. It was on this night that Woodson would bring up the topic of marriage. Green, enjoying his bachelorhood and the bounty of women that came with his success in the music industry, refused to commit. Distraught, Woodson put on a pot of Cream of Wheat and as Green was about to take a bath, appeared in the doorway and threw the hot cereal mixture on him. He suffered second-degree burns on his arms, chest, and back. A few minutes later Williams and Green heard a loud *boom*. Tragically, Woodson had taken Green's .38 caliber pistol and shot herself in the head. A suicide letter in her purse read: "All I wanted to do was be with you and love you until I die. I love you, Al. I'm not mad, just unhappy because I can't be with you."

After her suicide, he learned that she was already married, with four children. A few months before her suicide, she had predicted that Green would give up singing about women and sing about the Lord and that one day he would lead his own church. He didn't believe her, but joked that he would only if she would come with him. She replied: "I can't do that. But just promise me one thing—that you'll save me a seat in the front pew." A few years later, he did just that, reserving an empty space in the front pew for the spirit of Woodson in his own church, Full Gospel Tabernacle, after becoming an ordained pastor in 1976. Rumors abounded that it was Green that had shot her. The police ruled it as a suicide.

When Marvin Gaye appeared on February 16, 1974, he also invoked the spirits and African ancestry. Gaye represented so much of what was on the minds of young people like the dancers that surrounded him. He was consumed with the social issues of the day—police brutality, the Vietnam War—and was emboldened as an artist who could produce topical works like the *What's Going On* album, his very commercially successful album and his most risky work artistically. Despite his success, he was still struggling, personally: his marriage was crumbling, his best friend had died, and his finances were in disarray. He continued to struggle professionally as he quickly outgrew Motown and grew increasingly stifled. This was his first television appearance after his four-year hiatus from touring after his best friend and singing partner, Tammi Terrell, died from a brain tumor that reoccurred after eight surgeries. She had first been diagnosed with a malignant tumor on the right side of her brain after she had collapsed in his arms three years before onstage at a concert in Virginia. Gaye felt that she had died for everyone who couldn't find love. He had deep, entrenched bags underneath his eyes and a skullcap in his vanity to cover a growing bald spot.

Gaye was supposed to be touring for the *Let's Get It On* album, but had promised himself not to tour after Terrell's death. Motown and his fans pressured him and he agreed to do his first tour within the four years following her death, starting at the Oakland-Alameda County Coliseum in January of 1974.

His next stop was a taping for *Soul Train*, scheduled to air in February. Dressed in a green shirt, and cable-knit plaid pants, Gaye looked melancholy as he told Cornelius, "I'm surprised I'm out performing again. I'm in a good frame of mind and I think I want to perform this year. I want to let the people see me—I think I'm ready to perform now."

"I was extremely apprehensive," he admitted to Cornelius. "I enjoyed doing the two numbers previously. I didn't lip-sync the songs too well, but I really enjoy the kids here," he said as he stood surrounded by Soul Train Gang members.

Cornelius laughed, slightly embarrassed, asking Gaye, "You had to say that, didn't you?" This was the first time an artist had admitted to the television audience that they had lip-synced on the show.

One dancer asked Gaye about his hobbies: "I am pretty sensual," he stuttered, "I enjoy people, I enjoy fooling around."

Regular dancer Fawn Quinones asked him, "How come you were away from the stage so long?"

"I had an unfortunate incident. Some of you all are old enough [to remember]," he said, struggling to get the words out. "Tammi and I recorded together years ago. When we lost her, it affected me psychologically and I didn't really care to record." Soul Train Dancers laid hands on him as he performed songs from the album *Let's Get It On*.

While some of the artists, like Marvin Gaye, looked at *Soul Train* as an exercise in coming home, many artists looked at it as an opportunity to teach young people who looked up to them, and to educate television audiences in a way that they weren't able to on shows that catered to a more mainstream audience.

When Lil' Joe, a regular dancer, asked Bill Withers if he would ever consider scoring a movie, Withers's answer reflected his ambivalence about the blaxploitation era. "I have been offered some movies to score. When I was young most of the images I got was what I held on to. I don't want to make any images of any hustlers or dope," Withers said. With his working-class roots installing toilets on airplanes for three dollars an hour, he was relatable, and he spoke to the dancers in a fatherly tone. "I'm kind of waiting on a movie—I'd like to see two folks in love with each other."

In a previous *Soul Train* episode with Withers in 1971, one high school dancer, a pretty petite teenager, asked him, "The songs that you play—do they play to any of your past experiences?" That pretty teenager would become the musical powerhouse, Patrice Rushen. Before she was known as Baby Fingers for her piano-playing prowess, she was strutting down the Soul Train Line as a dancer and would later become a part of the jazz-fusion movement that Roy Ayers helped spearhead.

"Some of them do," Withers answered her. "I have one about suicide, but I never shot myself," he joked. "But I try to use things that have happened to me or to someone close by."

Another dancer asked him, "What inspired you to write "Ain't No Sunshine?"

"I met some students from Thailand that were very humble men, very masculine, but they didn't have that American male ego," Withers answered. "I used an Orient sound on top and stuck our music underneath: the blues. I decided to forego my American male ego and admit to a situation of losing—rather than do what American males do and say, 'I'm glad the broad split!'"

When James Brown introduced a young, up-and-coming preacher and activist named Al Sharpton to Don Cornelius, that impressionable nineteen-year-old Sharpton, who looked up to Brown as a father figure, would never forget what Brown said as he introduced him: "The thing you got to understand about

Mr. Cornelius," Brown said in a reverential tone, "is most blacks are in show—he's in *show business*."

Cornelius had given Brown a full hour to perform. "The James Brown story is far deeper than we can ever go into in this one-hour, but we intend to go deeper than anyone else has ever gone before on television," Cornelius intoned.

Just two years before, in October of 1972, Brown had been booed at a show in Baltimore where only 2,500 people showed up at an arena that held 13,000 seats. Five hundred people outside the venue became rowdy and smashed windows. Fifteen people were arrested. People thought of Brown as a political sellout because of his affiliation with the Republican Party.

During the *Soul Train* question and answer session, a dancer, Lamont Peterson, asked Brown, "You, among black people, have voted for President Nixon. What advantages would you say he could offer towards black people?"

"I'm really glad you asked me that, because I really wanted to get into it all day," Brown answered. "For so long we've been told we gotta be one thing, but we gotta be a part of the whole system in order to get the best out of it. If a cat can get in, then he can do a lot of things for us. The country cannot survive unless everybody is making it."

Before Cornelius introduced Sharpton, he asked Brown's opinion on violence occurring in black communities. "All of the things people died for and the marches and the revolution are in vain if we are going to kill each other," Brown answered. In another segment Brown talked about his program to get the curriculum in black colleges up to par so that they could compete with universities around the world.

"We have a young brother in our studio who is outstanding because of his youth and how much he has accomplished," Cornelius says, looking into the audience. "And he's here to make a presentation to James Brown. We want to welcome him warmly. His name is Al Sharpton, the national director of the National Youth Movement Incorporated."

Sharpton comes out to the stage dressed in a white suit, his hair parted on the side, in salute to James Brown's hairdo, and presents the man he would adopt as a father figure with an award. Sharpton had been close friends with Brown's son, Teddy, who died in a car accident, and after Teddy's death Brown promised to support Sharpton's youth movement by giving him money from his concerts and showing Sharpton how to earn his own money for it. About a month later, Brown offered to take Sharpton to *Soul Train*. For a nineteen-year-old who was making a name for himself around New York, this was the venue that would catapult him to the national audience he needed.

At first Cornelius resisted giving out an award on the show. He told Brown, "You know I don't do awards on the show."

"You gonna do it on this show," Brown told him.

Brown and Cornelius argued with each other like an old married couple, but there was mutual respect and admiration. Cornelius knew he would do anything Brown asked, and he was familiar with Sharpton's work with Operation Breadbasket in New York.

"We know that in the recording industry they give a Gold record for those that achieve a million seller," Sharpton said with a preacher's voice, as he showed the plaque to Brown on the show. "But we view your million seller, 'Payback,' as a black record. It says many things that young blacks have tried to say and could not. We feel like 'Payback' is the theme song of young black America in 1974."

Nixon was in office and social and youth programs were getting cut, left and right. The country had entered the Vietnam War and Sharpton thought that "Payback" captured the spirit of the time—that if the country was taking everything away, then you gotta be ready for the big payback. By the next year, the payback wouldn't come in the form of riots or even political rhetoric. It would come in the form of cold, green cash.

5

JUST BECAUSE I'M AN OLD CAT DON'T MEAN I'LL GET SCRATCHED BY A KITTEN

The music business is a cruel and shallow money trench, a long plastic hallway where thieves and pimps run free, and good men die like dogs. There's also a negative side.
—Hunter S. Thompson

Soul Train Records wasn't even a twinkle in the future record mogul Richard Gilbert "Dick" Griffey's eye as he pushed against the glass sliding door, standing as he put his thick finger toward the handle of one of a bank of phone booths at the gas station near the intersection of La Brea and Coliseum Streets. He thumbed the receiver as he confidently finished a pitch to a record executive.

"Okay, call me at the office," he insisted, hanging up, his eyes darting over just a few inches to confirm the number of the phone in the booth next to him. He sat on top of his briefcase and waited by the bank of phones he had relegated for incoming calls. On any given day, his forceful, rumbling baritone induced the unlikely trifecta of fear, respect, and love. His imposing six foot two barrel-backed frame sparked intimidation. Today was one of those days.

The crunch of aimless footsteps and eager catcalls surged around him as he waited for the phone in the booth next to him to ring. The area surrounding him had been nicknamed "The Jungle," originally named by people in the area because of its lush foliage—banana trees and begonias that thrived among postwar apartment buildings. The name didn't change but the meaning did, when the 1980s crack era brought in a bloody gang-warfare menace. Griffey couldn't afford a telephone in his apartment, so daily he ambled into this makeshift office. It's here that his business, booking top acts for the nightclub Guys and Dolls, began to take root.

He opened Guys and Dolls, located at 3617 S. Crenshaw Boulevard, in partnership with his buddy and schoolmate from Tennessee State, Dick Barnett, who had moved to Los Angeles to play basketball for the Los Angeles Lakers. Originally a billiard parlor, the club would be referred to as Dick Barnett's Guys and Dolls, with the slogan, "The Haven for the Greatest Athletes and Celebrities." The club attracted all of the players from the Los Angeles Lakers, and all of the hangers-on, pretty women, fans, and celebrities that accompanied them.

There were other competing clubs along the Crenshaw Strip, like Maverick's Flat at 4225 S. Crenshaw Boulevard, a hip club on par with the Apollo Theater on the East Coast for its popularity. It was a space both for A-list acts to play and for fledgling acts to test out their material. Songwriter John Daniels opened the club (which formerly housed the Arthur Murray Dance School) in 1966, intending for it to have a Playboy Club feel, with psychedelic colors, glass-tile tabletops, and an exclusive members-only air. The club operated without a liquor license, and many teenage patrons were welcome.

But it wasn't all kid-friendly. Patrons needed a membership in order to bring in their own liquor and place it inside their lockers at the club. Wild, electric mood lights and psychedelic coloring set the anything-goes tone of the club. When Norman Whitfield came to the club, he was inspired by its interior design to write the song "Psychedelic Shack" for the Temptations. Groups like the Commodores and Earth, Wind and Fire got their start there, along with the Seven Souls, who operated as a kind of house band with Bob Welch as the lead guitarist, who would later become a member of the British blues and rock band, Fleetwood Mac. The club had occasional appearances from actor Marlon Brando and football star and actor Jim Brown—who would invest money in the club.

Another club along the Crenshaw Strip was Lonnie Simmon's The Total Experience, at 5428 Crenshaw Boulevard, an R&B venue for up-and-coming artists. Acts that were unproven started here. The club eventually inspired Simmons to start a record company by the same name, Total Experience Records. The Gap Band would be the club's first act.

On 54th and Broadway sat black America's West Coast precursor to New York's Studio 54—the Five-Four Ballroom. But by the mid-'70s, the club was losing some steam. It had been the premier destination for the black rich and famous in the '50s and '60s—a playground for A-list celebrities like Jackie Wilson, Sam Cooke, Lou Rawls, and James Brown.

What set Griffey and Barnett's Guys and Dolls apart from other clubs along the Crenshaw Strip was that they would get their liquor license—something that wasn't an easy feat. In order to get a liquor license, you had to know someone with clout. A jazz connoisseur named John T. McClain, a consummate gentleman, likeable and gregarious, was able to get the license for Barnett and Griffey, which gave the club status and exclusivity. McClain acted as a father figure to Griffey. He owned a number of hotels and nightclubs in the city, and infamously ran with Benjamin "Bugsy" Siegel. McClain eventually ran many of the clubs, hotels, and restaurants he owned from jail. McClain had the right mix of people skills to bring in money, and he looked to pass them on to develop Griffey as a promoter.

Under McClain's tutelage, Griffey was well on his way to becoming the most well-known black promoter in the business—cajoling with his straight-talk charm, strong-arming, and demanding to managers of some of the biggest acts including the Impressions, Ike and Tina Turner, and Jackie Wilson. Griffey eventually moved into concert promotion, seeing the greater returns with larger venues booking tours for the likes of Stevie Wonder, Aretha Franklin, and James Brown.

Griffey had long burned the ears of anyone who would listen about the obstacles black promoters faced booking top black acts. Some clubs and venues were off-limits. Others charged higher rates to black promoters. And once the artists became famous and more established, white promoters snatched them, guaranteeing them an escape from the boxed-in limitations of the Chitlin' Circuit with larger, more lucrative venues.

With this dilemma in mind, Griffey approached a young reverend out of Chicago. Jesse Jackson, who was operating off-shoots of Operation PUSH all over the country, helped Griffey to form a coalition of black promoters to work in a de facto union. It was a marked departure from Griffey's solo tactics, which included, but were not limited to, threatening club owners with burning down their clubs if they didn't comply with his needs. Jackson also introduced Griffey to a guy from Chicago— a tall, cerebral man with a mellifluous voice, someone who was fast becoming a power broker in the entertainment industry, a man named Don Cornelius.

Around the country Griffey was gaining name recognition in the music industry and a reputation that caused people to whis-per his name in admiration and unease. These two mavericks, Cornelius and Griffey, together and apart, would become bigger than life.

At times Cornelius was a deadpan jokester. At other times he walked with a reserve that kept everyone but his closest friends at a distance. In public and in business, he could be contradictory; he was serious and always about business, but always late. He was generous and cultivated friendships with people that had nothing to offer him. However, he was hardly warm. He could be laid-back and cool but a worrier, thorough, methodical, nerdy and stiff, someone who was never in a rush to do anything. What was clear with his move from the cool pose of Chicago to La La Land was that he was an ocean of ambition on an island where he was trying to learn the language.

He insisted on playing by the rules in the almost exclusively white television industry, wary of taking risks or making mistakes. Promoting black acts wasn't easy at the time, and television opened up a whole new world that he wasn't about to blow. Cornelius, with his six foot five frame, his no-nonsense gaze, and his ability to curse with poetic prose and gangster charm, earned the respect he deserved on the streets. When he met Griffey, Cornelius focused closely in the mirror and knew he had met his match.

If there's one thing Griffey hated, it was weakness. Cheery "Good mornings!" got answered with, "What's so good about it?!" He waited for the response and, instantly, respect was lost for anyone somehow intimidated by that gruffness.

Griffey had consummated his street smarts in the projects of Nashville, where he became alternately known around town as much for his talent as a drummer as his prowess on his first job—as a lookout for a prostitution ring. When he found success as a music promoter, his popular refrain became, "I don't mind losing money, cause I can make it again. That's how sure I am of me!" He would boast that he could spend a million dollars on a Monday, and make it back the next day.

"I'm the baddest motherfucka you'll ever meet!" he told the Whispers singing group when he met them after a concert, and sold them a bill of goods on why he should manage them. At the time Louis Chin, a Chinese version of Griffey's no-nonsense style, was managing them.

Lead singer Wallace "Scotty" Scott's first reaction was, "When somebody comes in with that kind of conviction, you either say, 'He's crazy!' or 'I gotta take this ride to see *if* he's crazy.'"

"He had the gift of gab and you believed the shit," Wallace's twin brother, Walter said. "He'd say, 'We're gonna fall off this bridge, and when we get down there, there's gonna be a million dollars waiting for you.' We'd be like, 'Okay, Dick.'"

Griffey called Walter and Wallace every day. One of the biggest acts at the time was Gladys Knight and the Pips, and Griffey convinced the Whispers that they would be bigger than Gladys and the Pips in two years. The Whispers took the ride with Griffey and he started booking them around the country. They kept Chin on as a manager, who would tell the Whispers, "Find a void and fill it!" But Griffey eventually eclipsed him.

Rumors abounded about Griffey's other unseemly characteristics—for example, threatening club owners who didn't pay, having dubious characters on the payroll, and being a womanizer. Once, a bodyguard came into the office with a bullet freshly lodged in his leg, ready for work; Griffey had to urge him to go to the hospital. Of course, no one had the balls to dare repeat the stories—not as long as Griffey was still taking in air. Not even as long as anyone who knew him was taking in air. Or even people who knew people who knew him.

Around the same time that Cornelius made his move to Los Angeles, Berry Gordy had succumbed to the allure of the klieg lights and finally moved all of Motown's operations out of the Motor City in 1972, taking with him the company's television subsidiary, Motown Productions, which branched out into film in Los Angeles. Many of Motown's top acts, like Gladys Knight and the Pips, stayed behind in Detroit. Others, like the Jackson Five, the Temptations, Marvin Gaye, and the Four Tops, would eventually take flight to other labels. While Gordy's ambitions would take them to new heights in the movie business, with his princess singer, Diana Ross, starring in films like *Mahogany* and *Lady Sings the Blues*, it would be at the expense of his record label, which was falling behind other labels that were capturing the musical explosion of '70s funk bands, more topical soul artists, and disco.

At a time when everybody was trying to make it, acts were hungry for exposure, riding in cars that barely worked, playing in local clubs to earn their reputation. Cornelius was struggling to do the same and was constantly on edge about keeping his show afloat.

"I can do that for you," Griffey said to him matter-of-factly, during their first meeting.

"What's that?" Cornelius asked him.

"I got the relationships," Griffey boasted. "I don't have to call the record label. I can call *Al Green* and get him here."

Cornelius hired him right away as a talent coordinator for the show. By then, Griffey had already branched out into concert promotion. He was booking acts at the Adams West Theater and the Forum in partnership with Forum owner Jack Kent Cooke— acts like Al Green, the Temptations, and Aretha Franklin, stoking a reputation by landing international tours for Richard Pryor and Whitney Houston. When he forged a relationship with Johnny Cash's manager, Griffey moved his office from a bank of telephone booths to Cash's management's office. He would eventually parlay with the power brokers of the industry. People like Irving Azoff and prolific musicians like James Brown and Stevie Wonder would answer his calls on the first ring, talk shit with him, and let him curse them out. They would curse right back and love him like a son. He lived by his belief that "Entertainers come and go, but business people will always be here."

As the coffers began to fill, more business ideas began to blossom. Still working as a talent coordinator for *Soul Train*, Griffey approached Cornelius about opening up a Soul Train club. Every week there were at least twelve acts that were booked for a weekend taping of *Soul Train*. Two episodes were taped on Saturday and another two on Sunday. Maverick's, Guys and Dolls, and Total Experience were the main clubs where acts could play in their downtime—either waiting for the taping or after the show was wrapped. Griffey thought that a Soul Train club would be a perfect pit stop for acts, a way to make money from the acts that offered them no immediate financial gains from the show. The Los Angeles market was saturated, so they looked toward the financial beacon along the high hills of San Francisco.

Cornelius and Griffey made a deal with the owner of a club, the Matrix, at 412 Broadway in the seedy strip-club district on the corner of Broadway and Montgomery in the North Beach section of San Francisco. Its owner was Louis Chin, the Whisper's former manager. The Matrix hosted Bob Marley and the Wailers for their first US date, to a packed house, showing Marley that he could be a success in the States. Before it had been the Matrix, the same space had been a supper club named Mr. D's (after Sammy Davis Jr.) operated by Tony Bennett.

Griffey and Cornelius renamed it the "Soul Train Club" and promptly started booking acts that were on the show. The club brought in a mixed crowd and was the only one in the area bringing in national acts like Harold Melvin and the Blue Notes. Griffey called Chuck Johnson, who had worked with him at Guys and Dolls, to come out to help him with the Soul Train Club. Johnson, a handsome man with an admirable talent for claiming pretty girls, was working back in Chicago at a high-end clothing store, dressing pimps, athletes, and celebrities. Cornelius hired him in 1974 to be a dance coordinator for the show.

In 1974, Richard Pryor played and recorded part of his third album, *That Nigger's Crazy*, live at the Soul Train Club, and would later host an episode of *Soul Train*, where he was presented with an award by Soul Train dancer "Lil' Joe" Chism for the album that had gone Platinum and earned a Grammy. Pryor performed a live, watered-down version of his skit from that album on *Soul Train*, about the differences between the black church, where the black preacher acts like he knows *Gaaaawd* personally, and the white church, with strange music, where you wonder if Dracula is going to jump out from under the pulpit.

That Nigger's Crazy on Stax Records (and later Warner Bros. Records when Stax folded) went Gold and won a Grammy. It was a culminating record in what had been a three-year turnaround for him—moving from mainstream, cotton-candy material to street, character-based comedy. His albums prior to *That Nigger's Crazy* featured street comedy, but they didn't garner the same mainstream attention because the executives didn't know how to market them. In his club shows, he was still emulating Bill Cosby, clean-cut and family-friendly, before he found his own voice and gained fame by talking about the characters of the underworld and their antics that informed his youth—prostitutes, winos, and pimps. Al Bell, president of Stax Records, couldn't get *That Nigger's Crazy* played on radio, so they marketed it in black barbershops, beauty salons, and restaurants that had pool halls where they played dominos, and they hung posters everywhere that read, "That Nigger's Crazy." The record sold half a million copies with no radio airplay and became the talk of the country.

===

Cornelius and Griffey would shutter the Soul Train club, after a year, as their energies became divided into several business ventures, but Griffey approached Cornelius with the idea of starting a record label. In addition to his other ventures, Griffey was still managing the Whispers and still held connections in the recording industry. The Whispers knew Cornelius from the time he was working at *Soul Train* in Chicago and they had appeared on the show. Both self-made and self-willed men, they thought, unequivocally, that their partnership and Soul Train Records was going to be the biggest thing that ever happened.

They figured they could triple the kind of profit Berry Gordy made with Motown Records. At the time, major labels had awakened to the financial viability of the black market in part because of a 1971 Harvard Report titled "A Study of the Soul Music Environment," created by Harvard University's Business School and commissioned by Columbia Records, to help major labels understand how to better situate themselves to benefit from soul music. Capitol Records, CBS (of which Columbia was a subsidiary), and Warner Brothers would open black divisions, competing against independents like Tabu, Total Experience, Motown, and Stax. But Cornelius and Griffey figured they could break the records from their label on *Soul Train* every Saturday and corner the market with acts on their label.

One of the first groups they signed was the Mystics, a funk band from Cincinnati that Cornelius had befriended back in the Chicago days. They used to play at the Skyway Lounge, located on Seventy-Ninth and Halsted on the South Side, where crowds would line up around the corner to get in and half of them would be turned away. Cornelius eventually met them one night when they opened for the O'Jays.

The Mystics consisted of the always suited-up, brown-skinned, bowlegged singer and model named Terry Brown; his younger brother, Gerald Brown—tall, with light-brown eyes and high cheekbones—sang tenor. Gerald was always asked by high school women he dated, "Why can't you look more like your brother?!" The third singer, who sang baritone, was an athletic math wizard named Bob Banks.

Terry, introspective and intuitive, had earned his master's degree in music at the Cincinnati Conservatory of Music at the age of twenty-three, and the next year began teaching at Hughes High School in Cincinnati. Terry's students included Antonio "L.A." Reid (who would later play drums with the group the Deele), Carlos Green (who would be one of the lead singers with the Deele), and Reggie and Vincent Calloway (who would later play with the group Midnight Star). When he and his brother decided to create the Mystics, Terry invited L.A. Reid to gig with them as a drummer in the band, along with Jimmy Macon on guitar (he later left to play in the Gap Band), and Banks to sing lead vocals. They were known around Cincinnati as the funkiest band in town.

When Cornelius moved to Los Angeles, he didn't forget the Mystics. He called record companies trying to land the band a recording contract, but none of them were interested. In 1974, he called the Brown brothers on the phone when he was looking to assemble his first act for Soul Train Records.

Cornelius only wanted Terry, but Terry refused, insisting he wouldn't come to Los Angeles without his younger brother. And when Griffey and Cornelius flew out to Cincinnati and signed them, it was news all over Cincinnati. Neither of Cincinnati's local favorites—teenaged Bootsy Collins, who was touring with James Brown and funk spearhead Roger Troutman, who was gigging with a group called Little Roger and the Dells—had signed with major labels yet.

Cornelius sent the brothers $50,000 for them to relocate from Cincinnati to Los Angeles. For a year he paid their $265 monthly rent for a one-bedroom apartment on Raintree Circle in Culver City. A year into their career on the label, he gave Gerald a 1968 two-seater 280 SL Mercedes-Benz convertible—a hand-me-down gift that his girlfriend didn't want.

Griffey and Cornelius held a nationwide audition for other members of the band and vocalists that would end up making up the Soul Train Gang. Over four hundred people were auditioned, but the Gang would consist of soprano Pat Williamson, a shapely woman who had grown up singing gospel and spoke in a high-pitched baby voice; classically trained dancer Mississippi native, Hollis Pippin; and a fair-skinned, green-eyed sixteen-year-old named Judy Jones.

The doo-wop vocalists, the Whispers, had already gained a following on the defunct Janus Records, before Griffey, as their manager, purchased their contract from Janus, and signed on to Soul Train Records. Other acts on the label were Carrie Lucas, Griffey's soon-to-be wife, who had a voice you could tune a piano to, and the soul/funk vocal duo Sunbear. The Whispers members—Walter Scott, who sang lead and tenor, twin brother Wallace "Scotty" Scott, who also sang lead and tenor, tenor Nicholas Caldwell, tenor Gordy Harmon, and baritone Marcus Hutson—put out the first song on the label, "In Love Forever."

Cornelius had a special affinity for the Whispers. He played basketball with them at his house with Griffey and Virgil Roberts, the lawyer who represented the group. The twins, especially, were athletic, performing flips and acrobatic feats at their stage shows. He admired their routines and choreography and was eager to see them succeed at the next level. He and Scotty became close friends.

Griffey and Cornelius created Hip Trip Publishing, and fought over who had the most musical talent and an ear for hits. One day, Cornelius, Griffey, and the Whispers were in the studio, recording a take for a song that Cornelius wrote for them, "You'll Never Miss the Water." Griffey and Cornelius were competing for the Whispers' approval of their musical prowess. When they got to the harmony, Scotty and Griffey couldn't agree and started arguing loudly. Griffey figured he was producing the record and he would prove his chops with the finished product. Cornelius busted through the door:

"Both of you motherfuckas got it wrong!"

The Whispers fell out laughing. Cornelius sang vocals on the demo, and the song wound up on the album the way Cornelius originally wrote it. Griffey thought it was ridiculous. "Don is trying to tell the Whispers how to sing!"

The Soul Train Gang's first album was titled *Don Cornelius Presents the Soul Train Gang* (Soul Train '75). Cornelius wrote a song on the album with lead vocalist, Gerald Brown, titled "Garbage Can," which was arranged by Stevie Wonder. Wonder wrote another song on the album—a duet with Pat Williamson and Gerald Brown that was a driving, bass-heavy soul ditty entitled "Baby Open the Door" (with the refrain "I'm gonna kick it down!"). Most of the Soul Train Gang's album was executive produced by Griffey and Cornelius, and arranged by Ron "Have Mercy" Kersey, who would write music for the soundtrack of the disco movie classic *Saturday Night Fever*. Most of the other songs on the album were covers of Motown hits. But the album was largely ignored.

Cornelius always wanted the best of everything, and Philadelphia International Records (founded by Kenny Gamble and Leon Huff) was the hottest label in the industry. The label eclipsed Motown as the major expression of black culture, with breakout artists like Teddy Pendergrass, Patti LaBelle, the O'Jays, Billy Paul, Harold Melvin and the Bluenotes, and Lou Rawls. Gamble and Huff's goal was to be the voice of black America, and they distinguished their label from Motown (considered the sound of young America) with "message" music, examining social issues specifically affecting the black community. The second album by the Soul Train Gang, entitled *The Soul Train Gang*, was produced by Gamble and Huff in 1976, but still didn't garner a hit. The duo had just scored a hit with MFSB's (Mother, Father, Sister, Brother's) "TSOP" (The Sound of Philadelphia), with vocals by the Three Degrees, which had been created as a theme song for the show in 1973.

The song "If It Takes All Night," from the *Soul Train '76* album, was reminiscent of the Delfonics' sound, with Terry singing the falsetto lead. The song made a small splash with fans, but didn't garner nationwide attention. The following year, "Soul Train '76" (with the refrain "Get on...get onboard!"), written by Terry Brown, would become one of the show's most recognized themes.

As everyone in the Soul Train Gang filled in as a lead singer, the group struggled to create a sound and an identity. Cornelius—not one to do anything unless it was top of the line, if he believed in it—had invested $200,000 in the label, and so far wasn't seeing any of that money being recouped. Some of the members of the Soul Train Gang were becoming frustrated.

Chuck Johnson had been hired as the dance coordinator for the show and as an assistant for the Soul Train label. He manned the door with a discerning eye. Mediocrity in looks or in dancing skills didn't get you in the door.

Dancer Tyrone Proctor brought style to the show by dancing to the instrumentals of the songs and creating a style of dancing called "waacking"—later reinvented by Madonna, and called "voguing." Proctor would become a regular on the show. One day Proctor snuck in his friend and roommate, a slim, tall dancer named Jeffrey Daniel, who glided like a ballet dancer. Daniel hid behind the bleachers until the set began and went unnoticed by the staff until they saw his dance moves—he performed the mechanical man, alternately stiffing his joints and gliding effort-lessly across the floor, like no one had seen before. He would become the premier dancer on the show, eventually working with Michael Jackson.

Johnson confronted Daniel afterward, but Johnson had already been impressed enough by Daniel's innovative dancing to know he would let him in the next day. Daniel began creating a fan base when he partnered with Jody Watley. Watley and Daniel began dating. They would dress alike on the show—wearing silver lamé shorts and T-shirts or jumpsuits, and getting top billing on the risers. They were fan favorites and two of the most talented dancers—moving effortlessly in unison. They in-corporated theater and costuming into their act. But behind the scenes their relationship had turned abusive and they were prone to physical battles, sometimes while performing.

Eventually Johnson tried to convince Daniel to join the group Shalamar, and one day asked him to come by the studio to dis-cuss the possibilities. Daniel answered that he had to go to work wrapping presents at a department store for the Christmas season, and maybe he could come over during his lunch break.

"If this takes off like I think it will, you'll never be wrapping anything ever again," Johnson told him. Daniel and Watley rounded out Shalamar as dancers and background vocalists, though Griffey was initially reluctant to have Watley onboard, because he was suspicious about whether she could sing. Cornelius and Johnson convinced him that she could.

Shalamar grew out of the 12-inch single "Uptown Festival," by the Soul Train Gang, recorded at the suggestion of a French producer named Simon Soussan, who had shopped the cut to Griffey. Soussan rechristened the Soul Train Gang as "Shalamar" (a name derived from the French perfume Shalimar, by Guerlain).

The single was recorded with studio musicians, including Daniel, Watley, and the Whispers on background vocals, and Cleo Williams and Gary Mumford on lead vocals. When it came time to tour, Mumford suddenly left the group to join the ministry, and Williams, a born-again Christian who was a member of James Cleveland's church, didn't want to perform secular music anymore. Cornelius and Griffey had to scramble to assemble a touring group. Gerald wasn't interested in touring as a background singer, but was eventually convinced to be the lead singer. The group toured but didn't see any money recouped from the tour—Griffey told them it was because they hadn't recouped their advances.

Meanwhile, Terry, who had lupus, was growing sicker and Gerald Brown was thinking about the lucrative engineering career he had left back in Cincinnati. They both sat around waiting for the next thing to happen. They ended up sitting around for eight months.

Cornelius was talking with his accountant daily, who was telling him in no uncertain terms to get out of the business. The record company was bleeding money and taking energy away from the television show.

By now, Cornelius had seen the seedier side of the record industry, and he wasn't interested in the shady business deals required to get records played. Television was a more high-profile, lucrative industry. Without warning, Cornelius decided to shut down the label.

Chuck Johnson, who was on vacation in Saint Tropez, picked up the phone to call Griffey about money for the Whispers tour.

"Operator, can you connect me to Soul Train Records?" he asked.

"That line is disconnected."

"Operator, you must have this shit wrong. C'mon, lady, give me the company!"

Around the same time, the Whispers were walking into the Soul Train Records office, located in the penthouse at 9200 Sunset Boulevard, coming fresh off of tour, and would find nothing but silence and a padlock on the door.

Scotty would call in later that day.

"Nah, the number is working," he insisted to the operator. He spoke slowly, enunciating each word like she spoke a foreign language. "This is Soul Train Records, you know, DON CORNE-LIUS!"

She didn't have a different answer.

"How long you been working for the phone company?"

Gerald would call Cornelius.

His answer was simple: "I'm out the record business, Gerald. I'm not fucking with the record business."

No forewarning and no explanations, other than that he was losing money. He told Gerald that Griffey was going to be han-dling the company. Gerald wasn't interested. Cornelius had taken care of them, treated them like celebrities before they had a hit. He felt like Griffey was taking them for a ride.

"RCA Australia gave him a $100,000 budget," Cornelius told him matter-of-factly.

"I'll give him a call," Gerald said without hesitation.

Griffey assured all of the groups that everything would be all right. Griffey told the artists, "Don't even worry about it. I got a whole other thing I'm doing." He was starting a new company. They would fold the old one, and Cornelius would sign every-thing over to him with a few hundred thousand dollars. The new company would be named, SOLAR—an acronym for the

Sound of Los Angeles Records. The label already had a hit with "Uptown Festival," which would roll over to SOLAR.

Gerald Brown knew that there was more money than what he had been receiving—from that hit, and from their touring, now and in the future. The group members weren't receiving any of their live performance money, and their contract stated they were entitled to 5½ percent of gross in royalties, and they hadn't seen a dime from it. They were receiving a $300 salary weekly and were paid hourly for session work. Gerald wasn't satisfied. He called up a lawyer, Abraham Saperstein—along with his accountant, Robert Brenner. Together they went to meet with Dick Griffey. He sat in his office.

"Ain't none of y'all really in the group, unless I say so. You ain't going to be taking the live performance money," was Griffey's angry reply when confronted about revenue from shows.

Gerald sat with his back stiffly against the back of the chair.

"You are going to have to pay me 5½ percent when the new album sells, according to our Soul Train agreement," Gerald said, trying to keep his voice even.

"It will cost me five thousand dollars apiece to get rid of you, you, and you!" Griffey deadpanned as he pointed to each person in the room. "Now get the fuck out of my office!"

The air in the room was dead. Saperstein looked at Griffey strangely and edged Gerald out the door. When they got on the other side of the door, he told Gerald, "Either he's serious or crazy. Or both," he said. "All I can advise you to do is to get as far away from him as you can."

6

I'M NOT FATTENING NO FROGS FOR NO SNAKES

They say that nobody is perfect. Then they tell you practice makes perfect. I wish they'd make up their minds.

—Wilt Chamberlain

Use what talent you possess: the woods would be very silent if no birds sang except those that sang best.

—anonymous

Even before the meeting between Griffey, Gerald Brown, Abraham Saperstein, and Robert Brenner, Griffey had begun looking for a new lead singer for Shalamar. He continued wearing many hats—managing artists like the Whispers on his label, working as a talent coordinator for *Soul Train*, and acting as the president of SOLAR. Like Julius Caesar, Griffey's ambition would be his greatest gift and his most enduring weakness.

Griffey's defense, like many record executives' when it came to paying artists what they were due, was that they hadn't yet earned out their advances. None of the artists in Shalamar could afford houses or cars. They leased vehicles through Griffey's leasing agency. And yet the group was steadily garnering hits and had become as popular in Europe as the Rolling Stones.

When Soul Train Records folded, one of the master's Griffey bought from the company was the hit "Uptown Festival." That was all he needed to get the ball rolling for SOLAR.

Now that Soul Train Records was defunct, so was Brown's contract. Griffey began auditioning singers from the ranks of the *Soul Train* dancers, but wasn't having much luck. "A hit can cure cancer," David Lombard, now the concert promoter for SOLAR, intoned. "In the record business that's all you need."

Rainey Riley-Cunningham, the former secretary for *Soul Train* who was working at Cornelius's new business venture, the Soul Train dance studio, told Griffey that her boyfriend, Howard Hewett, was a singer.

"You can see him at Maverick's," she told him. The Soul Train dancers knew him and his talent very well—he and his group, Disco Inferno, performed at Maverick's, singing mostly Top 40 hits.

But Hewett had not gone unnoticed within the industry, and in the spring of 1979, Hewett was on the 15th floor of the Motown building on Sunset Boulevard and Argyle Avenue in the middle of negotiations with Motown executives Jeff Bowen and Angelo Bond, when suddenly the phone rang.

"It's for you," Bowen handed Hewett the phone looking perplexed.

"If it's my lady, tell her I'll call her back," Hewett said. He had been in negotiations with the company for months and was finally making some headway toward getting his group a deal.

"It's a guy and it sounds like it might be long distance," Bowen told him.

It was Jeffrey Daniel from Shalamar. He had tracked Hewett down through Hewett's girlfriend. Shalamar was in New York in the middle of a tour when Gerald Brown walked out, upset with Griffey because the money from performing that he was sending back to the company could not be accounted for. "We want to offer you a position as the lead singer," Daniel said eagerly. "Where are you in the Motown building?"

"On the 15th floor."

"SOLAR has an office in the same building on the 9th floor. We already talked to Dick," Daniel told him.

When Hewett hung up he told Bowen and Bond about the phone call.

Don Cornelius in his classic attire. (Soul Train Holdings, LLC)

Marvin Gaye, 1974. (Soul Train Holdings, LLC)

B. B. King, James Brown, and Bobby Blue Bland. (Soul Train Holdings, LLC)

Patti LaBelle in her platform shoes. (Soul Train Holdings, LLC)

Minnie Riperton. (Soul Train Holdings, LLC)

Chuck Berry.
(Soul Train Holdings, LLC)

Elton John. (Soul Train Holdings, LLC)

Gladys Knight. (Soul Train Holdings, LLC)

Early dancers. See Superman on the right. (Soul Train Holdings, LLC)

Right: Patricia Davis. (Courtesy of Patricia Davis)

Above: Damita Jo Freeman. (Courtesy of Damita Jo Freeman)

Left: Dancer Sharon Hill was known for her creative hairstyles, from intricately styled braids with beads to Afros, perms, and curly styles. (Courtesy of Sharon Hill)

Cheryl Song.
(Soul Train Holdings, LLC)

The pilot show of the hip-hop dance
show *Graffiti Rock* gave the audience
definitions for the latest slang terms
like *fresh*. (© Martha Cooper)

New Edition: Ronnie DeVoe, Michael Bivins, Ricky Bell, Ralph Tresvant, and Bobby Brown. *Soul Train* would be one of their first television appearances. (© Oggi Ogburn)

Surrounded by dancers, Stevie Wonder creates an original song about *Soul Train*. (Courtesy Everett Collection)

Donna Summer, the Queen of Disco, performing at Roseland. (© Allan Tannenbaum)

The iconic Grace Jones. (© Allan Tannenbaum)

"Shalamar is nothing but a fly-by-night disco group that will never amount to anything," Bowen warned him.

"I hear what you're saying," Hewett started and paused. "Listen, I'm parked on the street. I'm gonna go put some money in the meter. I'll see you guys later."

Hewett hauled ass to the 9th floor. It was a Friday. Hewett explained to Griffey that although he hadn't signed a contract with Motown, his word mattered more than anything else. When he went home he called Bowen and left a message with his secretary saying, "If you guys want to work this out, call me." Hewett's phone sat silent. They never called.

The next morning he went to Griffey's house and watched a videotape of a Shalamar show. He sat in a rocking chair and listened to Griffey's gruff voice.

"Jeffrey and Jody say you're a great singer. Sing something."

"Right here? A cappella?"

"Yeah."

Hewett started singing Peabo Bryson's ballad "Feel the Fire." As he got to the hook Griffey stopped him.

"I'll be right back," Griffey said as he ambled up the stairs. When he came back down he reached into one pocket and pulled out five one hundred dollar bills and handed them to Hewett. Then he went into his other pocket and pulled out an open airline ticket to New York.

"Catch the red-eye tonight and meet the group tomorrow. Practice the choreography and lip syncing for 'Take That to the Bank,' 'cause you got a television show to do on Monday."

The new group featuring Hewett performed on *The Dinah Shore Show* that Monday.

Meanwhile, while they were garnering hits, Jody was still taking the bus to rehearsal. The artists were still struggling financially. They worked with Leon Sylvers for their next album, *Big Fun*, which included the hit "Second Time Around" and landed at No. 8 on the pop charts. They sold out Wembley Arena in London. Gerald Brown fielded offers from other labels, but his career stalled after Shalamar, and he never received the money he was owed. He went back to Cincinnati and taught high school math.

Even though the group meshed musically, they didn't personally. Watley and Daniel had been lauded on *Soul Train* for being one of the cutest couples. But with all their cute matching outfits, gauchos and plaid shirts, props and immaculate choreography, there was a darker side. On the Soul Train Line they once choreographed a number that was a make-believe fight scene. Two Soul Train dancers rushed from the sidelines, broke them apart, and picked them up and brought them down the line as everyone on the line laughed. But the laughing stopped when in real life their high kicks and acrobatics were aimed at each other—physically fighting in dressing rooms, onstage, and on set.

Daniel would eventually marry R&B singer Stephanie Mills for a short period of time, but that only increased the tension between him and Watley.

Hewett and Watley didn't hit it off well, either. Hewett wasn't getting along with too many people—he came across to everyone he came in contact with as arrogant and self-absorbed. The first time he met Watley, he tried to hit on her. Their relationship tanked for the rest of the time in Shalamar, culminating in a fight, and they requested to film a video for the single "Dead Giveaway" in separate takes.

It wasn't just within the group that tension existed. Shalamar was appearing on *Soul Train* with regularity—their disco, roller-skating hits wouldn't stop coming. Sometimes Watley and Daniel returned to dance on the show. But now the dancers who they had once hung out with behind the bleachers and shared KFC boxes with now looked at them with green-eyed hatred.

Meanwhile, other groups on the SOLAR label were making it big. A background singer in the group the Deele, named Kenny "Babyface" Edmonds, was seemingly content to be a shrinking violet, singing background and writing hits for the Whispers and other groups on the label. But during a practice session, Griffey kept hearing one voice surging above the others. He moved in closer and realized it was Babyface, and promptly put him up front.

SOLAR had quickly become the Motown of the late '70s and early '80s, and *Soul Train* was benefiting from all of their hits.

As fast as they were being produced, they were performing them on *Soul Train;* in most cases, SOLAR artists appeared multiple times on the show. Some had records that were heard first on the show. It wasn't unusual to have five or six SOLAR singles on the charts at the same time. Some of the label's biggest hits that were in heavy rotation on the show were the Whispers' "It's a Love Thing," "Chocolate Girl," "Rock Steady," and "And the Beat Goes On'; Midnight Star's "Slow Jam" (one of Babyface's first hits as a songwriter), "Freak-a-zoid," "No Parking on the Dance Floor," and "Operator"; Lakeside's "Fantastic Voyage"; Babyface's "It's No Crime"; and Klymaxx's "The Men All Pause." Everybody was making money and excess abounded.

Despite their success, all of the members of Shalamar were still griping about receiving royalties. The relationships between them had soured to the point that they were taking separate limos to perform at gigs. When they performed their last album together, a discrepancy about their ride to the event would finally implode the group. The dispute ended in a heated argument between Hewett and Watley that nearly got physical, and their tour manager, Stanley Dillard, had to break up the fight. Watley quit the group on the spot. When Griffey threatened to sue her for breach of contract, she consented to appear for the video shoot for the single "Dead Giveaway," with the requirement that she and Hewett would not appear on the set at any given time together. Stand-ins were used to accomplish this. Even with this consent, according to a contractual agreement, Griffey was entitled to a portion of her royalties for her first solo album on the MCA label.

When she came back to perform on *Soul Train* as a solo act, Cornelius told her that he was proud of her. She had long looked up to him as a father figure, and with his endorsement she knew she had arrived.

Hewett and Cornelius had also built a friendship from Shalamar's frequent appearances on the show. Cornelius, always striving for perfection, would offer him advice about his career and his personal life as they sat in his convertible Rolls Royce Cornice. They would talk for hours. One day, Hewett ran into

Cornelius as he was leaving Larrabee recording studio. He told Hewett: "I never claim to be 100 percent right. But I am about 80 to 85 percent right all of the time," he said. "I'll take that 80 to 85 percent. He knew talent. Plus, he thought he had his hands on the next Donny Hathaway or even Prince. *Soul Train* was at the pinnacle of success by 1975, airing in 100 top U.S. markets, Canada, Puerto Rico, the Caribbean, Japan, and parts of Europe, and Cornelius, buoyed by its achievements, believed he could do anything.

Tyrone Garfield "Ron Have Mercy" Kersey, former keyboardist for the Trammps, had suddenly been catapulted to worldwide fame after winning the Grammy Award for the soundtrack to *Saturday Night Fever*. And his wife, Melanee Kersey, had discovered a male singer in the young adult choir at their Second Baptist Church in Sneads Ferry, North Carolina. She approached him about introducing him to her husband, and when Kersey called the young singer, the kid impressed him with his uncanny mimicking of Peabo Bryson when he sang "She's a Woman" over the phone to him.

O'Bryan McCoy Burnette would end up shortening his stage name to just O'Bryan, and Kersey, who was in the midst of trying to start his own group, recruited O'Bryan into the band, which included a medley of jazz musicians: Melvin Davis, Chuck Norris, Michael Norfleet, and Levi Caesar.

The group disbanded a few months later, but Kersey had an idea. Kersey and Cornelius were good friends and had talked for years about ways they could go into business together. He told O'Bryan he wanted to introduce him to Cornelius.

A few days later eighteen-year-old O'Bryan rode in the passenger's seat to Cornelius's house with Kersey, coming up over Cold Water Canyon, getting dizzy as the roads swung around in curve after curve. O'Bryan was impressed with Cornelius's house and his lifestyle. A Lucite piano was the centerpiece—a baby grand piano inspired by Elton John's request to have one when he performed on *Soul Train*. He had a pool in the backyard and a classic grey Bentley from overseas with a right-hand drive, a 12-cylinder Ferrari Daytona, and a cream-colored convertible Rolls Royce Cornice in the garage. He was dating a beautiful Mexican-American woman named Vicky Avila, and plenty of other models on the side.

Cornelius would listen to music daily, on his McIntosh stereo system with six-foot-tall speakers that sat on either end of his fireplace. At Kersey's urging, O'Bryan sang a song he wrote, entitled "Passion," as an audition. He could tell that Cornelius had been touched, when he finished singing it. Cornelius sized him up.

"He's got the look," Cornelius told Kersey.

"So, you ready to be a star boy?" Cornelius asked O'Bryan.

Cornelius became his manager, getting him started with $200,000 and eventually pouring more than a half a million dollars into his career. He signed him to Don Cornelius Productions, and as his production manager, was the go-between for O'Bryan's record label, Capitol Records, where Cornelius had signed him. Cornelius provided O'Bryan with the same benefits he would receive under the direction of an executive in Artist and Repertoire (for example, working as a liaison between O'Bryan and Capitol Records, overseeing the recording process, helping O'Bryan find producers and songwriters, booking studio time, choosing songs for albums, marketing, and promoting). Kersey acted as the producer and corralled musicians, many of whom were members of the R&B group LTD. The group's leader, Jeffrey Osborne, sang backup and was on the cusp of releasing his first self-titled debut album that same year.

The first thing O'Bryan bought with his advance money was a Mercedes-Benz 190E from a dealership on Sunset Boulevard in Hollywood. It was the bottom-of-the-line model for a Mercedes-Benz. When Cornelius found out about the car, he looked at it disgustedly and said, "This is not what you should be in." He gave the car to his girlfriend, Avila, and bought O'Bryan a Porsche 930 Turbo.

O'Bryan wrecked the car after having it for a week. One day he turned the key in the ignition while the car was already in gear, and the car slammed into the back of another car, totaling it. O'Bryan thought Cornelius, who was prone to giving people a piece of his mind, would lose it. He blew it off. "Shit happens," Cornelius shrugged.

Because of Cornelius's generosity and devotion to O'Bryan's talent, rumors began that the two were lovers. But O'Bryan, a pretty boy who occasionally wore hazel contacts and, like Prince, clothing that wasn't gender specific, was a lady's man, scoring the most beautiful women, and having bundles of children. The rumors continued, but went unfounded. There were other inappropriate rumors floating around—of executives from *Soul Train* sleeping with underage dancers and abusing women at parties, but no one ever approached the police.

O'Bryan's music was a mixture of new wave, R&B ballads, and funk tunes. Every album Cornelius and O'Bryan worked on would be a collaborative effort. Cornelius would write the lyrics to O'Bryan's melodies. They wrote the next theme song for *Soul Train*, "Soul Train's-A-Coming," which would run on the show from 1983 to 1987—a tune so funky you could smell it, and which became the most popular theme song for the show. Then one day, O'Bryan, who had never dared touch Cornelius's piano, was suddenly inspired. They were sitting together listening to music.

"You mind if I play the piano?"

"Nah, go ahead," Cornelius said.

As O'Bryan was playing, he heard something in his head. That something turned into the hit single, the quiet storm ballad "Lady, I Love You."

The single would go on the *Be My Lover* album, which peaked at No. 3 on the R&B charts, his highest charting album in 1984. The postdisco era of the '80s had welcomed a contradictory mix of soft love ballads, pop music, heavy metal, and hip-hop. O'Bryan, who wore an s-curl hairstyle, cornered the market in love ballads and pretty women he attracted. When it came time for O'Bryan to tour, a pretty, curly-haired high school singer came to audition for him to go on tour as his background singer. Her name was Karyn White. She was intimidated by Cornelius when she came to audition, but he winked at her to calm her down, letting her know there was nothing to worry about. He would come to believe in her talent. So much so, that he would send her checks when they were off the road. She and her boyfriend, who ended up working as the drummer in the band, would check their mailbox and checks for a few grand from Cornelius would come randomly, for no apparent reason. When he believed in talent, he was generous.

As Capitol demanded more, O'Bryan and Cornelius had their creative differences. For O'Bryan, it was hard to take direction from someone who wasn't a singer, and as always, Cornelius was heavy-handed and wanted perfection. He found it necessary to control all parts of a creative project. They would disagree on what was a funky sound. O'Bryan would tell him, "That note is flat," and Cornelius would think it was just fine. There were other times in the studio where O'Bryan would be insistent on fixing a melody and Cornelius would say, "You can't do it any better than that." Sometimes their creative differences were reduced to shouting matches.

By O'Bryan's fourth album, Kersey and Cornelius had fallen out. Cornelius was being pushed out as the middleman between the record company and O'Bryan. The record company figured they didn't need a production company; they had an A&R department that could handle all of O'Bryan's needs.

Cornelius would sign other artists—a one-hit wonder artist named Glenn Edward Thomas, who in 1982 had his *Take Love* album produced by Cornelius. The single "Turn Around" was the only bright spot on the album that tanked.

A funk/soul artist named Rosie Gaines was introduced to Cornelius by Levi Caesar, who was in O'Bryan's backing band. Gaines lasted with Cornelius for a year before she got an opportunity to work with Prince after she met him while singing a demo of a song for the Pointer Sisters.

Cornelius and the dance coordinator for *Soul Train*, Chuck Johnson, also found an up-and-coming comedian who spoke in the blunt, street-wise style reminiscent of Richard Pryor at a jazz club called the Pied Piper, and couldn't stop laughing at every word that fell from his lips. The comedian, a protégé of Redd Foxx, was named Robin Harris. Cornelius signed him to a three-year contract, before Harris moved on to greener pastures. Meanwhile, Cornelius moved on from artist management to other business ventures.

Supremely ambitious, Cornelius was determined to seal a place in history in the world of Hollywood. His next venture would set the stage for a young comedian that had appeared on his show, a teenager named Arsenio Hall, to host his own show.

The Tonight Show Starring Johnny Carson in 1975 was NBC's golden child. The show was ninety minutes long and had just moved three years before from its home in New York City to taping at Studio One in Burbank, California. Cornelius saw yet another void that needed to be filled. No one was interviewing black guests in a late-night television format. He thought he would be the one to do it.

As with all of his ventures, Cornelius dipped into his own pockets to fund the pilot program, a talk show he titled, "Don's Place." He hired Stan Lathan, who had worked as a director on the WNET program *Soul!* Lathan had also worked on network sitcoms like *That's My Mama* and *Barney Miller*.

Soul Train's set designer Anthony Sabatino created a *Tonight Show*–styled set with aluminum, copper, neon, and art deco furniture. Aida Chapman, Cornelius's "right and left hand," booked the talent for the pilot: Redd Foxx, Stevie Wonder, Denise Nichols, and Hank Aaron. The house band, the Bruce Miller Band, provided funky and hip music. And the announcer was KDAY radio deejay and program director, Steve Woods. Cornelius was committed to inviting and featuring the best people available, regardless of color.

On the pilot, there was one joke segment where audience members were challenged to tell a joke that would make the reserved Cornelius laugh. If they succeeded they would receive $100 dollars. Chapman was armed with five $100 dollar bills to deliver to audience members. Not one person made Cornelius laugh. Chapman used the money to go shopping for herself.

In his quest for excellence, Cornelius had all of the right ingredients: great guest stars, the finest producers and behind-the-scenes talent in the industry, and as a host, he was now a household name.

But his delivery didn't work. His reserved manner that came off supercool in the presence of artists he chatted with for three- to five-minute stretches worked for *Soul Train*, but his wooden delivery didn't work for the required outsized personality of a late-night talk-show host. It didn't help that there had never been a black host to dominate late-night television. Even with his track record with syndicators for *Soul Train*, not one syndicator bought the show.

His next venture, three years later, was more practical and filled another void—the Soul Train Dance Studio. There was Juilliard and the Joffrey Ballet and other prestigious schools for the dancing elite, but black dancers, for all their creativity, had not had a dance studio to call their own. Chapman paid hundreds of thousands of dollars for the wood floor and mirrored walls for the new studio. Choreographers who had danced with Alvin Ailey worked alongside the Soul Train dancers to teach dance classes. Cicely Tyson became a student at the studio.

The Soul Train Dance Studio opened with much fanfare in July of 1978, with a Hollywood star-studded party with guests like actor Eliot Gould, singer Thelma Houston, musician Hugh Masekela, and actor Lawrence Hilton-Jacobs. Cornelius, who had dazzled at basement parties, cut a rug at the party, dressed in a white suit, dancing with instructor Hope Clark. With the opening of the studio, Cornelius had opened his mind about disco music. "While our emphasis is on disco dancing, we're into other aspects of dance. After all, it is a valid art form," he told *Soul* magazine. A year later the club would close down for lack of interest.

SOUL FORFEIT

Disco music is funk with a bow tie.
— trombonist Fred Wesley, from the JB's

Disco is from hell, okay? And not the cool part of hell with all the murderers, but the lame-ass part where the really bad accountants live.
— Hyde, from *That '70s Show*

As the strobe lights flashed, dancers—gay, black, white, Chinese, teenagers and parents alike—ran toward the six-foot speakers straddling both sides of the stage. A large fountain offered free punch to the exhausted and thirsty. The sound system was like no other in New York. An extended version of Unlimited Touch's "Searching to Find the One" was booming, bouncing off the walls, merging with sweat, writhing bodies, ecstatic screams, and a shaking floor. It was otherworldly—a tent revival full of sin.

It was nearly noon and club-goers had been partying since midnight the night before. The Paradise Garage, the New York underground playground for dance music, was the starting point for black disco—breaking records from Grace Jones, Chaka Khan, Barry White, Madonna, Sylvester, Jocelyn Brown, and Taana Gardner. Frankie Crocker, the "Chief Rocker," took the reins from the deejay at the Garage, Larry Levan, playing the records he broke in the club on New York's radio station WBLS (the call letters stood for Black Liberation Station—the country's first black-owned radio station), introducing funky intonations of Manu Dibango's Afrobeat anthem "Soul Makossa" to the masses. Madonna, still a virtual unknown, came up to Crocker's station, after having her record pressed and played at the Paradise Garage with the help of her then-boyfriend, Jellybean Benitez. She autographed her record to Crocker, signing it with bravado: "From one star to another."

There was no other more enduring image that personified the disco era than that of Crocker galloping in on a white stallion through the front entrance of the famed disco nightclub, Studio 54, as part of a promotional kick. He was disco's biggest celebrity—proof positive that black folks had arrived post-civil rights and that the black middle class could dabble in the luxuries of escapism, unattached sex, and an abundance of drugs as carefully and carelessly as anyone else.

Crocker became famous for breaking rules. Unlike most deejays at WBLS, he didn't wait for record labels to bring him the latest 12-inch dance records—he searched for them himself at the three biggest dance clubs in New York: deejay Larry Levan's Paradise Garage, Leviticus, and the world-famous Studio 54.

He delved outside of the three-minute radio format, bringing the more playful disco scene to radio, playing extended records like MFSB's "Love Is the Message" in full length. As radio was resegregating, Crocker was integrating. He mixed up genres, playing Barry White and following it with Led Zeppelin or Bob Dylan, alongside jazz, rock, and pop standards.

Cornelius became good friends with Crocker when he came to Hollywood and would share a scene with him in the blaxploitation flick *Cleopatra Jones*. Cornelius, Crocker, and Howard Hewett would hang out frequently canvassing the disco scene. Crocker had a cameo appearance on *Soul Train* in 1976, wearing a button-down red shirt with a butterfly collar and an earring in his left ear, to promote his album *Frankie Crocker's Heart and Soul Orchestra Presents the Disco Suite Symphony Number 1 in Rhythm and Excellence*. He became a de facto competitor to Cornelius when he began a gig as the short-lived host of *Solid Gold*—a cheesy disco dance show made popular by the Solid Gold dancers, who danced, shook, and performed acrobatics in skimpy costumes made of gold lamé and sequins. The show aired on Saturday nights and was an instant hit.

By the mid-to-late 1970s, the concept of the "nightclub" where live music was played had changed over to the anything-goes, drug and sex-filled discotheques, where deejays exclusively spun recorded music. Patrons decided how hip a club was based on how skilled the deejay was—how well he or she mixed, found new records, and kept the crowd on its feet. Beat-heavy, up-tempo music was the standard fare, with an emphasis on propulsion rather than substance. Some radio stations reverted to all disco programming. Special 12-inch records were being produced, with extended versions of disco hits where the beats went on and on and on. By 1977, there were 10,000 discotheques around the country. These discos had grossed $4 billion.

The angst of the late '60s—exemplified by concept albums like Marvin Gaye's *What's Going On*, singles like Stevie Wonder's "Living for the City," and protest albums like Sly Stone's *There's a Riot Going On*, Edwin Starr's *War*, and Curtis Mayfield's *Superfly*, had given way to lighter fare. As things grew better for the black middle class and they danced their workweek troubles away at weekend discos, things were growing worse for poor black people—isolated in pockets of poverty as factory and union jobs faded in working-class towns and a crippling recession took hold in the late '70s.

The lush instrumentation and insistent rhythms of Gamble and Huff's Philadelphia International label helped usher in the sounds of disco. Patti LaBelle, Donna Summer, and Rufus represented some of the best beginnings of the genre.

There was no way Cornelius could ignore disco and not give it top billing. With the help of Crocker on the East Coast, Cornelius presented the best of black disco on *Soul Train*, though he was resistant to the vapid nature of the genre. He brought its biggest stars onboard the train—KC and the Sunshine Band and B.T. Express (who both had singles—"Do It Till You're Satisfied," and "Get Down Tonight," respectively—that created the model for the 12-inch, extended-play disco single), The Village People,

Cheryl Lynn, George McCrae, Gwen Guthrie, the Hues Corporation, Barry White (who had the first disco track to become a No. 1 pop hit, with 1973's "Love Theme"), Gloria Gaynor, and Van McCoy.

Even with his endorsement of disco, Cornelius remained a reluctant convert. The simple four-on-the-floor beat was a watered-down version of the polyrhythm innovations of the self-contained funk bands that had preceded the genre. It ensured that anyone could dance to it. It brought gay clubs and culture, always on the cutting edge of new music and fashion, into a new spotlight. Disco's strongest message was that anyone was welcome and anything goes. But Cornelius was still married to the soul sounds of the early '70s.

By now all of the black bands during those years were begrudgingly (often at the behest of their labels) recording requisite disco songs—at least one or two on their albums. Cornelius, though still unimpressed, thought some of the best songs in the genre were being recorded by black artists, and he eventually resigned to book them on the show. The set of the show got a flashy new look, dimmed lighting for a club atmosphere, with a sparkling disco ball rising above the floor as the centerpiece.

The queen of disco, Donna Summer, came on *Soul Train* in 1976, showcasing some salacious vocals with her hits "Spring Affair," "Love to Love You" (a 17-minute-long sonic witness to multiple orgasms and her first single off the Casablanca label), and "I Feel Love," which was popularized as the gay anthem in the clubs. Giorgio Moroder designed it for Summer with a completely synthesized backing track—a constant thumping that began the techno movement. Johnnie Taylor performed "Disco Lady" on the same episode.

For Summer it was the best of times and the worst of times—as much as she accepted the role as the queen of the era, she was also symbolic of its demise. In the summer of 1979, WLUP, a station in Chicago, played her hit "Last Dance" for twenty-four hours straight before pronouncing disco dead and switching over to their Top 40 format. Summer's image as the queen died with it. Summer switched over to new wave with her single

"The Wanderer" on the Geffen label, before she scored with her biggest hit, "She Works Hard for the Money."

In December of 1982, an ever-ambitious Cornelius would finally have to slow down. He had been plagued by recurring, debilitating headaches for much of his adult life. His girlfriend, Avila, and O'Bryan, were the only two people who sat by his side as he underwent a brain operation at Cedar Sinai Medical Center that lasted twenty-one hours. Without the surgery, he would have run the risk of sustaining possible leakage or hemorrhaging of blood vessels in his brain.

Doctors ordered him to rest, but his reprieve didn't last for long. After a rest period of just six months, Cornelius stubbornly began taping new episodes of *Soul Train* in March of 1983.

At some point, Cornelius had to decide if *Soul Train* was going to continue to be a soul-music dance show or a disco show. A reluctant disco convert he was, but it would be the genre that would maintain *Soul Train's* status through massive changes in the music industry.

No matter the changing trends, Cornelius had the longest-running first-run syndicated show on television. He owed his success to the fact that the show followed the patterns of the music. As long as the music was successful, the show would be, too. The music from the decade of the '80s would be a very lucrative time for the show. Cornelius didn't think he had any reason to worry.

By the early '80s the dream had come true: SOLAR Records had become a hit-making factory of Motown proportions, with a SOLAR artist gracing the stage of *Soul Train* nearly every week. But Michael Jackson had defined the decade with his indispensable album, *Thriller*, in 1983. He broke the color barrier on a new youth-oriented cable music station—MTV—and had become the king of pop. Once he reached this worldwide superstardom, like many other crossover artists who yearned to reach a larger market, Jackson never performed on *Soul Train* again. His last appearance was after his acting debut in the Motown production of the movie *The Wiz*, scored by Quincy Jones.

"Ease on Down the Road" from *The Wiz* had earned a nomination for a Grammy Award and an Academy Award, and Cornelius focused his interview on Michael's acting debut on the show in February 1979. "There's a difference in your scarecrow and the original *Wizard of Oz* and the Broadway play—it's a little hipper and funnier," Cornelius says. "Yeah, that's true, it has a little more razzamatazz," Michael says, his voice still at the high octaves of his youth.

Michael would have fewer and fewer television appearances, period, as his fame grew. His inaccessibility added an air of mystery to his persona that would only catapult him further into stardom.

Artists like Luther Vandross, a mainstay for black audiences, continued to appear on the show. White artists like Teena Marie almost exclusively performed on *Soul Train*, because they catered exclusively to a black market. When Madonna released her eponymous first album, she garnered three hits that resonated in gay discos and in the black community: "Holiday," "Borderline," and "Lucky Star." But Cornelius didn't feel that she had the chops to make it very far, so he never invited her on the show.

Prince was reluctant to come on *Soul Train* when he started having success in the '80s—eager to cross over, he, according to popular opinion, thought performing on the show would harm his image. Cornelius invited him on the show in the '90s, when he had changed his stage name to an unpronounceable symbol (known as the "love symbol") and was promoting "The Most Beautiful Girl in the World."

Michael Jackson, Prince, and Madonna would come to define the music scene for the next decade, as crossover success became the brass ring. By 1978, the listenership for FM stations exceeded AM stations and Top 40 stations abandoned AM radio altogether. Slick-sounding production, synthesizers, and technologically advanced sounds would dominate the airwaves. The concept of the group act returned with groups like New Edition, Boyz II

Men, Mint Condition, and Guy—with a slicker presentation and sound than their doo-wop predecessors from the 1960s. New jack swing was the new sound for urban youth. Everything was new, polished and perfect.

As a result of the Harvard report called "A Study of the Soul Music Environment," more black executives were hired at mainstream labels—and everyone started making a ridiculous amount of money.

There were annual conventions like the Black Record Executive conferences and Jack the Rapper, named after disc jockey Jack Gibson, who opened the first black-owned and black-operated radio station at WERD in Atlanta and founded the National Association of Radio Announcers. These gatherings were necessary for black executives to share secrets and celebrate their success.

At one of these conferences in Miami, BRE, an acronym for the trade magazine, *Black Record Executives*, record and industry executives partied with Cornelius in his hotel penthouse. There was cocaine bought from New York, so unrefined it still had bugs in it, and so strong you could smell it across the room.

"Man, where'd you get this shit from?" Cornelius asked one executive.

"Can you get some more of this?" Cornelius asked.

"No, I got it from New York."

The blow was so good Cornelius insisted on having one of his assistants travel from Los Angeles back to New York three times in one weekend, first class, just to get more. He always had to have the best product available.

—

"Who does that high-yellow bitch think she is?!"

Cheryl Song heard the whispers behind her, just below her on the floor. After having been on the show just a few times, dance coordinator Chuck Johnson had elevated Song—known as "the Asian chic with the long hair" by most television audience viewers—onto the risers, a coveted spot for dancers because it had the highest visibility for television viewers. Dancers who had been there for years, and were stuck on the floor with little chance of getting camera time, weren't afraid to express their displeasure.

Song, one of the first Asian dancers on *Soul Train*, was catching it from all angles. A petite woman who stood five feet with hair that hung to the middle of her behind, she was sexy and sensual when she danced, and was known to fling her long hair around at will. She immediately got top billing—but was afraid the first time she got on the riser she was going to get jumped and beaten by some of the women on the show. At home, her strict, stereotypically non-emotional Asian parents were upset because she was dancing on a black show, asking her what they were going to tell relatives.

Regular dancer Myron Montgomery had brought her on the show as a dare, and was surprised when the dance coordinator and audience members took to her. Eventually, the regular dancers did, too, when she proved that she could dance.

Song had a traumatic childhood, molested from the time she was four until she was a teenager by an uncle who lived with the family. She loved to dance as a release, studying dance in high school, and watched *Soul Train* religiously, admiring dancers like Damita Jo Freeman and Pat Davis. A graduate of the predominantly black Susan Miller Dorsey high school, Song felt soon enough that she had finally found a family and a place where she belonged at *Soul Train*, doing what she loved to do. She considered herself incredibly fortunate to be the first Asian dancer on the show.

In December of 1978, she and her regular dance partner, Randy Thomas, were practicing to dance for a Christmas party they were performing in. As he did a lift, picking her up toward the ceiling, he accidentally dropped her and she hurt her back bad enough for a trip to the hospital. She stayed in the hospital for a few weeks, and was on bed rest for several more weeks, before she got a call from Cornelius offering her an opportunity to work in the office. That's when she really got to know her soon-to-be boss.

There was a whole new crop of dancers who became characters that viewers looked for in the '80s. Derek "Fox" Fleming was a high-energy dancer with model looks, and at six foot three was the peacemaker of the crew. He got along with everybody, particularly the ladies, and brought new girls to audition for the show every week after partying at clubs like Moody's, Club Paradise, Danceteria, and 24K Club. The *Soul Train* staff requested often that he choreograph the openings for the show. He wore a foxtail on his belt, and had a different hairstyle and look on each show.

Nieci Payne, a beautiful fair-skinned beauty with a thick hourglass figure and a long ponytail, had been dancing since she was six years old and had danced on the original show in Chicago. The local show held dance contests daily and she won one of them—the prize was a new pair of shoes from Campbell's Department Store. By the time Payne was seventeen, she was touring with the Commodores. When the group sang "Brick House" in concert—*she knows she's got everything that a woman needs to get a man/how can she lose with the sex she use, 36-24-36, what a winning hand*—she was the "brick house" girl that came onstage and danced.

When the Los Angeles version of the show came on, Payne met another dancer, Thelma Davis, who took her on the show. Payne dazzled the audience with her million-dollar smile and sexy, colorful outfits. On her first appearance on the show, she wore tie-dyed powder-blue balloon pants, a matching tie-dyed T-shirt, and carried pom-poms, while she pop-locked.

Another dancer that joined the ranks was a five foot one buxom Bronx bombshell named Rosie Perez. Perez, looking to get a break as an actress, spent time in Los Angeles and landed on *Soul Train*. She electrified viewers at home with her East Coast energy, overtly sexual dances and clothes, and her brash New York charm. Cornelius was wary of the sexual suggestiveness—she would pump her back, her breasts jiggling, pantomime her hands on her behind, and wear tight, skimpy clothing. Cornelius was worried about the direction in which the show was heading, and about the direction in which black music was heading—with its increasingly shallow lyrics and technologically enhanced sounds. (Though he joined the bandwagon as the revenue continued to increase.)

Another dancer, Odis Medley, wore Halloween-style masks as he danced down the line. Five dancers from this period would go on to be stars in their respective fields: Jermaine Stewart, a flamboyant R&B singer who became good friends with Watley and Daniel and auditioned for Shalamar, but lost to Howard Hewett; Vivica Fox, who had moved to California to attend college and later became an actress; and MC Hammer, who would become a multi-Platinum artist and create iconic fashion statements with his balloon pants and dance moves. There were other fan favorites that didn't make it to stardom like Fantasy and Diesel, two handsome, chiseled dancers who specialized in body snapping and waving, flipping, always breaking the rules, and wearing costumes (like pirate costumes) or appearing in trash cans as fat kids with their bellies padded with cotton. Fantasy and Diesel started dancing in local clubs, winning so many dance contests that they were able to buy twin Corvettes with the cash they made. They used their winnings to buy clothes to appear on Soul Train—to them still the most desirable place to be even though they didn't get paid.

Since the show first took off in the '70s, dancers couldn't get on without a recommendation. There were just too many people and not enough space to accommodate them. Chuck Johnson would pick the attractive girls and the gay guys who were regulars and could dance. Straight guys had to come with a gimmick. Diesel got in by wearing baggy pants, a tight Capezio shirt and stretching like a ballerina doing pirouettes and twirling around in the line of dancers waiting to get in. Johnson assumed he was one of the gay dancers that could dance and came to the show regularly, and let him in.

But it was Louie "Ski" Carr, a six foot five black Mexican, who would resonate with the thugs, boy bands, future hip-hop heads, and women of every hue for years to come. Carr was movie star handsome with chiseled features. When he first came on Soul Train he had long, black curly hair styled in a jheri curl (which he traded for a short cut). He donned 1920s-style white suits, fedora hats, and sunglasses, rivaling only Don Cornelius himself in his sartorial choices. Carr won over dance coordinator Chuck Johnson as he waited in line hoping to gain entrance to the show by wearing a black tuxedo, a bow tie, and holding a cane.

He mesmerized audiences, with skits, with subtle cool posing. He leaped like a ballerina from one riser to another, which garnered him the nickname "Ski." He stood and posed. He pointed toward the ceiling in a signature move he dubbed the "Cutty Finger Salute." Influenced by James Brown and Elvis Presley, he would imitate Michael Jackson's signature kicks and glides with perfection. But mostly, as he danced he sweated out cool. Men idolized him and girls would kill for him.

In 1983, fresh from the Orchard Park housing projects in Boston, the R&B group New Edition featuring Ronnie DeVoe, Bobby Brown, Ricky Bell, Michael Bivens, and Ralph Tresvant were the hottest progenitors of the rekindled boy band phenomenon of the '80s. Melding the style of the Jackson Five and the Temptations with bubblegum funk, they had created a crazed fandom made up of teenage urban girls. Their precise choreography, a definitively energetic take on the Temptations, was modeled after the soul group Blue Magic, a favorite of their choreographer Brooke Payne, Ronnie DeVoe's uncle. They carried the baton of Cholly Atkins from Motown and added hip-hop. Payne, who was a drill sergeant with their choreography, named them the New Edition to signify that they were a "new edition" of the Jackson Five.

The consummate bad boy and standout, Bobby Brown, told the group that one day they would make it to the pinnacle: they would dance on *Soul Train*. None of the other members believed him, even when they got their first record deal—a prize for winning a talent show—on Arthur Baker's independent label, Streetwise Records. New Edition's first album, entitled *Candy Girl*, launched them into instant stardom. They performed the title track (which shot to No. 1 on both the American R&B singles chart and the UK singles chart) on *Soul Train*. For them, performing on the show meant they had made it. Even when they made their first video for the single "Popcorn Love," to them it wasn't as significant as performing on *Soul Train*. This would be their first national performance on television.

While they waited to go on, someone told Louie "Ski" Carr that the group members were fans of his and they had wanted to meet him for years. They had watched his signature moves and cool posing for years on the show. Carr went over to the teens and shook their hands.

"Where are y'all from?" Carr asked.

"Boston," they answered apprehensively.

"Well, welcome to the train," he said to wide smiles.

They told him that they had talked about him for years and promised that if they ever got on the train, they would make it a point to meet him. They had been intrigued by him and his California style. They said they were told his name was George by someone back in Boston, and every time they saw him on television they would point and say, "There's George!" They bought suits like his and waited for the day they would meet him in person.

On the set, they asked Carr if he could come onstage when they performed their hit, "Candy Girl." Excited about the opportunity to get onstage, he told them he would, but only if they didn't tell Cornelius—because Carr knew Cornelius would have stopped it.

Dressed in white outfits and dazzling with high-energy choreographed steps, they were infectious performers. During the last minute of New Edition's performance on the show, Carr emerged from the side of the stage, doing a hop-skip behind the teens, towering over them, wearing a black leather suit, sunglasses, and a black derby hat. Effortlessly, he moved in sync with their choreography before he ended in a lifted-leg Michael Jackson–style kick, momentarily stayed frozen in place, and exited as miraculously as he took the stage. Cornelius sauntered onto the stage looking befuddled: "Big Louie!" he said, making his voice deeper than it already was, "Don't come on stage no more."

He turned to New Edition: "I realize you guys asked Louie to do this. You like Louie?"

"Yeahhhh," they answer as if he had asked if they liked Santa Claus.

"Well, Louie can't dance too well," Cornelius says.

"Yeah, yeah," they say incredulously. "I like his style."

"You like that style?" Cornelius asks. "He can't pop or lock."

"But he can George, though," Ricky Bell says.

"What are your names?" Cornelius turns to Brown.

"Bobby Brown, I'm fourteen." "Ralph Tresvant, I'm fifteen years old."

"You don't look like you're fifteen—you on some Jackson Five stuff," Cornelius teases him.

"Michael Bivins, fifteen."

"Ronald DeVoe, fifteen."

"Ricky Bell, I'm sixteen."

"You are aware that you are compared to another group—is that good or bad or are you indifferent?" Cornelius asks.

"That's good, we take it as a compliment, knowing that people compare us to the Jackson Five," Tresvant says.

"What are you gonna do with all the money you make?"

"I'm gonna invest my money," Michael says. Ralph, Ricky, and Ronnie agree, nodding their heads.

"Absolutely," Don says.

"I'm gonna spend my money," Bobby says quietly. The Soul Train Gang hears him and laughs.

"Hope you come back later and do a song for us," Cornelius says.

Carr's relationship with the group wouldn't end after he danced with them onstage. He went on to have a cameo in their *My Secret* video (filmed at the LA Forum and featuring Magic Johnson as a guest) and tour with them around the world.

But in the next year, 1984, Carr would lose and gain some major cool points during one episode. He decided to walk blindly to the edge of the stage with his back facing the television audience. He was going to embark in the circle of trust—fall backwards into the Soul Train dancers and surely someone would catch him. The problem was no one was told *they* would be the one to catch him.

As he began to fall backwards, none of his usual crew was there to catch him—just five perplexed dancing young ladies were within reach.

WHAM!!!!!!

He fell directly onto the floor and like on a cartoon, just the soles of his shoes were visible. The cameramen cut to another angle and panned in on Cheryl Song and Randy Thomas. Song didn't flinch, though Carr was still on the ground, as she saw the camera coming toward her. No one wanted to ruin their sole camera time, and she wasn't going to be the first to do it. Thomas stopped and said, "Oh no!" He tapped her, like, "Look!" Song kept dancing. The camera came back to Carr, who instantly jumped onstage and did a magnetic pose, wordlessly conveying: *I'm not hurt, nothing to see here, people.*

At the same time, on the opposite end of the floor, Pat Davis was engaged in a salacious dance where her hips were wrapped around her dance partner's pelvis. In the next second, magically, she and her partner appeared on camera near Carr. No one seemed to care that Carr could have broken his neck. This scene was either a testament to Cornelius's insistence on perfection or a window into the importance of dancers getting and staying in the spotlight, at all costs.

———

At the *Soul Train* offices, Song answered phones, screened guests who came in, helped to get the show ready, traveled to record companies to obtain new music, and penned write-ups about who would be on the show for people in the business. It was the second golden era of the show; money was rolling in, and everything was at their disposal.

Cornelius was still dating a Bob Mackey model, Vicky Avila. On the side, he dated a blonde model. One Valentine's Day, Song was given the task of getting them both Valentine's Day gifts. She was instructed to buy them the same gift for fear that she would deliver the wrong gift to the wrong woman. There would be a revolving door of other models that Cornelius would entertain while Avila remained his steady girlfriend.

There was so much money being made that eventually people were having a hard time keeping up with it. Cornelius's accountant worked in the office with Song, signing the checks. Nothing came through the office without her approval. She was always dressed in the best clothes, and she would take lavish vacations overseas and to the Caribbean. No one questioned why she was always flush with cash because she was always right beside Cornelius. People assumed that he paid her a handsome salary to do all of his bidding. He entrusted her with everything—from what artists to put on the show to staging to writing the checks. Because she handled the books, it took several years for Cornelius to realize that she had steadily been embezzling money from him.

After Cornelius realized what was going on and cursed out the entire staff, his assistant was never heard from again. Cornelius stopped trusting anyone that had been friends with her, including his protégé O'Bryan, who was tight with her. He cut back on the crew. He and Pam Brown fell out and she quit. Before long, he stopped trusting everyone and stopped speaking to much of the staff.

There were other changes Cornelius would have to adjust to in the music industry. As a music connoisseur, he had always enjoyed the music as much as meeting the guests he had on the show. Suddenly, a new genre of music had emerged from the ashes of concrete in the Bronx, and Cornelius, with his Chicago cool, gangster pose, and race man sensibilities would not be able to relate.

8

A BEAT LIKE THIS MIGHT TEMPT ME

This is not Michael Jackson, and this is not "Thriller"!
—from "King of Rock," by Run-D.M.C.

By 1979, the music industry was changing fast, and *Soul Train* and Don Cornelius were struggling to keep up. On July 12, 1979, Comiskey Park became the receptacle for rock and roll fans' revulsion, as the end of the disco era was inaugurated with mass burnings of disco albums in the park; the event became popularly characterized as "the night disco died." Led by shock jock Steve Dahl, tens of thousands of disco records were blown up on the field between games of the doubleheader. Part of the backlash against disco stemmed from the presumption of gay culture associated with the music, but also grew from what some thought about the music itself—too mechanical and simplistic.

Black pop, led by superstars Michael Jackson and Whitney Houston, exploded—and Houston and Jackson, both now on mainstream labels, became the forbearers of crossover success. Prince and Madonna were showcasing a new sexual freedom. A new blue-eyed soul invasion led by artists like Boy George and Hall and Oates were giving a new face to race-based soul sounds. The conglomeration of radio companies led to the segregation of radio and the new radio format became Top 40.

In the next year, President Ronald Reagan would ride in like the grim reaper and cut federally funded programs for the poor, dismantle tax incentives for investing in the arts, and fire air traffic control strikers, which helped to weaken the power of unions. With a commitment to big business over social programs, government expected individuals to pull themselves up and out. The less the government aided people through welfare strategies to provide food and housing, the more likely the poor were to become dependent was the philosophy. The income gap between rich and poor widened, budget deficits increased, and a recession was inevitable. The black poor became more isolated. By 1982, the unemployment rate among black men had soared to twice the level among whites, passing 21 percent in 1983. Amidst the misery, in the poorest neighborhoods of New York City, a musical cultural renaissance was happening. Dubbed "hip-hop" it impressed with colorful graffiti, captivated with "b-boying," and had people dancing to a new creative style of deejaying, where "turntablists" reconfigured breakbeats so the rhythms were continuous. The last element, rapping, happened largely over gritty funk and soul samples from disco, R&B, and soul icons like James Brown. Though hip-hop was the antithesis of disco—disco music was sampled without irony.

It wouldn't be long before someone thought to package it for a national television audience.

A young, mixed-race ex–Wall Street junior investment banker, a New York kid named Michael Holman, had been a fan of *Soul Train*, *Hullabaloo*, and *Shindig!* as much for the music as the dancing and fashion culture.

In a *Soul Train* format, Holman created a pilot for a hip-hop dance show and called it *Graffiti Rock*. The show took a much more heavy-handed, didactic approach than Cornelius's "live and let live" approach to showcasing culture. But it was the only approach Holman could use to explain this new curiosity to the mainstream.

Holman had long been giving artists a venue to expose their work. He cocreated graffiti art events, which helped to establish a then-obscure graffiti artist named Jean-Michel Basquiat.

Holman helped to nurture another graffiti artist named Fab Five Freddy (who modeled his early art after Andy Warhol) and Puerto Rican political graffiti artist Lee Quinones. Quinones's quote from one of his pieces, "Graffiti is art and if art is a crime, please God, forgive me," would be used in the Harry Belafonte-produced, Stan Lathan–directed hip-hop movie *Beat Street*, released in 1984.

Holman worked with the b-boying group, the NYC Breakers, and became the manager for the Rock Steady Crew. Before that, he had worked with the b-boying dancing crew International Break Masters. He would be one of the first to record hip-hop culture in print, writing one of the first profiles on deejay and godfather of hip-hop, Afrika Bambaataa, and the Soulsonic Force for the *East Village Eye* newspaper.

Bambaataa, who grew up in the Bronx River Housing Projects and was raised by an activist mother, was the perfect representative for hip-hop's beginnings. Through his mother, he bore witness to the black liberation movement. Despite her influence, he ended up becoming a warlord for the gang the Black Spades. The Black Spades cleared out drug dealers, assisted with community health programs, and fought, often to the death, with other gang members for turf. When Bambaataa won a trip to Africa as a prize for a school essay competition, it changed his consciousness, as he saw the solidarity of the Zulu. He came back to the States, and along with Jamaican-born deejay Kool Herc and Brooklyn-born Kool DJ Dee, began hosting hip-hop parties and organizing block parties around the South Bronx.

Holman would introduce former manager of the Sex Pistols and British musician, Malcolm McLaren, to this strange new world, along with RCA executive Rory Johnston, when Bambaataa invited him to a block party at the Bronx River Projects. Holman picked up Malcolm and Rory at Malcolm's hotel room at the Le Parker Meridien Hotel in Midtown at 119 W. 56th Street. They flagged down a gypsy cab driven by a Puerto Rican woman at 57th Street and Sixth Avenue. When Holman, McLaren, and Johnston got out of the cab and walked toward the Bronx River Projects, the first thing that struck them was that all of the streetlights had been shot out. Fights were breaking out left and right. Lights from project windows cast eerie zigzags on the concrete. Funky beats wafted through at a frenzied pace as Bambaataa and another deejay, Jazzy Jay, spun records. McLaren was scared.

But he couldn't deny the infectious energy around him. Bambaataa was playing the Monkee's "Mary Mary," mixing it with Jimmy Castor Bunch's "Just Begun," while hundreds of junior high kids—kids who weren't old enough for the downtown clubs—danced. He would switch from the live version of James Brown's "Give It Up or Turnit a Loose"—mixing the beats, segueing into the theme song of the television show *I Dream of Jeannie*. Among his many talents, he was a turntable artist—who would find the backbeat or chorus or a riff to use to merge into another song, mixing it manually until it became a collage—often extending the songs until it became another sound altogether. Everything was acceptable as long as it had a groove. It was the summer of 1982.When McLaren saw all that was going on, he started talking about showcasing it at The Roxy in Manhattan. Holman thought much bigger. He wanted to take it to television.

Holman talked to a few investment bankers from Paine Webber who had invested in New Edition's first record label, Streetwise Records owned by Arthur Baker, and they immediately believed in the idea of *Graffiti Rock*. Holman wanted to hire New York radio deejay Mr. Magic to work on the show, and Debbie Mazur, a dancer who was part of the downtown club scene, to dance on the show. Afrika Bambaataa would serve as the music consultant.

On the pilot, the show's title appeared in colorful graffiti bubble letters, as a sparse crowd danced on the risers. Kool Moe Dee, from the group the Treacherous Three, dressed in white and gray leather and a Kangol cap, and Special K, dressed in burgundy leather from head to toe, rapped during the introduction about the merits of the show that the audience was about to see. Right after they finished, Holman magically appeared between the two of them, dressed in a black shearling vest and Cazal sunglasses with the lenses out. He started rapping with a jerky lack of rhythm: "Party people in the place to be—this is a crazy fresh show called *Graffiti Rock*...now you know why the show is number one, 'cause we are all about having fun."

The show started out with a jaw-dropping display of breaking by the New York City Breakers. Before commercial breaks and during breaks between acts, a slang term written in graffiti appeared on the screen along with a definition. The slang term *fresh* was defined as the "hippest, newest, most together, most unique." Two teenage dancers, a boy and a girl, were interviewed specifically about their fashion—the girl sported a Le Coq Sportif shirt and Adidas with fat laces, while the teenage boy explained his Kangol and Cazals. The dancers, wearing name belts and chains, Sasson jeans, Izod and Le Coq Sportif shirts, and sweat suits moved in b-boy and b-girl style, popping and moving their bodies effortlessly, doing the wave to the latest club 12-inch single hits—"Let Me Love You," by the Force MDs, and "Hey! DJ," by the World's Famous Supreme Team. Run-D.M.C. performed "Sucker M.C.'s" live and then battled Kool Moe Dee and Special K in a contrived rhyme fest.

Holman took the show to the National Association of Producers of Television Entertainment Conference in Las Vegas. Some showed interest, but most of them had no idea what they were seeing. Many of them didn't see the difference between his show and *Soul Train*. Others thought hip-hop was a passing fad. One producer for a New York station promised to put it on the air if they were paid in cash $10,000 under the table per episode. Holman refused.

The same year that Holman was turned down for *Graffiti Rock*, in 1984, he and the New York City Breakers appeared on *Soul Train* on May 5. Cornelius, who had been leery of allowing his dancers to participate in breaking on the show would devote a portion of a segment devoted to honor Dionne Warwick to the NYC Breakers as the Soul Train dancers gathered around them in a circle of amazement, watching them uprock, glide, and head spin.

Cornelius looked worried as they prepared to make magic on the floor in just black bodysuits and Puma sneakers.

"Let me get everybody's name before you break the place up!" Cornelius said, his voice hot with frustration. As they spun on their hands, performed windmills, backspins, head spins, and the wave effortlessly, the Soul Train dancers stood around them in a circle of awe and clapped. After the breakers performed, Cornelius talked to Holman about his work with the movie *Beat Street*, with Harry Belafonte and Stan Lathan, and the coming-of-age teen-angst film, *Sixteen Candles*. He and the NYC Breakers had cameos in both.

Graffiti Rock didn't see the light of day—at least not beyond that first pilot episode. The similarities to *Soul Train* were striking—even the tone followed the same *Soul Train* format, with the camera zooming in and out on the dancers and back to the performers on an elevated stage, breaks for interviewing guests and dancers, and a focus as much on educating as it was on entertaining. Though it didn't succeed on the airwaves, it would pave the way for *Yo! MTV Raps* as a successful vehicle that featured hip-hop exclusively. There would be fiercer competition for *Soul Train*—music videos and BET and MTV, shows like *Video Soul*—that were coming to take over in the dawning of the niche market.

Though Cornelius may have been a skeptic, *Soul Train* was one of the first shows to give b-boying this space and time. He was a trailblazer, if not a reluctant convert to hip-hop's brash attitude.

In the winter of 1979, Curtis Walker, who would become famous by his sobriquet, Kurtis Blow, was gripping a pen nervously. He was about to become the first rapper to sign a major-label deal with Mercury Records. Two former *Billboard* magazine writers, Rocky Ford and J. B. Moore, had recorded his demo with money saved from Moore's first novel. Curtis's demo had been shopped to twenty-two different record labels, and without reservation everyone proclaimed that they hated the song. Even black executives at major labels like Atlantic and Columbia were befuddled by the demo. Cory Robbins, an A&R representative for Panorama Records, would be one of the few that liked it, and offered them $10,000 for the single and the request to retain half of their publishing royalties. They agreed to the deal reluctantly. Then something strange happened.

Though Kurtis had lived in Harlem all of his life, his fandom would begin overseas. John Stainze, an A&R director at Mercury in London, loved the record and offered them a contract that would allow them to keep their publishing. All of a sudden, Kurtis became an international sensation, all the while sitting in a tiny apartment in Harlem.

By December of that year, Kurtis's debut rap song "Christmas Rap" was blasting through boomboxes and climbing over barred Harlem project windows. The deal he signed was only for two records, and only if the first record sold more than 30,000 copies and the second sold more than 100,000 copies would he get the chance to do an entire album. Few believed the record would sell, especially the executives at the label. The first single sold 370,000.

The next single was "The Breaks," an infectiously comedic take on life's disappointments, with a hard-driving original funk beat: "If your woman steps out with another man...and she runs off with him to Japan/And the IRS says they want to chat and you can't explain why you claimed your cat..."

It would be the hottest song of the summer of 1980 and would become the first certified Gold rap song. The 12-inch version became the second 12-inch record in music history to reach Gold status behind the duet with Barbra Streisand and Donna Summer, entitled "No More Tears (Enough Is Enough)." The single was on Streisand's *Wet* album and Summers' *On the Radio: Greatest Hits, Volumes 1 & 2.* (The third 12-inch single to go Gold was Madonna's "Angel/Into the Groove.") Mercury signed them for a four-album deal. Kurtis, at twenty-one years old, was becoming accepted in the upper echelon of the music industry. He was suddenly thrust into the best clubs, onto the cover of magazines, and performing with top disco artists who still commanded huge audiences, including The Village People and Donna Summer.

If any rapper were to be the first to be thrust into the mainstream, Kurtis was the perfect poster boy—articulate, young, good looking, clean cut, and charismatic. He was a born hustler, driving a cab, working at the liquor store, working as a party promoter for Russell Simmons, and going to college at City College of New York, studying communications. Underneath his clean-cut image was a past marked with drug abuse, gang life, and poor choices. After getting jumped by a gang in high school, for protection he joined a gang called the Peace Makers. It was a temporary plan, so he wouldn't get beat up again, but when his brother became the leader, he became the warlord for the Manhattan division of the gang. When his brother eventually went to jail, that was the impetus for him to stop gangbanging. Once Kurtis signed his first label deal, he didn't rap about his delinquent past—those days dried up like ink. He would rather, he told everyone who would listen, "celebrate the positives in life, not backtrack to how life was like in Harlem."

Kurtis had already honed his stage presence by rapping in parks, ballrooms, churches, and gyms around New York City, learning how to rock the crowd at clubs like the Disco Fever in the Bronx and the Hotel Diplomat Ballroom in downtown Manhattan. He created skits to warm up the crowd and get them engaged through call-and-response, the way his idol Cab Calloway did. To Kurtis, it was important that the few rappers who had made it to the big stage did well. He knew that all eyes were on him.

Rap's biggest vocal opponents were mainstays in the black middle class—seemingly a reminder of the lifestyle they would long rather forget. It would be college radio stations that would put hip-hop on the map. Stations like Columbia University's WKCR-FM featured *The Stretch Armstrong and Bobbito Show*, which featured unsigned hip-hop artists freestyling. Some artists sent in demo tapes that were played on the air, while major commercial radio was still hosting "No Rap Workdays," where stations promised listeners that rap wouldn't be played from nine in the morning until five in the afternoon.

The Sugarhill Gang made history with the party rap "Rapper's Delight"—the year before Kurtis signed his major-label deal. The cut was a playful ode to street corner braggadocio and lighthearted partying: "Ya see, I'm six foot one and I'm tons of fun and I dress to a "T"/Ya see I got more clothes than Muhammad Ali and I dress so viciously."

The record would go down as the first rap tune in history (though it wasn't—the Fatback Band's "King Tim III" is largely considered to be the first, but "Rapper's Delight" was the first commercial hit). "Rapper's Delight" was performed over a thumping bass line boosted from Bernard Edwards and Nile Rodgers of Chic's disco hit "Good Times." There was an eight-bar limit in using the line. Rodgers and Edwards would sue the group for using their song without their permission, which ended in a settlement that actually set a precedent for how similar disputes were handled in the years to come. Rodgers's and Edwards's names would be added as cowriters.

Sugar Hill Records was started by Sylvia Vanderpool Robinson (who sang as part of the duo Mickey & Sylvia) and her husband Joe Robinson, a numbers runner from Harlem. The label received financial funding from Morris Levy, owner of Roulette Records, who had ties to the Genovese crime family. Artists like Sequence, the Treacherous Three, Funky Four Plus One, and Grandmaster Flash would put not just the label but also hip-hop on the map.

The group Grandmaster Flash and the Furious Five was convinced to come to Sugar Hill Records after the success of "Rapper's Delight," and scored with their 1982 hit, "The Message." Groups like Grandmaster Flash and the Furious Five, the Treacherous Three, Sequence, and Afrika Bambaataa were making noise underground, but hadn't reached the international appeal that Kurtis did right off the bat.

Beverly Paige, the head of publicity at Mercury, was booking Kurtis for audiences who didn't have any idea about rap. Shows like *Top of the Pops* in London (which rarely played R&B, let alone rap) and *Don Kirschner's Rock Concert* were the kind of shows that Kurtis performed on early in his career.

Paige would book Kurtis for *Soul Train* and *American Bandstand* on the same weekend in September 1980. He and Paige were more excited about being on *Soul Train* than *Bandstand*. When

Paige called Kurtis and told him they got *Soul Train*, he knew that in order to be on the show, he had arrived.

When he stepped onto the set, he was anxious to meet the dancers and nervous about meeting the iconic Don Cornelius, an intimidating musical father figure to him. He relaxed temporarily when he was in the makeup room and he saw Irene Cara and knew for sure that he made it. He said to himself, "I'm a star."

But he lost his enthusiasm when he found that the tradition for *Soul Train* was for artists to lip-sync. His whole performance was dependent upon audience participation, call-and-response, feeling and responding to the energy of the crowd—it was the foundation of the art. He would never stoop so low.

"Look, let me have a live mic—just put this on the B side and play the instrumental," he asked, showing Cornelius the single as he stood outside of Cornelius's office.

"No, you have to lip-sync—that's our policy," Cornelius answered without looking up from his desk.

Then Kurtis raised his voice several octaves.

"Oh no, this ain't hip-hop! This ain't real performance! You mean to tell me all these years y'all been in here LIP-SYNCING? People ain't been singing live on *SOUL TRAIN*?! What kind of shit is this? *James Brown* was lip-syncing?!"

Cornelius came out of his office and looked at him.

"Look, this is rap—it has to be live," Kurtis tried to explain calmly. "I have to connect with the audience."

"Okay, whatever," Cornelius dismissed him and let them do a run-through with the B side.

Standing by himself without any of his deejays, Kurtis was dressed in a blazer, his carved chest exposed, a gold medallion bouncing off it. Onstage he had the crowd chanting back at him, "That's the breaks!! That's the breaks!!!" Every time he asked, the crowd delivered. Still, he was nervous. Known around New York for his breaking skills, his live show wasn't complete without splits and acrobatics, but on *Soul Train*, he was nervous and danced conservatively in between rapping.

Even with his comparatively reserved performance, the crowd was into him and cheered when he finished. He had achieved another first—becoming the first hip-hop artist to rap live on *Soul Train.*

Before Cornelius began his interview with Kurtis, he leaned over and told Kurtis into the mic, "I don't really understand what you guys are talking about, but everybody seems to love it." Kurtis attempted a weak smile, but he was clearly crestfallen. He couldn't believe the godfather of black show business just insulted his music. "It doesn't make sense to old guys like me. I mean I don't understand why they love it so much. But that ain't my job—my job is to deal with it," Cornelius went on, oblivious to Kurtis's reaction.

After Kurtis's performance on *Soul Train,* his celebrity skyrocketed. He couldn't walk down the street without getting asked for his autograph. He needed a crew of people with him when he went out in public. "Before, I could walk down 125th Street and shake a couple of hands, but after *Soul Train* everybody wanted an autograph," he remembered.

Kurtis was the answer to the cynicism surrounding hip-hop. *Soul Train* had presented and packaged it to the mainstream. That next year, he opened for the Commodores and Bob Marley at Madison Square Garden, a few months before Marley's death in May of 1981. Marley would shake his hand and tell him he liked what he was doing. That same year he would star in a Sprite commercial.

In 1982, Paige booked Kurtis to open for the British punk rock group the Clash at Pier 84, a floating stage next to the Intrepid, in New York City. Rock and rap were still distant cousins (Kurtis would later feature Bob Dylan as a guest on his single "Street Rock"), related by a rebellious spirit. But many rock purists didn't understand or accept hip-hop.

The Clash was an intimidating group and often drew a crowd that was difficult to open for—many newbies were barraged with bottles and beer cans. Gregory Isaacs was infamously booed. Many top-rated artists didn't make it opening for them unscathed by empty bottles.

Kurtis had a different idea. As an emcee he had grown used to pumping up a crowd, prepping them with anticipation.

"Are you ready to hear the Clash?" he asked the impatient crowd.

"AAAAHHHHHHHHH!!!!!" they screamed.

"Well, ladies and gentleman—my name is Kurtis Blow, and the Clash asked me to come out and sing one song for you. Can I sing one song?"

"RAHHHHHHHH!!!!" they roared as he launched smoothly into "The Breaks."

After "The Breaks" he asked: "Are you ready for the Clash? "If you're ready, say HOOOOO!!"

"HOOOOOO!" they answered.

"Everybody scream!"

"AHHHHHHHHHHHH!!!!!!" He had them in the palm of his hand. Or so he thought. He heard a surge of booing coming from the ground.

"Okay, one more song and then the Clash will come out," Kurtis played this game with them for another thirty-five minutes. He did this for three nights and had everybody up in the stands dancing and didn't get beer bottles thrown at him. The Clash ended up taking him on tour doing thirty shows around America, introducing hip-hop to a hardcore rock 'n' roll crowd.

—

Sylvia Robinson had gained fame with her sexually charged hit song "Pillow Talk," a song she had written and performed on *Soul Train* in 1976. After her performance she became close friends with Cornelius. When she, along with her husband, Joe, put together the Sugarhill Gang, she called Cornelius to see if they could perform on the show.

When the group came to *Soul Train*, all of a sudden the ever-cool, hip Cornelius was struggling to fit in. He was awkward, trying to make jokes with these new brash pioneers, and he was drowning.

The episode aired in May of 1981. The group performed "Rapper's Delight," which when released sold 50,000 copies per day, rose to No. 4 on *Billboard*'s Hot R&B/Hip-Hop songs chart and No. 36 on the *Billboard* 100. In Europe, Israel, and South Africa it went to No. 5.

The Sugarhill Gang was honored to be on the show. In the dressing room, Cornelius came in and made sure they were comfortable. Within two days time, they were going to perform for tapings of *American Bandstand, Solid Gold,* and *Soul Train.* A grueling schedule, but all they could do was wonder whether Damita Jo Freeman would somehow be coming back to the show that day. And where was Pat Davis with her slanted eyes and aloof, mysterious attitude? They were trying to pay attention as Cornelius interviewed them after their performance of "Rapper's Delight," but they were looking at all of the dancers they recognized.

After they performed "8th Wonder," their second hit, where they were dressed in blazers, ties, prep-boy sweaters, and Master Gee was shirtless with a blue suit and a white bow tie around his neck, Cornelius came onstage with his three-piece suit on and starts off jokingly, "Alright Hill...Sugar."

Master Gee begins to give an answer to Cornelius's question about what "this rap thing is all about."

"A rapper is a cat who rhythmically raps under any given beat."

"You did it in discos back East?" Cornelius asks.

"Anywhere we could."

"Parties?"

"Anywhere."

"The street?"

"Anywhere." They all laugh. Cornelius is bemused, if not clueless—as is most of the world about rap. It shows in his awkward questions and nervous laugh. He asks, "Have you found that the idea of rapping has spread here in the United States?"

"We toured Europe and South America, and the response was just as good as it is here," Master Gee answers.

"How has it changed your life," Cornelius asks Wonder Mike.

"It took me to places I never thought I'd go. I found myself in different worlds, trying to speak the language of the people."

"You guys seem educated," Cornelius says, surprised.

Master Gee retorts, "What did you expect?"

Master Gee's response is edited out of the segment.

━━

Run-D.M.C., the rap group from Hollis, Queens, composed of Joey "Run" Simmons, Darryl "D.M.C." McDaniels, and their deejay, Jason "Jam Master Jay" Mizell, would come together in 1981 and become the most influential group in hip-hop's history. They became the first hip-hop act to perform on *American Bandstand*; their album, *King of Rock*, went Gold, and MTV played their video, *Rock Box*. Hip-hop had officially reached the mainstream. But after they had appeared on *Soul Train* in June of 1984, they described Cornelius to Lee Bailey on his syndicated radio show, *Radioscope*, as "the uncle that invites you to his house and complains about you putting your feet on the coffee table." They received a much warmer reception from Dick Clark.

On October 25, 1986, Run-D.M.C. fresh off of a tour in England, performed "Hit It Run" from their *Raising Hell* album. McDaniels dressed in their customary black leather jackets and pants and Adidas sneakers and Jam Master Jay rocking the turntable behind them, and deejay Hurricane (then Run-D.M.C.'s bodyguard) standing onstage mean mugging with his arms folded. The crowd—many dressed in conservative '80s suits and ties—jumped up and down madly during the whole performance, waving their arms, screaming in ecstatic celebration, while they rhymed back and forth bouncing off of each other's words like an old married couple: "I leave all suckers in the dust, those dumb muthafuckas can't mess with us/Beats flow from Joe and never stop, better get yourself together, let's rock, HIT IT RUN!"

The group had out-cooled the coolest man in show business—Cornelius was left speechless. The dancers wouldn't stop screaming.

"Welcome to the Run-D.M.C. show, okay!" Cornelius says. "It's called popularity, huh?"

140

"Something like that," Run says.

Cornelius was equally flustered when rap pioneers Eric B. & Rakim came on for their first national television debut and performed "I Know You Got Soul," which featured the line, "Grab the mic like I'm on *Soul Train!!*" The Soul Train dancers screamed in unison when Rakim got to the line and were so hyped that they were jumping up and down the whole time they were onstage.

Cornelius came out to another awkward interview.

"Rakim, you don't smile too much."

"I ain't no joke," Rakim answers, a line from the group's second single, released on his *Paid in Full* album. Cornelius laughed. Rakim didn't.

"Yeah, I gathered that," Cornelius says. "I see Eric smiles," he said, trying hard to relate, turning to Eric. "What's the matter with your brother, he don't smile?"

"It's a strong positive image. That's our image, Eric B. and Rakim," Eric answers.

"I don't like the way Rakim is looking at me," Cornelius says to a deadpan expression from Rakim. Then he tries to save face: "You fellas have a lot of charisma. It is something about the way you play and Rak-*eem* has a low pitch that's unusual for me. We'd like you to come back, and you don't have to smile a lot. I don't smile a lot either, and I ain't no joke. Let's hear it for Eric B. and Rak-*eeem!*" Cornelius says, turning to the audience and mispronouncing Rakim's name.

He was no less awkward with progressive rappers. When Arrested Development, an Afrocentric, alternative hip-hop group came on in December 1992, they were taken aback by the women dancing in skimpy clothes.

"We have this whole grassroots movement, these women have their dresses up to here," said Speech, Arrested Development's lead vocalist, pointing to his thigh as he started to tell Cornelius, who was moving around, overseeing the set, towering over him.

"Excuse me, Mr. Cornelius!" said Speech.

Don finally looked down at him.

"We have a different type of thing," Speech started again. "We have our own dancers."

"Oh, you want the dancers off?" Cornelius asks nonplussed. "Get the bitches off the stage!"

When the sex symbol of rap—a dark, handsome, six foot one emcee named Big Daddy Kane—came on *Soul Train*, he also insisted that he wouldn't lip-sync. Kane was a big fan of the show and was so inspired by it that when he broke his arm in a motorcycle accident, he insisted on going on tour with his arm in a sling because he saw Al Green perform on *Soul Train* with a broken arm. He compromised with Cornelius, telling him that he would record the vocals in the studio with no reverb, much louder than the track to make it sound like it was being performed live. He even recorded the ad-libs, "Put your hands in the air!" and "Somebody say HO!!!!"

When the people in the studio heard it, they called in Cornelius.

"So, brother Kane, are you going to remember all of this?" he asked slowly.

"I've got it, this is what I do onstage every night for this song."

"Well, impress me."

Kane performed splits, stepped into his two dancer's hands and jumped down into a split, then switched sides to do another split.

The group, Public Enemy, performing "Rebel Without a Pause," came onboard—along with an eighteen-year-old LL Cool J wearing his customary thick gold rope chains and a Kangol, Whodini, and Eric B. & Rakim—one weekend, as they shot two episodes. It was October of 1987, and *Soul Train* was a stop along the Def Jam tour that included all of them. At the time, radio stations weren't playing Public Enemy, and they had been banned from *Soul Train* because Flavor Flav had jumped onstage during a taping of another performance. But Cornelius came to understand what the group was about and invited them to perform in October to promote their debut album, *Yo! Bum Rush the Show*. At the end of their performance of "Rebel Without a Pause," Cornelius responded with, "That was scary!" The second time they appeared later that year in December, Flavor in a moment of clarity asked for a moment of silence for Redd Foxx and Miles Davis to realize the magnitude of the contributions of these icons. Cornelius gave him the time. *Soul Train* would be the promotional vehicle that would catapult them to become a national sensation. By 1991, when they appeared again to perform "Can't Truss It" and "Shut 'Em Down" from the *Apocalypse 91...The Enemy Strikes Back*, Cornelius had become a convert to the group. "I don't know much about rap, but Public Enemy, I like them," Chuck D remembered Cornelius telling them, "Even crazy ass Flavor." "We relished in that," said Chuck about getting validation from Cornelius.

The Beastie Boys were made up of three white emcees— Michael "Mike D" Diamond, Adam "MCA" Yauch, and Adam "Ad-Rock" Horovitz—and originally formed as a hardcore punk band and came to be a hip-hop trio in 1983. They released their first album, *Licensed to Ill*, in 1986 on Rick Rubin's (their former deejay) Def Jam Records, and appeared on *Soul Train* on March 7, 1987. They took over the show, slam dancing into the audience of Soul Train dancers.

It was clear that the *Soul Train* where Cornelius called all the shots and artists felt honored to be in his presence and on the show was something of the past. *Soul Train* wasn't ahead of the curve anymore, and it was starting to show. But Cornelius had a new idea that would prove to be more lucrative than the weekly show.

9

MAKING A FORTUNE SAWING NICKELS IN HALF

"Mr. Van Peebles, how did you get to the top?" I told him the truth: No one would let me in at the bottom.

—Melvin Van Peebles

By the late '80s, Cornelius had changed his sartorial choices from the colorful suits, wide neckties, knee-length boots, sunglasses, and perfectly coiffed Afro to a supremely more conservative three-piece suit, a neatly tapered jheri curl, and reading glasses. His movements were slower, and the sharp clip at which he spread his profound bass around the studio was dragging, more measured than it had ever been. He was getting older, while everything around him was blossoming, moving at breakneck speed, changing and renewing itself.

In June of 1981, Robert Johnson's Black Entertainment Television Network had launched a new video show, *Video Soul*. It catered to R&B artists and was hosted by a handsome, dreamy, hazel-eyed, local Washington, DC, deejay named Donnie Simpson. Later that summer, in August of 1981, the cable music channel, MTV, launched. It was initially conceived as a channel that would air music videos specifically for rock music stars. Three months later Home Box Office (HBO) launched a music video show, *Video Jukebox*, on its network, which reached more households than MTV.

Two years later, SuperStation WTBS launched its own video show, *Night Tracks*, which boasted fourteen hours of music videos played each day. But while *Night Tracks* aired videos by black artists, MTV continued to reject them.

Soon after, NBC also launched a music video show, *Friday Night Videos*, an hour and a half show (later cut down to an hour) that aired at twelve thirty in the morning. Frankie Crocker was the first of many hosts for its nineteen-year run. The show was produced by Dick Ebersol and Burt Sugarman. Sugarman had also produced *Midnight Special*, the music variety show that ran in the '70s, where celebrity artists were allowed to play live music. Meanwhile, Ralph McDaniels, a New York deejay and hip-hop pioneer, created another music video show, *Video Music Box*, in 1983. Though the show aired only locally in New York City on public television station WNYC-TV, it enlightened networks to the untapped urban audience as it grew in popularity. *Yo! MTV Raps*, hosted by Fab Five Freddy, Ed Lover, and Dr. Dre, followed *Video Music Box* in 1988 on MTV. The channel featured hip-hop music videos exclusively—a first on television, and a colossal success.

By 1989, *American Bandstand* had gone off the air. And by 1990, Cornelius also began playing music videos on *Soul Train* as one of the segments on the show.

All of these shows cut into *Soul Train*'s sponsorship—particularly shows like *Video Soul*, which ran during prime time and courted bigger sponsors. As sponsorship dried up, Cornelius searched for answers. Some of the personnel suggested that they start making cuts. Cornelius was insistent that it keep going as is, if for no other reason than they employed so many people; layoffs would affect hundreds of livelihoods. As he searched for new revenue streams, a gift from an angel, "his black angel," as he referred to him, would appear.

Don Jackson, the former advertising director for WVON, had moved on from the radio station and created his own company, Central City Productions, at the same time that Cornelius was launching *Soul Train*. Jackson had once refused to work with Cornelius, predicting that the "show would never work."

Since leaving WVON Jackson had focused his efforts on building his company, which specialized in marketing, promotion, sales, and the production of media and television programs for black Americans. As *Soul Train* became successful over the years, Jackson would come to eat his words over his initial skepticism about the program. But pride didn't get in his way when he noticed that his old friend's advertising numbers were beginning to dwindle. Cornelius revealed to him that he wanted to start an awards show in the same vein as the American Music Awards—hoping to fill a void where black artists were routinely neglected on music award shows like the Grammy Awards and the American Music Awards. Jackson suggested partnering with Capital City Productions. Cornelius was underpriced and losing coverage, losing time periods, and represented by people who didn't have his best interests at stake. Broadcast television, at the time, was more inclined to seek paid television advertising, rather than independently produced programs like Cornelius's syndicated program.

At the time, Johnson Products was also losing steam. By the early '70s Johnson had received $10.2 million when the company became the first black-owned firm to trade on the AMSE. George Johnson had a mansion in Glencoe, Illinois, houses in Jamaica and Paris, and two cattle ranches in Mississippi and contributed to a number of black charities. He bought his wife extravagant gifts—she owned twenty fur coats, a Rolls-Royce convertible. Barbecues at their farm featured private air shows for friends.

People in the business world started taking notice, particularly his competition. Revlon, a white-owned hair-care product company, was interested in paying $60 to $70 million for Johnson's company, but he wasn't interested. His rebuke caused the ire of Revlon executives. They fought back, hiring a black sales force and marketing similar relaxer products. By 1975, the Federal Trade Commission ordered Johnson Products to warn customers on their packaging about the dangers of using lye. The FTC didn't require Revlon to do the same until twenty-two months later, and only after a lawsuit by Johnson Products. But the damage had already been done—Johnson's sales had fallen by 14 percent. By 1989, he and his wife, Joan Johnson, his high school sweetheart, were engaged in a bitter divorce. His wife received his controlling share of the stock in the company in 1989 to dissolve their thirty-eight-year marriage. Johnson had wanted to keep the company in the black community, but two years later his ex-wife sold the company to Ivax Corporation for $37.5 million in stock and a one-year annual salary of $300,000. Cornelius's loyal national advertiser was no more. The year before the sale of Johnson Products, Motown had also been sold from black interests to MCA and Boston ventures for $61 million; it was the second-largest black-owned corporation after Johnson Publications (unrelated to Johnson Products, Johnson Publications, owned by John H. Johnson, publishes *Ebony* and *Jet* magazines) to be sold.

Meanwhile, Jackson told Cornelius that he had a distribution deal with the Tribune Company, and he shared a strategy to get the weekly show on prime-time slots in top markets. Cornelius couldn't refuse the offer. Jackson distributed, syndicated, and sold advertising—generating more than twenty million dollars in advertising over two to three years. His company earned more than five million dollars in commissions. They had enough money to launch the Soul Train Music Awards in 1987. Big-name advertisers, particularly car advertisers who refused to advertise on the network show, were more willing to take a chance with the award show because it aired during prime time and attracted a more diverse viewership.

For the first few years of the awards show, Cornelius had no problem booking acts. On March 23, 1987, the Soul Train Music Awards made its debut. For reporters with the black press, it was as enthralling as the thought of covering the first black president. Lee Bailey, reporting for Radioscope, described it as the "highlight of my career." For such a long time black talent had courted recognition, only to be ignored on mainstream award shows despite hefty sales and popularity. This would be a place for them to finally be honored—in a venue that was equal parts coming-home ceremony, family reunion, and professional

Hip-hop group Salt-N-Pepa. Cheryl "Salt" James, DJ Spinderella, and Sandra "Pepa" Denton. (© Ernie Paniccioli)

Members of the b-boying group Rock Steady Crew. (© Ernie Paniccioli)

Hip-hop star Big Daddy Kane started his career as a member of the Juice Crew. (© Ernie Paniccioli)

Hip-hop star Kurtis Blow—the first hip-hop artist to rap live on *Soul Train*. (© Ernie Paniccioli)

Songstress Anita Baker began her career with the funk band Chapter 8. (© Oggi Ogburn)

Whitney Houston. (© Oggi Ogburn)

Don Cornelius at the Soul Train Music Awards. The awards show garnered advertisers that the weekly show had courted for years with no success. (Courtesy Everett Collection)

Jody Watley and Don Cornelius. (© Tribune Entertainment/Courtesy Everett Collection)

Soul Train dancers Derek Fleming and Vivica Fox. (Courtesy of Derek Fleming)

Soul Train dancers Rosie Perez and Louie "Ski" Carr. (Courtesy of Derek Fleming)

Soul Train dancers Deniese Payne, Rick Carson, and Cheryl Song. (Courtesy of Derek Fleming)

Dancer Derek Fleming demonstrating some flexibility. (Courtesy of Derek Fleming)

Soul Train dancers, circa late 1980s. (Courtesy of Derek Fleming)

Journalist and dancer Stephen McMillian was a dancer on the show until the show ended in 2006. (Courtesy of Steve Mac)

Don Cornelius and Arsenio Hall during the Seventeenth Annual Soul Train Music Awards Nominations at Spago in Beverly Hills, California. (Steve Grayson/WireImage/Getty Images)

In 2012 former L.A. Lakers star Earvin "Magic" Johnson bought the rights to *Soul Train*. He danced on the show during an appearance in the 1970s. (Getty Images)

Soul Train host Dorian Gregory, 2003. (© Don Cornelius Productions, Inc./ Photofest)

Don Cornelius being honored with a street sign during the forty-year anniversary of the show in Chicago. (Paul Natkin/WireImage/Getty Images)

Don Cornelius on-site at an exhibition for *Soul Train* at the Expo 72 Gallery on East Randolph Street in Chicago. (Paul Natkin/WireImage/Getty Images)

production. For members of the audience who were at the Santa Monica Civic Auditorium where it was taped, and for those at home watching their televisions, they were about to bear witness to Cornelius-style excellence.

The soul/funk band Cameo was the headliner for the first show. Larry Blackmon donned his trademark nearly foot-tall flat-top, wearing a red cup over his groin, doing a rendition of their hit, the title track from the album *Word Up!*, which had landed at No. 6 on the *Billboard* Hot 100. Whitney Houston sang "You Give Good Love." In tribute to Stevie Wonder, host and hostess Luther Vandross and Dionne Warwick sang a medley of hits: "My Cherie Amor," "All in Love Is Fair," and "You Are the Sunshine of My Life," before Stevie came out and sang and played the harmonica with Houston, Vandross, and Warwick, in a wail fest of "That's What Friends Are For."

There wasn't a dull moment or a minute wasted on this first show. During the finale, gospel artists Cissy Houston, Edwin Hawkins, Shirley Caesar, Vanessa Bell Armstrong, Doug Williams, Lynette Hawkins, and Ronald Hawkins wrapped their voices around the auditorium, bringing down the house in a raucous church roar.

For the first time, artists who didn't necessarily have crossover success but were widely regarded in the black community were being recognized for their achievements. Artists like Luther Vandross, a virtual unknown by mainstream standards (though he had sung background vocals for Carly Simon, David Bowie, and Roberta Flack)—but a mainstay in the black community for his love ballads—was recognized, awarded and celebrated in this venue. Teena Marie, the Ivory Queen of Soul, a white artist well known for her soulful ballads and revered in the black community, started her career with her 1979 album, *Wild and Peaceful*, on Motown Records. Neither the album nor the packaging had her picture on it for fear that blacks wouldn't buy it if they knew she was a white artist. Many radio programmers assumed she was black during the first months of her career. When she performed "I'm a Sucker for Your Love" with Rick James on *Soul Train* in 1979, for many of her radio fans this was the first time seeing her in person. She became the first white female guest on the show and would end up appearing on it more than any other white act. She would be embraced by the black community, which christened her with the nickname Vanilla Choc, while continuing to go virtually unnoticed in mainstream circles. She rose steadily on the pop, Top 40, R&B, *Billboard* Hot 100, black singles and albums charts, but still went virtually unnoticed in the mainstream for much of her career. Despite a Gold album and widespread popularity and success, she would be nominated for a Grammy, but the only awards she would receive were Soul Train Awards.

The show continued with much success, but Cornelius found that as artists grew used to it, they began using it as a stepping-stone to crossover success. The R&B group Destiny's Child, which featured a young, rough-cut Beyoncé, was still relatively unknown when they were nominated for a Soul Train Award. When they paraded down the red carpet, the media didn't know who they were. Pop-rock singer Pink would get her first television break and media attention at the Soul Train Awards—at the time she was considered more of an R&B act before she became part of the mainstream.

Eventually, Cornelius would call artists to whom he had given their first break performing for the Soul Train Awards and they would avoid him, not returning his calls when he needed artists to fill performing slots for the awards show. Then he would see them performing at the Grammy Awards and the American Music Awards.

During the Soul Train Music Awards in 1989, Cornelius's protégé, R&B singer Karyn White, didn't show up to the show because she assumed she had no chance of winning because she was up against Janet Jackson. When White ended up winning, and her seat was empty, Cornelius gave her a tongue-lashing and angrily took back the award.

There were many acts broken at the award shows, as well as loves ignited, fights instigated, and disappointments inflicted. In 1989, Zoro, the drummer for New Edition and later for Bobby Brown, was working with Brown at the Soul Train Awards at the Shrine Auditorium. Whitney Houston came up to Zoro after Brown, dressed in all white, including a white silk trench coat and white shoes, performed "My Prerogative," and had the crowd on its feet. Houston stood at the side of the stage.

"Come here," she directed Zoro, curling her finger toward herself. "Do you think you could introduce me to Bobby?" Zoro said it seemed that she wasn't attracted to him so much as she was a huge fan. Zoro introduced them that night and they began dating soon after.

In the '80s, if Michael Jackson had become the king of pop, Whitney Houston was the queen—but it was a title taken with some derision by some blacks, who thought she was watering down her music to appeal to a crossover market. These sentiments culminated in her being booed on the 1989 Soul Train Music Awards show. Two schools of thought prevail as to why. Some people in the audience say it was because, unlike Janet Jackson, who at the time was dominating audiences with her dance moves touring for her 1986 album, *Control*, Houston came onstage and embarrassed herself with jerky dance movements lacking rhythm. She was parodied on the Keenan and Damon Wayans's variety show *In Living Color*, in a skit portraying Houston performing a new video, entitled *The Rhythmless Nation*. Kim Wayans, acting as Houston, struggles to dance *and* sing as she squeaks out lyrics: "There's music on my mind/which really helps me hide/plus the fact that I can't sing."

Other members of the audience claim that she was booed because she went up against soulful jazz singer Anita Baker and won the award, much to the consternation of audience members who didn't feel that she had the same chops as Baker. Moreover, many felt her sound just wasn't "black enough."

The Soul Train Music Awards continued to be a huge success and began to eclipse the weekly show. As the mid-'80s approached, Cornelius found it harder and harder to book acts for the weekly show. Always business minded and buoyed by the success of the Soul Train Awards, he branched out with the first Soul Train Comedy Awards (which lasted only a year), The Lady of Soul Awards, and the annual Christmas Starfest, where artists would perform their holiday favorites. Each show sought to fill a void—celebrating black comedians who were infinitely the most popular but least appreciated, and giving a spotlight to female artists, who often played the background to black male artists. The only one of these shows that would remain a constant would be the Soul Train Awards, eventually outlasting *Soul Train*.

By 1993, Cornelius was revamping the television show to reflect the growing popularity of hip-hop, commissioning a new hip-hop song by the New Jersey rap group Naughty by Nature. He called on Brent Rollins, a designer for the hip-hop magazine *Ego Trip*, to update the Soul Train logo.

In February of 1994, Cornelius was called to participate in a series of hearings before the House Subcommittee on Commerce, Consumer Protection, on "gangsta rap" lyrics and their effect on American youth. The hearings were called by Rep. Cardiss Collins (D-IL), who chaired the subcommittee. Many people in the entertainment industry were called to investigate the subject of controversial recording lyrics that had occurred in the previous ten years. There were three overnight hearings to investigate the production, sale, and distribution in interstate commerce of music that was alleged to contain lyrics that were violent, misogynistic, and homophobic. Collins called the hearings as a result of discussions with a number of black groups and individuals.

Though Cornelius participated and was adamant about his displeasure about much of hip-hop music, he remained business savvy. He always courted advisors who would keep him abreast of what was happening in the music industry. Despite his personal reservations, he would feature acts on his show and on the Soul Train Music Awards that would be considered "gangsta rap" by the mainstream. He even featured Ice-T., who had become a vocal opponent of *Soul Train's* snub of rap music.

Some hip-hop artists aware of Cornelius's reluctance to embrace rap retaliated in clandestine fashion. When De La Soul came on the show in 1993 for their Platinum album, *Buhloone Mindstate*, they switched around who would do the vocals. A line in the song "Pass the Plugs" was a direct dis' to the show:

"Will end this season/The soul reached high plains/We didn't reach Soul Train/But Don don't like rap/So that won't happen"—a nod to them reaching Platinum status without the help of iconic black institutions like *Soul Train*. Years later, when Questlove (from the Roots) came on—once with Common, for his production work on his album *Like Water for Chocolate*, and another time playing live with the Roots—he swiped the letter *Q* both times from the Soul Train Scramble Board.

By the mid to late '90s and 2000s, many of the dancers felt the end of the show was near. There were no longer couples coming down the Soul Train Line with choreographed routines, there were no more characters like Louie "Ski" Carr or cute couples like Jody Watley and Jeffrey Daniel. Dancers came down the Soul Train Line solo, and were more outrageous every week. As the women dressed more provocatively and danced salaciously, the cameramen would follow suit, zooming in on their breasts and staying steady on a dancer as she gyrated. Suddenly, more than anything else, *Soul Train* was beginning to lose its class.

On June 26, 1993, Cornelius handed over the hosting reins, in part because of his illness—complications from the twenty-one-hour brain operation he underwent to correct a congenital deformity in his cerebral arteries—but also because he felt that he just didn't sound cool anymore reciting the latest slang. The artists and dancers were getting younger as he was getting older. In the '70s, he was supercool, using the latest street lingo of his generation. Now, he was awkward, his language stilted.

"The show was so modern looking that we needed to try something new in the hosting area," Cornelius said during a television interview. "People want to see people who look like them—that they can relate to. I could be like, 'Yo, what's up?!' but I would look stupid."

There was no warning given to the television audience or even to the staff when he turned over the reins to a series of guest hosts (including Steve Harvey, Jamie Foxx, and Cedric the Entertainer) before hiring three different long-term hosts—comedian Mystro Clark, actor Dorian Gregory, and actor Shemar Moore.

The last episode he hosted, on June 26, 1993, featured the musical groups the Commodores, II D Extreme (featuring Randy Gill, Jermaine Mickey, and D'Extra Wiley), and Mahogany Blue. As Cornelius gave his signature introduction, forcing an energetic persona, it was difficult to hear what he was saying, as dancers around him screamed and talked over him. It was a far cry from the early days when the dancers were kept at a distance and everyone hung onto Cornelius's every word. The end of Don's reign was anticlimactic, business as usual.

Dancers wore biking pants, tank tops, and skimpy outfits as they did dances like the Cabbage Patch, the Smurf, and the Snake down the Soul Train Line. The dancers who wore the most revealing outfits received the most camera time. The new dance coordinator, Eric Casem, insisted that the dancers come down the line looking sexy. They would blow kisses into the camera.

The next episode, featuring H-Town, Keith Washington, and Xscape would feature Cornelius only in the beginning, introducing the guest host, comedian Kim Wayans. He offered no explanation for the guest host. As he introduced a different guest host each week, he peppered his speech with the latest slang: "Come back and kick it with some fat grooves and some totally cool music guests," he said on an episode that featured the artist formerly known as Prince. On another episode, wearing sunglasses and leather pants, he said, "We're gonna hear some slamming, hype, cold chillin' music." He was trying hard and it showed.

There were still great artists: Alicia Keys performed, her first time on television performing live. The Roots performed with Jill Scott—live in a set reminiscent of *MTV Unplugged*—and Scott, the original writer and singer for the single "You Got Me," performed it on a set with lighting taken straight from an intimate club scene.

Cornelius would still be on set, even as other hosts took over. He would walk slowly with his hands in his pockets, talking slowly, conferring with Casem about who was putting out energy, and which girls were considered eye candy.

The show was becoming increasingly disjointed and erratic.

The end would come abruptly and unceremoniously.

On April 1, 2005, Casem told dancer Stephen McMillian, who traveled from New York to Los Angeles once a month to dance on the show, about the next taping dates. Other dancers received word about the taping via email. But when McMillian showed up to the studio, no one would open the door.

The email that other dancers received said that the taping was cancelled and that they would be shooting again in May, but that May taping would be cancelled. Back at home, McMillian was clicking his remote and rather than finding a new episode of the show, he stumbled upon a *Best of Soul Train* rerun featuring guest artist Barry White and Love Unlimited. He got a tight feeling in his stomach as he sat with his mouth clenched, realizing they were rerunning shows from the '70s vault.

By March of 2006, the end finally came. There would be no more first-run episodes of *Soul Train*. The show aired reruns until September 20, 2008, and would go down in history as the longest-running first-run syndicated show in history. Many syndicated shows didn't last more than a few years; Cornelius's had lasted thirty-five, and if he had chosen to, could have gone on longer. And still, there was only a brief mention of his talents and contributions during the Grammy Awards ceremony held a little over a week after his death. While other celebrities were honored in memoriam (including a rousing tribute to Whitney Houston, whose death ten days after Cornelius's stole the celebrity spotlight), there was only a brief mention made of his legend, by Questlove and LL Cool J, a few minutes right before a commercial break. His life had been reduced to a sound bite.

10

ON A NEW TRACK

Yeah, I hear voices, I see people, I hear voices of many people/
Saying everything is everything

—Donny Hathaway

In 2008, after nine months of negotiations, Cornelius sold *Soul Train* and its offshoots to three young black men who had been introduced to him by his good friend, Clarence Avant. They were Anthony Maddox, Kenard Gibbs, and Peter Griffith, partners in the entertainment company MadVision. The deal had gone off the table a dozen times throughout the nine-month negotiation process. Cornelius didn't have a problem saying no. He had protected the *Soul Train* brand more fiercely than he had his own children. The biggest factor in the negotiation was what Cornelius assessed the value as being—a treasure trove of 1,100 episodes of four decades of the best performances in soul, pop, R&B, jazz, hip-hop, and rock music.

After he sold it—for an amount never disclosed by either party—Cornelius remained onboard as a consultant, with a six-figure income.

The three new owners intended to repurpose the brand—licensing some of the best episodes to BET's cable channel Centric to be rerun, creating a Broadway play and a feature film about *Soul Train*, and embarking on a cruise with a *Soul Train* theme. The trio partnered with Time-Life to produce the DVD collection *The Best of Soul Train*, featuring interviews with Cornelius, music executives, music guests, and *Soul Train* executives, and a hand-picked selection of some of the best shows—Al Green singing "Jesus Is Waiting," with his arm in a makeshift sling, Smokey Robinson refereeing a game between Cornelius and Marvin Gaye, and Smokey and Aretha Franklin playing the piano and talking about growing up together—and hours and hours of footage from the best in music. They created a documentary in partnership with VH1 about the show that was nominated for an Emmy. They talked about creating a new version of the show.

Like Dick Clark, Don Cornelius had always wanted to expand his repertoire beyond *Soul Train*. He tried his hand at acting in cameo roles in movies like 1973's *Cleopatra Jones*, 1976's *No Way Back*, 1980's *Roadie*, and 1988's *Tapeheads*. He starred in an ad campaign for Reebok, playing a "godfather" character, with Pam Grier, Richard Roundtree, and Fred Williamson. Each spot had a Reebok athlete asking "the Don" for a favor and having to swear an oath. He also made some bad cinematic business decisions—investing in a porn movie, a trashy remake of *Cinderella*. He entered into one of the first black partnerships with Qwest Broadcasting, a minority-controlled broadcasting company that purchased television stations in Atlanta and New Orleans for $167 million, establishing it as one of the largest minority-owned broadcasting companies in the States. The diverse partnership included music producer Quincy Jones, television journalist Geraldo Rivera, businesswoman Sonia Gonsalves Salzman, and Hall of Fame football player Willie Davis.

But by October of 2008, as *Soul Train* was shutting down, Cornelius's personal life would come undone. He was arrested on a felony domestic-violence charge against his wife—the much younger, green-eyed, red-haired Russian model, Viktoria Chapman-Cornelius. He had threatened her with a gun, according to police reports. He was charged with spousal abuse and dissuading a witness from filing a police report and pleaded guilty and was ordered to stay away from his estranged wife, who had filed two restraining orders against him. He accused her of pepper-spraying him multiple times. In March of 2009, he changed his plea to no contest and was placed on thirty-six months of probation. A bitter divorce put a dent in his multi-millionaire-dollar enterprise that included three condos in Chicago, an art collection from Jean-Michel Basquiat, and a home for Viktoria worth $1,095,000, that supposedly she could move into before divorce proceedings began. That's when Cornelius stayed in his home on Mulholland Drive in Sherman Oaks—a place where lavish parties filled with blow and beautiful women regularly took place after *Soul Train* tapings.

During his marriage to Viktoria, Cornelius had adopted her daughter, also named Viktoria. He would be required to pay his ex-wife $10,000 monthly in spousal support, $18,000 in fees for her lawyer, and up to $16,000 per year for her daughter's college tuition. The relationship had turned violent, with threats and a restraining order that Viktoria filed against him. In a letter to the judge, Cornelius wrote, "I am 72 years old. I have significant health issues. I want to finalize this divorce before I die."

In the settlement agreement, it also stated that he make his ex-wife a beneficiary of both of his life insurance policies—totaling around $300,000 in benefits.

There were other problems. After his surgery in 1982, seizures would dog him for the next fifteen years—a complication from the brain operation he underwent to correct a congenital deformity in his cerebral arteries. He was never quite the same after the surgery, and that factored into his consideration of giving up hosting duties in 1993.

By the turn of the century, the music industry and the television industry had changed drastically. If teenagers wanted to see their favorite performers and didn't have the money to see them in concert, they could watch a performance on YouTube. There was a proliferation of cable shows that catered exclusively to music programming. *Soul Train* had become something your parents watched. The show had lasted as long as it did, Cornelius had always reiterated, because it followed the trends of what was happening in the music industry. As long as the music was good, the show would last. As the music industry began to focus less on artist development and more on the bottom line, the quality of the music bottomed out. *Soul Train* kept rolling, using the best artists of the time period, but Cornelius had lost his enthusiasm for the show and for the music.

Still, in his last days, he was in good spirits. One day in late January of 2012, in a Century City doctor's office, R&B singer Karyn White bumped into him. She had not seen him in over twenty years. He looked sharp—turned out as usual—in a gray and white suit with mauve colored shoes, a silk scarf, and John Lennon shades. When he saw her he hugged her and reached for his cell phone: "Guess who I'm with?!" he said into the receiver. They talked for half an hour—reminiscing—Cornelius lamenting that O'Bryan should have been as big as Prince. He was in a great mood. Five days later everything would change.

Bowlegged Lou, a singer from the '80s family R&B group Full Force, talked to Cornelius daily. Cornelius would complain to him that people had amnesia—when *Soul Train* was declining and people couldn't use him to promote their acts, they stopped calling. Lou would continue to call and check on him regularly.

"Yo, brother, you're really sincere," Cornelius said one day when he called him. "All these years you call me to check on me. You're really just a sincere brother. Why do you like me so much? Why do you respect me so much?"

Lou would just laugh. "Come on D-man, I love you—we all love you."

Lou and his brothers wanted to arrange a tribute to Cornelius at the Apollo Theater. He and his brothers called and began working with Cornelius's assistant Lisa Fortune on making it happen. Cornelius declined the offer. On some days Lou, a prankster, would call him and disguise his voice as a woman. Cornelius caught on, "Oh, is this *Lou*—isa?" He always had a sense of humor, even if it was hiding his pain.

When Full Force was a featured act on the television show *Unsung* (a show catering to underappreciated R&B acts from the '70s and '80s on Cathy Hughes's cable network, TV One), Lou asked if Cornelius would be interested in being interviewed on the show about the group. Executives had called Cornelius to participate in previous episodes, but every time he declined.

But this time he accepted the offer, only because Lou had kept in touch with him.

A party to celebrate them wrapping the episode of *Unsung* was set for the Savoy in Inglewood, California. Cornelius had become increasingly reclusive, but he promised he would be there. Lou and his brothers had a plaque made to honor him. At the last minute, Cornelius called and said he couldn't make it. Lou called Cornelius's assistant again and arranged to have it delivered it to him in person.

═══

Cornelius and his son Anthony also spoke to each other that day, the afternoon of January 31, 2012. In the years before his death, the only visitors Cornelius entertained at his home were a maid, Juanna Jovell, who came daily at 11 a.m., and his oldest son, Anthony, with whom he talked daily and who visited him regularly. Anthony, as physically intimidating as his father, was always a calm, competent, quiet presence. He had followed in his father's footsteps in the business, starting as a cameraman in Chicago where he lived with his mother, while his father went out to Los Angeles to begin the national show. Anthony eventually followed his father to California to work on the show, but their relationship bent toward the emotionally volatile at times.

The *Soul Train* staff watched with horror when, with little provocation, his father would curse him out on set. There were many years when silence formed their relationship. But lately they talked or saw each other at least once a day.

Don told Anthony he didn't know how much longer he could live—that he couldn't stand the pain. Anthony assured him that they would get new medicine, get the right dosages, they could fix this. But the seizures were coming on stronger and with more frequency. He couldn't do the things he loved—play golf, he couldn't drive his cars. His balance was off, and periodically he would take spills. His vision in his right eye was impaired. There was constant pain, incontinence. It was the pain—the debilitating physical pain and the uncontrollable seizures that dogged him. And every day it all was growing worse.

Cornelius called his son at three in the morning on February 1 and told him that he didn't want to do this anymore.

"I don't know how long I can take this," he told him.

"I'll be right over," Anthony told him, reassuring him that everything would be fine.

Cornelius told him not to come, but Anthony insisted. Cornelius told him he would leave the back door open. It took Anthony a little over half an hour to get to the house. As Anthony opened the back door, the smell of gunpowder coming from inside the house rested heavily on his heart. The television was on. His father, in his black pajama top and pants, his hand resting on his chest in his armchair, was still clutching a 9 mm Smith and Wesson. He had shot himself through the right temple. The bullet had pierced through the window into the backyard. Splattered brain matter gave little hope for a positive outcome.

Paramedics, members of the media, fire engines, and police squads from Van Nuys Division surrounded the house fourteen minutes later. Anthony had been instructed by 911 operators to remove his father's shirt, wet with blood, and lay him on his back on the carpet. Cornelius's larger-than-life frame at six foot five was bare-chested as they attempted CPR and put in a tracheal tube for him to breathe. There wasn't much hope. But when asked, Anthony agreed to have him transported to the hospital, in hopes of reviving him. But halfway along the winding road to Cedars-Sinai Medical Center, daylight had spread along the cliffs and seventy-five-year-old Don Cornelius was gone.

At the private funeral, artists and entrepreneurs came to pay their respects—Magic Johnson, David Winfield, the Whispers, Debra Lee, George Duke, Donnie McClurkin, Stevie Wonder, the Reverend Jesse Jackson, who had been given a platform back in Chicago in the early days of the show before anyone knew either of them. Artists recognized publicly that without him they wouldn't have had careers. Friends like Smokey Robinson joked about how refreshing it was being interviewed by a black host and about Cornelius's off-the-wall humor—during interviews sometimes Cornelius would ask Smokey about his music, other times he would ask him if had eaten Roscoe's Chicken and Waffles that day.

"To this day, nothing like that exists," said Jody Watley after the service about *Soul Train*'s impact. "He opened the door for new artists and that may have been your only television exposure. The show opened so many doors. I remember looking at the cameramen, the women on staff. He employed people of color. Going on other shows, you saw how different it was."

His six-foot stunner granddaughter, Christina Cornelius, poised, poignantly talked about him as her "smooth-voiced loving grandpa." At the reception she talked about how they would watch *Dancing with the Stars* and *American Idol* together. "He pretended not to like them, but he loved those shows," she said with a smile, as she talked about how he would teach her how to do "silly" dances like the Mashed Potato.

Stevie Wonder joked about how the dancers made the show a hit: "As much as I couldn't see the dancers, I could feel them," he said pausing. "And from what I felt," he joked, "I thought, Don, we got a hit!"

Magic Johnson talked about meeting Cornelius for the first time at the Forum Club when he had just begun playing for the Lakers.

"First thing he said was, 'Baby, you sure can play that basketball!'" Johnson said that when he first met Cornelius he could see the strength of his fight against segregation in the industry.

For nearly three hours mourners celebrated his life in song and words as Reverend Donnie McClurkin and Reverend Jesse Jackson alternated as pastors.

Cornelius had always had difficulty working for other people. He charted his own course, right down to his final breath.

Cornelius had told reporters, "My father taught me you need to work with your brain and not your back. When I have a job to do, time means nothing. I lose patience with people who work on a clock."

Cornelius made many mistakes, both personally and professionally. There were many that disliked him; others were indifferent. He could come off as brash, aloof, unlovable. Lee Bailey described him as "funny as hell when he was in a good mood, but like Jekyll and Hyde, 99 percent of the time he was serious and gruff. He was so protective of the brand—it guided how he treated people. He would call you up and curse you out if you reported something negative about the show or the awards. But he never denied access."

Most spoke of him in terms of his work and his legacy, not his personal charm.

In the months after the funeral, the whispers of silence filled the room when Cornelius's name was mentioned—perhaps because the subject of suicide in black community circles, particularly black religious circles, is taboo. Black depression—misunderstood. People who had endured slavery were considered weak to succumb to the pressures of daily life and commit suicide. Black Christians saw it as a violation of a spiritual contract—the ultimate selfish act.

But eventually, some began to talk. Damita Jo remembered when dancer Lil' Joe Chism died from AIDS, penniless and alone. She went to Cornelius, who Lil' Joe considered a close friend. If someone had a bad word to say about Cornelius, Lil' Joe would walk out of the room. Damita asked if Cornelius could put up half of $375 to pay for Lil' Joe's headstone. Cornelius responded that everyone would start asking him for money if he agreed to do that. He refused and Damita ended up paying for the entire amount.

Many of the dancers craved his recognition more than they wanted to get paid for their efforts. Tyrone "the Bone" Proctor adopted his nickname proudly because Cornelius had given it to him. Many of them—kids from the streets with a dream, not the pretty, glamorous Hollywood fare, just ordinary kids looking for direction—ended up feeling used and disrespected as they saw Cornelius's wealth grow. Cornelius felt as though he gave them a platform, giving them a spotlight on the show to choreograph their own routines, which could lead to bigger opportunities.

More so than money, they were looking for a father figure. Many dancers who started as kids just wanted him to smile at them, say hello, and tell them he was proud. No one asked as much of Dick Clark, but the expectations were higher for a black man who had paved the way—a hero of sorts—as were the pressure, loneliness, and responsibilities that came with it.

Much of the staff felt indifferent toward Cornelius—some hated him.

Maybe he worked too hard and loved too little. Or maybe it was the other way around. It's always hard to tell about anyone's life.

By the mid-'90s the golden age of *Soul Train* had come and gone. The end of syndication, where popular first-run syndicated shows like *Star Trek* could become classic appointment television did not exist anymore. In the '70s and early '80s, the local affiliates showed old kung fu and classic movies or cartoons during their least popular time slots. It was a tremendous benefit for them to receive a brand-new, innovative show like *Soul Train* to fill up that dead time. But with the onset of cable and niche marketing, *Soul Train* was no longer an anomaly or a cheap alternative with the potential for a large profit for the affiliates.

Cornelius was able to create the kind of show he wanted without censorship because it was syndicated programming. *Soul Train* was a show for young America. It helped to redefine segregated business. On the dance floor everyone was the same—they all sweated from the same places. Cuba Gooding Sr., from the Main Ingredient, once called Cornelius a calming presence: "It was so comfortable talking to another person with a great big Afro." Bobby Womack gushed: "I always loved coming [on *Soul Train*]; it's like coming home."

Soul Train came around at a time when America needed it the most. It exported great music around the world and changed the culture. Nick Puzo, a thirty-year-old who started the fan club/website SOULTRAINFANS.com, describes the show's impact simply: "People on *Bandstand* were dancing *to* the music; people on *Soul Train* were dancing *in* the music."

Cornelius had received numerous awards and recognition, including the coveted Hollywood Walk of Fame. Though he was unable to attend, the Smithsonian Institute for the new African American Museum held a celebration announcing two *Soul Train* installations—in the forthcoming museum and the existing one. But it was a street named in his honor in his modest hometown of Chicago that meant the most to him.

Sometimes we get everything we want. And then we look back with wistfulness—cynical, tainted—wanting what we had before. It is the fate of the afflicted, the crippled, the physically weak and mentally challenged who learn early in life that if you live long enough, your body will fail you, people will overlook you, your looks will fade. That no matter your contribution or how bright your light shined, everyone living in a society that celebrates youth will one day be rendered irrelevant—a "has been." In 1990 on the Wayans brothers' comedy show *In Living Color*, they created a spoof called "Old Train," where a long-haired Asian dancer strolled slowly down the Old Train Line with a walker, while "Don Cornelius" couldn't remember the name of the artists—or much of anything. During the BET Awards in 2009, that spoof was nearly reenacted when Cornelius took the stage and gave a tribute to the O'Jays in a painfully slow monotone, a shadow of his authoritative baritone. His entrance onto the public stage for the first time in years was muddied by the sympathetic looks of older audience members and the silent snickers of younger patrons, saying with their eyes, "It's time to hang it up, old man!"

Things had changed since the heyday of *Soul Train*. There were no longer just three major networks; there were hundreds of different cable channels—and two networks devoted exclusively to black programming. In a media-saturated society, reality television had become king and had shown success to be more about marketing than capturing culture organically or developing good storytelling. Lyrics had lost subtlety. Women had lost their clothes. Groups like the Jackson Five didn't have to slave away, practicing in their basement for years to hone their craft and hope to be seen at local talent shows. YouTube had made any and everyone a reporter, a filmmaker, a musician, an instant celebrity. Time—moving at breakneck speed—was always *now*.

It wasn't always this way, for Cornelius or for any of us. The pilot for the first national episode of *Soul Train* was filled with energy, with aspiration—with the triumph of overcoming odds from the South Side of Chicago. Cornelius walked with measured steps onto the set. "Hi, I'm Don Cornelius," he said, "and what you're about to see is a very special program."

Culturally, *Soul Train*'s mission was about celebrating life, often despite bleak circumstances, and creating something new—in the way of New Orleans second-line celebrations and the improvisational nature of jazz and hip-hop. Nothing like the *Soul Train* we witnessed will likely ever exist again. It came at a time when America, coming out of the turmoil of the '60s, needed it the most. The show educated at the same time it entertained. It uplifted the image of black people and employed blacks behind the scenes. This was Cornelius's sole intention, to give black people pride, opportunities. But mostly, it was all just good, clean, unbridled fun.

At a broadcasting luncheon at the Waldorf Astoria in New York in October of 2012, Cornelius was honored posthumously with an award for being a giant in broadcasting. His son, Anthony, accepted the award and spoke about the foundation he started in his father's name to bring about suicide awareness. He spoke about the first time he asked his father for a raise when he worked on the show, and his reply was, "Do good work and the money will come."

His father did good work weekly by making good on his promise: "You can bet your last money, it's all gonna be a stone gas, honey!"

AFTERWORD

WHEN SATURDAY WAS EVERYTHING

Maybe I was eleven or twelve years old. It's hard to remember now, but Don Cornelius introduced *Soul Train* into the living rooms of America in an era of creative and political expansion. There was the peace movement, the feminist movement, the environmental movement, and the black power movement. Don changed the cultural landscape on the strength of body movement.

It was the age of John Shaft, Priest from Super Fly, and Foxy Brown–film characters who were armed, dangerous, colder than ice, and exhibited sufficient self-reliance and agency to overthrow "the man" by the end of the third act of their revenge fantasies. Their adventures were often paired with Asian martial arts films, in the long-ago programming staple of the independent cinema house—the double feature. Independent film pioneer Melvin Van Peebles started the fire with *Sweet Sweetback's Baadasssss Song* and flipped the movie game on its ear. An effort by an industry that had largely ignored the black community's tastes and buying power attempted to replicate Van Peebles's success by replicating his formula.

More "responsible" segments of the black community labeled these films that featured actors who shared my skin tone as negative. Historically, this strain of middle-class cultural over-seer rears its head whenever some new form of valid creative expression emerges to represent the taste of the masses in a more urgent way than was previously thought of as appropriate. These "responsible" cultural watchdogs had ideas and tastes that had been formed in a previous era and were the inheritors of a tradition maintained by those who had previously decried the legitimacy of the blues and rock 'n' roll, and they were also the progenitors of the haters who would later show disdain for hip-hop.

You would have thought they'd never listened to funky soul classics on an 8-track tape while riding in a Lincoln, a Caddy, or an Elektra 225 (more colloquially known as a "deuce and a quarter"), or that they'd never spent a portion of Saturday afternoon at the barber shop chopping it up cross-generationally, while everyone discussed the latest heroic feats—from their favorite athletes to the current news from Jet magazine—and repeated jokes from the previous Thursday night's *Flip Wilson Show*.

Isaac Hayes scored one of the more important films of this derided genre, and for his efforts he was awarded an Oscar on national prime-time TV that he accepted while wearing a blue tuxedo trimmed in rabbit fur. The fur was baby blue and the bow tie matched. Judging from his fashion choice, he had obviously known the sublime pleasure of hearing his funk while cruising in a gas-guzzling luxury model from Detroit.

At about the same time, across the country, on the radio stereo FM broadcasting was supplanting the network of old AM stations that dotted the nation and formed the main network of information for black folks and were the primary source of exposure for Southern soul singing and working-class rhythm and blues. Suddenly Bobby Womack, Curtis Mayfield, Aretha Franklin, funk, and Motown could be heard in stereo at any time of day for free, and the sound of a people's joyful, consciousness-raising melodies and grooves were felt in crisper fidelity. Change was in the wind.

With few exceptions, the television industry was lagging and hadn't begun to participate in this cultural explosion until one man saw an opportunity and seized it. I'm not certain that he was inspired by the entrepreneurial spirit of Van Peebles, Berry Gordy, or Stax Records' Al Bell, but Chicago native smooth daddy Don Cornelius had vision that was grounded in that era's contemporary zeitgeist. As it is with most ingenious ideas, his was fiendishly simple: play a few hot records, book a couple of hot acts, give some kids who danced a sandwich for shaking their groove things to the current sounds, and pay the acts scale in exchange for television exposure. It was a concept that was older than Alan Freed and Chubby Checker, and America's "oldest living teenager" Dick Clark had already amassed a fortune by doing the same thing. But Cornelius would add one major innovative twist: make it black. Until then, no one had thought to feature the styles, moves, and fashion of young blacks while playing the most current releases with the deepest grooves.

In my home, this brilliant concept became available around the time my mother bought our first color television. Every Saturday, funkiness for free. The combination of youth culture, contemporary soul, funk, and Afrocentric messaging was stronger than a Long Island Ice Tea. The animated train, puffing smoke and fueled by economic self-empowerment, aspiration, and creative self-expression rhythmically chugging at you; the late Sid McCoy's sonorous voice-over inviting you to take "the hippest trip in America"; the montage of that week's guest lineup; the wide shot of the dancers putting it down and the pulsating theme music combined to create an almost Pavlovian response. *Soul Train* brought the elements of a strong house party into your living room every Saturday afternoon. All other activity was suspended or delayed when the show was on because you knew you were about to see some shit that could not be seen anywhere else on the television landscape. I was an early adopter.

Because of his time spent in radio, Don had loads of the only currency that's important in entertainment circles—relationships. He knew many of the early acts and their managers; they were veterans of the standup vocal-harmony tradition and some had even gotten their start in doo-wop. Top-tier performers frequented the show in those days, too. The Curtis Mayfields, Marvin Gayes, and Stevie Wonders appeared in living color and rocked it. But the records that were chosen for the dancers to get busy with were dope, and among the most cutting-edge at the time. This authentic cultural choice separated the show from everything else that was happening on television and positively linked it with black radio and the newer, hipper FM broadcasting. Kool & the Gang's "Jungle Boogie," Herbie Hancock's "Chameleon," the Ohio Players' "Skin Tight," and the Staple Singers' "Respect Yourself" were but a few examples of the aural "love, peace, and soul." My record collecting was tremendously influenced by the way *Soul Train*'s playlist was curated.

That was from the early days of the show's history, when it quickly changed from barely wanted syndicated stepchild to bona fide cultural phenomenon. Of course, it all seems somewhat quaint and old-fashioned now. In the age of Barack Obama and in an environment of OWN, BET, Hulu, Love & Hip-Hop, DVRs, and On Demand, the idea of a syndicated dance show owned and operated by one black man doesn't seem like much. But back then, Don Cornelius was the future.

When you heard "TSOP (The Sound of Philadelphia)" (what I believed to be the definitive theme music from the several used during the show's thirty-five-year run)—the tune that Gamble & Huff produced for the show with the thumping baseline, the lush strings, the insane saxophone solo, the organ fills and Three Degrees shouting the commanding and unifying lyrics: "People all over the world/let's get it onnnnn.../It's time to get down"—you knew what was up. I miss those days and the hipper-than-hip Cornelius. He inspired a revolution.

—Gary Harris/insideplaya

LIST OF EPISODES

SEASON 1 (1971–1972)

1. 1. Gladys Knight & the Pips / Eddie Kendricks / The Honey Cone / Bobby Hutton; originally aired October 2, 1971.
2. 2. Charlie Wright & the Watts 103rd Street Band / Carla Thomas / General Crook; originally aired October 9, 1971.
3. 3. Chairmen of the Board / Rufus Thomas / Laura Lee; originally aired October 16, 1971.
4. 4. The Staple Singers / Freda Payne; originally aired October 23, 1971.
5. 5. Bill Withers / Al Green / Viola Wills; originally aired October 30, 1971.
6. 6. Lou Rawls / The 100 Proof / The Emotions; originally aired November 6, 1971.
7. 7. Martha & the Vandellas / The Intruders / G. C. Cameron; originally aired November 13, 1971.
8. 8. Friends of Distinction / Clarence Carter; originally aired November 20, 1971.
9. 9. Chambers Brothers / The Five Stairsteps; originally aired November 27, 1971.
10. 10. Jr. Walker & the All Stars / Bobby Womack / Thelma Houston; originally aired December 4, 1971.
11. 11. Jean Knight / The Delfonics / Maurice Jackson / Ralfi Pagan; originally aired December 11, 1971.
12. 12. The Chi-Lites / Joe Tex / The Originals; originally aired December 18, 1971.
13. 13. Gene Chandler / Simtec & Wylie / The Free Movement; originally aired December 25, 1971.
14. 14. B. B. King / O. C. Smith / Patrice Holloway; originally aired January 1, 1972.
15. 15. Dennis Coffey / The Detroit Emeralds / Jesse James; originally aired January 8, 1972.

16. 16. Little Richard / The Undisputed Truth / Nolan F. Porter; originally aired January 15, 1972.
17. 17. Curtis Mayfield / The Honey Cone / The Persuaders; originally aired January 22, 1972.
18. 18. The Impressions / Merry Clayton / The Three Degrees; originally aired January 29, 1972.
19. 19. The Dells / Kim Weston / Luther Ingram; originally aired February 5, 1972.
20. 20. Jerry Butler & Brenda Lee Eager / Joe Tex / Hodges, Smith, James & Crawford; originally aired February 12, 1972.
21. 21. Al Green / The Whispers / Denise LaSalle; originally aired February 19, 1972.
22. 22. The Four Tops / Jackie Wilson / Kool & the Gang; originally aired February 26, 1972
23. 23. Gladys Knight & the Pips / The Ohio Players / Garland Green; originally aired March 4, 1972.
24. 24. Rufus Thomas / The Bar-Kays / Laura Lee; originally aired March 11, 1972.
25. 25. The Chi-Lites / Edwin Starr / James Gadsen; originally aired March 18, 1972.
26. 26. Wilson Pickett / Curtis Mayfield / War / Soul Train Dance Contest (Special Guest: Fred Williamson); originally aired March 25, 1972.
27. 27. Joe Tex / Gloria Lynne / The Independents; originally aired April 1, 1972.
28. 28. Lou Rawls / Otis Clay / The Peaches; originally aired April 8, 1972.
29. 29. The Isley Brothers / Love Unlimited / Millie Jackson; originally aired April 15, 1972.
30. 30. Ike & Tina Turner / Jerry Butler & Brenda Lee Eager; originally aired April 22, 1972.

Season 2 (1972–1973)

1. 31. Bobby Womack / The Bar-Kays / Candi Staton (Special Guest: Fred Williamson); originally aired September 9, 1972.
2. 32. The Isley Brothers / Luther Ingram (Special Guests: Melba Moore & Heshimu); originally aired September 16, 1972.
3. 33. Gladys Knight & the Pips / The O'Jays / Major Lance (Special Guests: Teresa Graves & Brock Peters); originally aired September 23, 1972.
4. 34. Eddie Kendricks / The Whispers (Special Guest: Bill Russell); originally aired September 30, 1972.

5. 35. The Jackson 5 featuring Jermaine Jackson; originally aired October 7, 1972.
6. 36. Johnnie Taylor / The Undisputed Truth; originally aired October 14, 1972.
7. 37. Bill Withers / Harold Melvin & the Blue Notes (Special Guest: Denise Nicholas); originally aired October 21, 1972.
8. 38. Billy Preston / Laura Lee / Johnny Williams (Special Guest: Jim Brown); originally aired October 28, 1972.
9. 39. Joe Simon / The Sylvers / Billy Paul (Special Guest: Wallace Terry); originally aired November 4, 1972.
10. 40. Friends of Distinction / The Persuaders / Doug Gibbs (Special Guest: William Marshall); originally aired November 11, 1972.
11. 41. The Temptations / King Floyd (Special Guest: Cicely Tyson); originally aired November 18, 1972.
12. 42. The Intruders / Betty Wright / True Reflection (Special Guest: George Kirby); originally aired December 16, 1972.
13. 43. Billy Paul / Barbara Mason / Anacostia; originally aired December 23, 1972.
14. 44. Tyrone Davis / Lyn Collins (Special Guest: Elgin Baylor); originally aired December 30, 1972.
15. 45. Curtis Mayfield / The Main Ingredient / Hank Ballard (Special Guest: Vonetta McGee); originally aired January 6, 1973.
16. 46. Stevie Wonder / The Moments / Fully Guaranteed (Special Guest: Judy Pace); originally aired January 13, 1973.
17. 47. Johnny Nash / Billy Butler & Infinity / Brighter Side of Darkness; originally aired January 27, 1973.
18. 48. The Dramatics / Syl Johnson / The Smith Connection; originally aired February 3, 1973.
19. 49. James Brown / Lyn Collins; originally aired February 10, 1973.
20. 50. The Four Tops / Otis Clay (Special Guests: James Brown and Teddy Brown / Soul Train Dance Contest Semifinals); originally aired February 17, 1973.
21. 51. The Spinners / Sisters Love; originally aired February 24, 1973.
22. 52. Al Green / Mel & Tim; originally aired March 3, 1973.
23. 53. Friends of Distinction / Timmy Thomas / The Independents (Special Guest: Richard Pryor); originally aired March 10, 1973.
24. 54. The Chi-Lites / The Honey Cone / G. C. Cameron (Special Guest: Pam Grier); originally aired March 31, 1973.
25. 55. The Impressions / Tyrone Davis / Billy Preston (Special Guests: Diana Ross and Brenda Sykes); originally aired April 7, 1973.
26. 56. Aretha Franklin (Special Guest: Cecil Franklin); originally aired April 14, 1973.

27. 57. The O'Jays / David Ruffin / Sylvia; originally aired April 21, 1973.
28. 58. The Sylvers / Ronnie Dyson / Archie Bell & the Drells (Special Guest: Rosie Grier); originally aired April 28, 1973.
29. 59. The Manhattans / Lyn Collins / Lee Auston (Special Guest: James Brown); originally aired May 5, 1973.
30. 60. The Supremes / Lloyd Price; originally aired May 12, 1973.
31. 61. Bobby Womack / The Whispers / Thelma Houston; originally aired May 19, 1973.
32. 62. Little Anthony & the Imperials / Edwin Starr / The Valentinos; originally aired May 26, 1973.
33. 63. Bill Withers (Special Guest: Steve Manning); originally aired June 16, 1973.
34. 64. The Miracles / Chuck Jackson / The Jackson Sisters (Special Guest: Smokey Robinson); originally aired June 23, 1973.
35. 65. Chairmen of the Board / Charles Mann / Sylvia (Special Guest: Jeffrey Bowen); originally aired June 30, 1973.
36. 66. Chuck Berry / Maxayan / Willie Hutch (Special Guest: Max Julien); originally aired July 7, 1973.
37. 67. "The Best of Soul Train," featuring James Brown, the Jackson 5, Chuck Berry, the O'Jays, the Temptations, Al Green, Curtis Mayfield, the Supremes, Teddy Brown, the Four Tops, and Stevie Wonder; originally aired August 11, 1973.

Season 3 (1973–1974)

1. 68. The Intruders / Foster Sylvers (Introduced by Edmund & Ricky Sylvers); originally aired August 25, 1973.
2. 69. The Whispers / Mandrill; originally aired September 1, 1973.
3. 70. Fred Wesley & the JB's / Lyn Collins / The Sly, the Slick and the Wicked; originally aired September 8, 1973.
4. 71. The Sylvers; originally aired September 15, 1973.
5. 72. The Isley Brothers / Betty Wright / Jr. Walker & the All-Stars; originally aired September 22, 1973.
6. 73. Eddie Kendricks / The Dramatics / Rufus; originally aired September 29, 1973.
7. 74. B. B. King / The Moments; originally aired October 6, 1973.
8. 75. The Four Tops / Bloodstone / Lee Charles; originally aired October 13, 1973.
9. 76. Barry White / Love Unlimited / The Temprees (Special Guest: Lola Falana); originally aired October 27, 1973.
10. 77. The Jackson 5; originally aired November 3, 1973.
11. 78. Curtis Mayfield / Millie Jackson / Natural Four; originally aired November 10, 1973.

12. 79. Tower of Power / The Pointer Sisters / Tavares; originally aired November 17, 1973.
13. 80. Smokey Robinson / First Choice / Al Wilson; originally aired November 24, 1973.
14. 81. The Temptations / G. C. Cameron; originally aired December 1, 1973.
15. 82. Bobby Bland / Ashford & Simpson / Barbara Jean English; originally aired December 8, 1973.
16. 83. Johnnie Taylor / Ann Peebles / Maceo & the Macks; originally aired December 15, 1973.
17. 84. Eddie Kendricks / The Persuaders / Eddie Floyd; originally aired December 22, 1973.
18. 85. Billy Preston / Creative Source / Eric Mercury; originally aired January 5, 1974.
19. 86. Johnny Nash / Kool & the Gang / The Originals; originally aired January 12, 1974.
20. 87. The 5th Dimension / Willie Hutch; originally aired January 26, 1974.
21. 88. Johnny Mathis / The Dells; originally aired February 9, 1974.
22. 89. Marvin Gaye / The Whispers; originally aired February 16, 1974.
23. 90. Harold Melvin & the Blue Notes / Billy Paul / Maxine Weldon; originally aired February 23, 1974.
24. 91. Jerry Butler / The Delfonics / Cecil Shaw; originally aired March 2, 1974.
25. 92. Curtis Mayfield / The Main Ingredient / Bloodstone; originally aired March 30, 1974.
26. 93. Al Green / The Impressions; originally aired April 6, 1974.
27. 94. The Stylistics / Bobby Womack / The Undisputed Truth; originally aired April 13, 1974.
28. 95. The Four Tops / Blue Magic / Barbara Mason; originally aired April 20, 1974.
29. 96. Eddie Kendricks / The Dramatics / Martha Reeves; originally aired April 27, 1974.
30. 97. Gladys Knight & the Pips / Lamont Dozier; originally aired May 4, 1974.
31. 98. Sylvia Robinson / The Moments / Ecstasy, Passion & Pain; originally aired May 11, 1974.
32. 99. The Spinners / The Independents / Leroy Hutson; originally aired May 18, 1974.
33. 100. Bill Withers / The Soul Children / Melvin Van Peebles; originally aired May 25, 1974.
34. 101. Tyrone Davis / Hugh Masekela / Black Ivory; originally aired June 1, 1974.

35. 102. The Staple Singers / Bunny Sigler; originally aired June 8, 1974.
36. 103. Kool & the Gang / Al Wilson / Natural Four; originally aired June 15, 1974.
37. 104. The O'Jays / Ramsey Lewis; originally aired June 22, 1974.
38. 105. Sly & the Family Stone / The Trammps; originally aired June 29, 1974.
39. 106. "The Best of Soul Train"; originally aired July 20, 1974.

Season 4 (1974–1975)

1. 107. Billy Preston / Rufus / George McCrae; originally aired September 7, 1974.
2. 108. James Brown and the First Family of Soul / Fred Wesley & the JBs / Lyn Collins / Sweet Charles; originally aired September 14, 1974.
3. 109. Johnnie Taylor / The Joneses / Syreeta Wright; originally aired September 21, 1974.
4. 110. The Miracles / Herbie Hancock / Yvonne Fair; originally aired September 28, 1974.
5. 111. Michael Jackson / MDLT; originally aired October 5, 1974.
6. 112. The Four Tops / The New Birth / Creative Source; originally aired October 12, 1974.
7. 113. The Chi-Lites / Bloodstone / New York City; originally aired October 19, 1974.
8. 114. Ashford & Simpson / Tavares / Little Beaver; originally aired October 26, 1974.
9. 115. The 5th Dimension / Al Wilson / Formula IV (Special Guest: Mark Gordon); originally aired November 2, 1974.
10. 116. The Ohio Players / Ecstasy, Passion & Pain / B. T. Express; originally aired November 9, 1974.
11. 117. Nancy Wilson / Johnny Bristol / Mighty Clouds of Joy; originally aired November 16, 1974.
12. 118. The Moments / Labelle / Carl Carlton; originally aired December 7, 1974.
13. 119. The Isley Brothers; originally aired December 14, 1974.
14. 120. Jose Feliciano / Minnie Riperton / The Dynamic Superiors; originally aired December 21, 1974.
15. 121. Johnny Nash / The Commodores / Lonnie Youngblood; originally aired December 28, 1974.
16. 122. Bobby Womack / Latimore / The Kay-Gees; originally aired January 4, 1975.
17. 123. Graham Central Station / Zulema / Leon Haywood; originally aired January 11, 1975.

18. 124. Ike & Tina Turner / Lonette McKee; originally aired January 18, 1975.
19. 125. David Ruffin / Shirley Brown / 9th Creation / The Lockers; originally aired January 25, 1975.
20. 126. Tower of Power / Hues Corporation / Garland Green; originally aired February 1, 1975.
21. 127. The Crusaders / The Whispers; originally aired February 8, 1975.
22. 128. Rufus featuring Chaka Khan / Gino Vanelli / Bohannon; originally aired February 15, 1975.
23. 129. Kool & the Gang / Charles Wright & the Watts 103rd Street Rhythm Band / The Jackson Sisters; originally aired February 22, 1975.
24. 130. Jimmy Ruffin / Buddy Miles / The Manhattans; originally aired March 1, 1975.
25. 131. Lou Rawls / The Main Ingredient / Gloria Scott; originally aired March 8, 1975.
26. 132. Bobby Bland / Tavares / Lyn Collins / Fred Wesley & Steam; originally aired March 15, 1975.
27. 133. Bloodstone / Carol Douglas / Syl Johnson; originally aired March 22, 1975.
28. 134. B. B. King / The Younghearts / People's Choice; originally aired March 29, 1975.
29. 135. Al Green; originally aired April 5, 1975.
30. 136. Blue Magic / Sister Sledge / Major Harris; originally aired April 12, 1975.
31. 137. The Dramatics / Barbara Mason / Ben E. King; originally aired April 19, 1975.
32. 138. Eddie Kendricks / L.T.D. / The Waters; originally aired April 26, 1975.
33. 139. Melba Moore / Eddie Harris / Bunny Sigler; originally aired May 3, 1975.
34. 140. Dionne Warwick / Greg Perry / The Futures; originally aired May 10, 1975.
35. 141. Elton John / Mandrill / (Comedian: Karl Grigsby); originally aired May 17, 1975.
36. 142. Barry White / Love Unlimited Orchestra; originally aired May 24, 1975.
37. 143. Curtis Mayfield / Leroy Hutson / Natural Four; originally aired June 7, 1975.
38. 144. Smokey Robinson / Betty Wright; originally aired June 14, 1975.
39. 145. Harold Melvin & The Blue Notes / The Southshore Commission (Guest Host: Richard Pryor); originally aired June 21, 1975.

SEASON 5 (1975–1976)

1. 146. The Supremes / Willie Hutch; originally aired August 23, 1975.
2. 147. Johnny Bristol / The Blackbyrds; originally aired August 30, 1975.
3. 148. Joe Simon / Millie Jackson / Choice Four; originally aired September 6, 1975.
4. 149. The New Birth / Blue Magic / Bobby Moore; originally aired September 13, 1975.
5. 150. The Impressions / Rance Allen Group / Soul Train Dance Contest; originally aired September 20, 1975.
6. 151. Eddie Kendricks / Tavares / (Comedian: Paul Mooney); originally aired September 27, 1975.
7. 152. The Pointer Sisters / B. T. Express / Ralph Carter; originally aired October 4, 1975.
8. 153. The O'Jays / Little Milton (Special Guest: Cholly Atkins); originally aired October 11, 1975.
9. 154. Labelle / Creative Source; originally aired October 18, 1975.
10. 155. Minnie Riperton / Twenty First Century; originally aired October 25, 1975.
11. 156. Ramsey Lewis / Fantastic Four; originally aired November 1, 1975.
12. 157. The Spinners / Merry Clayton; originally aired November 8, 1975.
13. 158. War / The Main Ingredient; originally aired November 15, 1975.
14. 159. Harold Melvin & the Blue Notes / Esther Phillips; originally aired November 22, 1975.
15. 160. The Miracles / Poison / Quincy Jones (Special Guest: Nat Adderley); originally aired November 29, 1975.
16. 161. Average White Band / The Undisputed Truth; originally aired December 6, 1975.
17. 162. Rufus featuring Chaka Khan / David Ruffin; originally aired December 13, 1975.
18. 163. Freda Payne / The Whispers; originally aired December 20, 1975.
19. 164. Billy Preston / The Sylvers; originally aired December 27, 1975.
20. 165. David Bowie / Faith, Hope and Charity / Jeff Perry; originally aired January 3, 1976.
21. 166. The Temptations / Edwin Starr; originally aired January 10, 1976.

22. 167. The Staple Singers / Bobby Womack; originally aired January 17, 1976.
23. 168. The Jackson 5; originally aired January 24, 1976.
24. 169. The Dells / Bloodstone; originally aired January 31, 1976.
25. 170. Bill Withers / The Soul Train Gang; originally aired February 7, 1976.
26. 171. The Jimmy Castor Bunch / Leon Haywood / The Southshore Commission; originally aired February 14, 1976.
27. 172. The Commodores / George McCrae; originally aired February 21, 1976.
28. 173. Joe Tex / The Chi-Lites / (Comedian: Tom Dreeson); originally aired February 28, 1976.
29. 174. Wilson Pickett / Betty Wright / The Modulations; originally aired March 6, 1976.
30. 175. Eddie Kendricks / The Temprees; originally aired March 13, 1976.
31. 176. Johnnie Taylor / Donna Summer; originally aired March 20, 1976.
32. 177. The Supremes / Al Wilson; originally aired March 27, 1976.
33. 178. The Dramatics / Dorothy Moore / Leon Thomas; originally aired April 3, 1976.
34. 179. Kool & The Gang / Ashford & Simpson / Ronnie McNeir; originally aired May 1, 1976.
35. 180. The Delfonics / D. J. Rogers; originally aired May 8, 1976.
36. 181. Billy Paul / The Trammps; originally aired May 15, 1976.
37. 182. Archie Bell & the Drells / Brass Construction; originally aired May 22, 1976.
38. 183. Rufus featuring Chaka Khan / The Checkmates / The Booty People; originally aired June 12, 1976.
39. 184. The 5th Dimension / The Brothers Johnson / Pat Lundy; originally aired June 19, 1976.

Season 6 (1976–1977)

1. 185. Johnnie Taylor / The Tymes; originally aired August 21, 1976.
2. 186. The Sylvers / Sun (Special Guest: Frankie Crocker); originally aired August 28, 1976.
3. 187. Melba Moore / The Whispers; originally aired September 4, 1976.
4. 188. The O'Jays / Thelma Houston; originally aired September 11, 1976.
5. 189. D. J. Rogers / The Lockers / Soul Train National Dance Contest; originally aired September 18, 1976.

6. 190. Labelle / Brother to Brother; originally aired September 25, 1976.
7. 191. The Spinners / David Ruffin; originally aired October 2, 1976.
8. 192. Jermaine Jackson / Tata Vega; originally aired October 9, 1976.
9. 193. The Emotions / The Rimshots / The Ritchie Family; originally aired October 16, 1976.
10. 194. Marilyn McCoo & Billy Davis, Jr. / Deniece Williams; originally aired October 23, 1976.
11. 195. The Undisputed Truth / Impact / Carol Douglas; originally aired October 30, 1976.
12. 196. The Four Tops / Vicki Sue Robinson; originally aired November 6, 1976.
13. 197. Aretha Franklin / Ronnie Dyson; originally aired November 13, 1976.
14. 198. The Manhattans / Brass Construction / Rose Royce; originally aired November 20, 1976.
15. 199. K. C. and the Sunshine Band / Dee Dee Bridgewater; originally aired November 27, 1976.
16. 200. The Ohio Players / Johnny Bristol; originally aired December 4, 1976.
17. 201. Average White Band / The Soul Train Gang; originally aired December 11, 1976.
18. 202. O. C. Smith / Dorothy Moore; originally aired December 18, 1976.
19. 203. The Moments / Donna Summer; originally aired December 25, 1976.
20. 204. The Supremes / Al Hudson & the Soul Partners; originally aired January 1, 1977.
21. 205. The Sylvers / Donald Byrd & the Blackbyrds; originally aired January 8, 1977.
22. 206. Billy Paul / Brick; originally aired January 15, 1977.
23. 207. Lou Rawls / L.T.D.; originally aired January 22, 1977.
24. 208. Billy Preston / Brenda Payton; originally aired January 29, 1977.
25. 209. Rufus featuring Chaka Khan / The Impressions; originally aired February 5, 1977.
26. 210. The Commodores / Thelma Houston; originally aired February 12, 1977.
27. 211. The Dramatics / Randy Crawford / Crown Heights Affair; originally aired February 19, 1977.
28. 212. Ashford & Simpson / Bootsy's Rubber Band; originally aired February 26, 1977.

29. 213. Latimore / Shalamar / Crown Heights Affair; originally aired March 5, 1977.
30. 214. Natalie Cole / Arthur Prysock; originally aired March 12, 1977.
31. 215. Al Green / Fatback Band; originally aired March 19, 1977.
32. 216. Melba Moore / Joe Tex; originally aired March 26, 1977.
33. 217. Roy Ayers Ubiquity / Lonnie Liston Smith / Gwen McCrae; originally aired April 2, 1977.
34. 218. B. T. Express / Letta Mbulu / Enchantment; originally aired April 9, 1977.
35. 219. Archie Bell & the Drells / Brainstorm; originally aired April 16, 1977.
36. 220. Teddy Pendergrass / Double Exposure; originally aired April 23, 1977.
37. 221. Smokey Robinson / Lakeside; originally aired April 30, 1977.
38. 222. Marvin Gaye; originally aired May 7, 1977.
39. 223. Harold Melvin & the Blue Notes / Side Effect; originally aired May 14, 1977.

Season 7 (1977–1978)

1. 224. O. C. Smith / Hot / Floaters; originally aired August 20, 1977.
2. 225. Jermaine Jackson / Switch; originally aired August 27, 1977.
3. 226. The O'Jays/ Al Jarreau/ Truth; originally aired September 3, 1977.
4. 227. Johnny Guitar Watson / The Whispers; originally aired September 10, 1977.
5. 228. Tyrone Davis / Dorothy Moore; originally aired September 17, 1977.
6. 229. The Dramatics / Tata Vega; originally aired September 24, 1977.
7. 230. The Emotions / Maze featuring Frankie Beverly; originally aired October 1, 1977.
8. 231. Lamont Dozier / Phyllis Hyman / High Inergy; originally aired October 8, 1977.
9. 232. Smokey Robinson / Dee Dee Sharp; originally aired October 15, 1977.
10. 233. Tavares / David Oliver; originally aired October 22, 1977.
11. 234. Johnnie Taylor / Millie Jackson; originally aired October 29, 1977.
12. 235. Teddy Pendergrass / Rose Royce; originally aired November 5, 1977.
13. 236. Barry White / Love Unlimited; originally aired November 12, 1977.

14. 237. Lou Rawls / The Ritchie Family; originally aired November 19, 1977.
15. 238. The Manhattans / Kellee Peterson; originally aired November 26, 1977.
16. 239. Deniece Williams / Mother's Finest; originally aired December 3, 1977.
17. 240. Ashford & Simpson / Ronnie Dyson; originally aired December 10, 1977.
18. 241. The Spinners / Hodges, James & Smith; originally aired December 17, 1977.
19. 242. Brick/ Sister Sledge; originally aired December 24, 1977.
20. 243. Philippé Wynne / Side Effect / Al Hudson & the Soul Partners; originally aired December 31, 1977.
21. 244. Brothers Johnson / Foster Sylvers; originally aired January 7, 1978.
22. 245. Freda Payne / Ronnie Laws / Morris Jefferson; originally aired January 14, 1978.
23. 246. The Sylvers / Lawrence Hilton-Jacobs; originally aired January 21, 1978.
24. 247. Bill Withers / Odyssey; originally aired January 28, 1978.
25. 248. L.T.D. / Michael Henderson; originally aired February 4, 1978.
26. 249. The Temptations / William Bell / Pattie Brooks; originally aired February 11, 1978.
27. 250. War / Eloise Laws; originally aired February 18, 1978.
28. 251. Billy Preston / Esther Phillips; originally aired February 25, 1978.
29. 252. Lonnie Jordan / Brass Construction / Pattie Brooks; originally aired March 4, 1978.
30. 253. The Four Tops / Con Funk Shun; originally aired March 11, 1978.
31. 254. Bobby Womack / Denise LaSalle; originally aired March 18, 1978.
32. 255. Marilyn McCoo & Billy Davis, Jr. / Cheryl Barnes / Stargard; originally aired March 25, 1978.
33. 256. Harold Melvin & the Blue Notes / Roy Ayers; originally aired April 1, 1978.
34. 257. Johnny Mathis / Deniece Williams; originally aired April 8, 1978.
35. 258. Enchantment / Wild Cherry / Bunny Sigler; originally aired April 15, 1978.
36. 259. Herb Alpert & Hugh Masekela / Aalon; originally aired April 22, 1978.

37. 260. The 5th Dimension / Mandrill; originally aired April 29, 1978.
38. 261. Smokey Robinson / Patti Austin; originally aired May 6, 1978.
39. 262. Cuba Gooding Sr. / Lenny Williams; originally aired May 13, 1978.

Season 8 (1978–1979)

1. 263. The O'Jays / Etta James; originally aired August 19, 1978.
2. 264. Brothers Johnson / The Dells; originally aired August 26, 1978.
3. 265.The Emotions / Randy Jackson / Hal Jackson's Talented Teens; originally aired September 2, 1978.
4. 266. The Sylvers / Kenny Brawner & Raw Sugar; originally aired September 9, 1978.
5. 267. Earth, Wind and Fire (in concert) / Heaven & Earth; originally aired September 16, 1978.
6. 268. Rose Royce / D. J. Rogers; originally aired September 23, 1978.
7. 269. Peabo Bryson / Stargard; originally aired September 30, 1978.
8. 270. Larry Graham & Graham Central Station / Charles Jackson; originally aired October 7, 1978.
9. 271. The Whispers / Gil Scott-Heron / Evelyn "Champagne" King; originally aired October 14, 1978.
10. 272. Melba Moore / Michael Henderson; originally aired October 21, 1978.
11. 273. Freda Payne / Atlantic Starr; originally aired October 28, 1978.
12. 274. The Trammps / Shalamar / Norma Jean Wright; originally aired November 4, 1978.
13. 275. Frankie Valli / Creme D'Coca; originally aired November 11, 1978.
14. 276. Jerry Butler / Rick James; originally aired November 18, 1978.
15. 277. Lenny Williams / Mother's Finest / Cheech & Chong; originally aired November 25, 1978.
16. 278. Johnny Guitar Watson / Jean Carne; originally aired December 2, 1978.
17. 279. Stylistics / Sun; originally aired December 9, 1978.
18. 280. Barry White / Danny Pearson; originally aired December 16, 1978.
19. 281. Switch / The McCrarys; originally aired December 23, 1978.
20. 282. The Temptations / Randy Brown; originally aired December 30, 1978.
21. 283. Marilyn McCoo & Billy Davis, Jr. / Lakeside; originally aired January 6, 1979.

22. 284. Roy Ayers & Ubiquity / Sarah Dash; originally aired January 13, 1979.
23. 285. Gene Chandler / Chic; originally aired January 20, 1979.
24. 286. Brass Construction / Peaches & Herb / Captain Sky; originally aired January 27, 1979.
25. 287. The Jacksons; originally aired February 3, 1979.
26. 288. Pattie Brooks / David Oliver / Michael Jackson; originally aired February 10, 1979.
27. 289. Joe Simon / Cheryl Lynn; originally aired February 17, 1979.
28. 290. Edwin Starr / The Jimmy Castor Bunch / Grace Jones; originally aired February 24, 1979.
29. 291. Bonnie Pointer / Dan Hartman; originally aired March 3, 1979.
30. 292. Gino Vanelli / Gloria Gaynor / Spotlight Dance Routine: Cheryl Song & Randy Thomas; originally aired March 10, 1979.
31. 293. The Bar-Kays / Arpeggio / Spotlight Dance Routine: Janice Carr & Abe Clark; originally aired March 17, 1979.
32. 294. Isaac Hayes / Tasha Thomas; originally aired March 24, 1979.
33. 295. Instant Funk / Cerrone; originally aired March 31, 1979.
34. 296. Billy Preston & Syreeta Wright / Chuck Brown & the Soul Searchers; originally aired April 7, 1979.
35. 297. Curtis Mayfield / Linda Clifford / Keith Barrow; originally aired April 14, 1979.
36. 298. Amii Stewart / Boney M; originally aired April 21, 1979.
37. 299. Hamilton Bohannon / The Raes; originally aired April 28, 1979.
38. 300. Third World / Danny Pearson; originally aired May 5, 1979.
39. 301. Tyrone Davis / Gary's Gang; originally aired May 12, 1979.
40. 302. Carrie Lucas / GQ / The Gap Band / Spotlight Dance Routine: Sherri Foster & Vince Carlos; originally aired May 19, 1979.

Season 9 (1979–1980)

1. 303. A Tribute to Minnie Riperton (featuring Stevie Wonder / Wintley Phipps / Professional Dance Routine: Lorraine Fields and Larry Vickers); originally aired September 15, 1979.
2. 304. Deniece Williams / Apollo / Professional Dance Routine: Frances Morgan and Michael Peters; originally aired September 22, 1979.
3. 305. Shalamar / Tata Vega; originally aired September 29, 1979.
4. 306. Bonnie Pointer / Switch; originally aired October 6, 1979.
5. 307. David Ruffin / Heatwave; originally aired October 13, 1979.
6. 308. Rick James & the Stone City Band / Teena Marie / Spotlight Dance Routine: Larry "Bobcat" Jeffries; originally aired October 20, 1979.

7. 309. Billy Preston / Creme D'Coca; originally aired October 27, 1979.
8. 310. The Bar-Kays / McFadden & Whitehead / Spotlight Dance Routine: The Eclipse / Spotlight Dance Routine: Jeffrey Daniel & the Eclipse; originally aired November 3, 1979.
9. 311. Herb Alpert / Dynasty; originally aired November 10, 1979.
10. 312. Salute to Smokey Robinson / Keith & Darrell; originally aired November 17, 1979.
11. 313. The Whispers / Vernon Burch / Comedian: Tom Dreesen; originally aired November 24, 1979.
12. 314. Salute to Aretha Franklin; originally aired December 1, 1979.
13. 315. The Commodores; originally aired December 8, 1979.
14. 316. Johnnie Taylor / Lakeside; originally aired December 15, 1979.
15. 317. War; originally aired February 2, 1980.
16. 318. Chic / High Inergy / Comedian: Dick Gregory; originally aired February 9, 1980.
17. 319. Lou Rawls / Narada Michael Walden; originally aired March 1, 1980.
18. 320. Shalamar / The Gap Band; originally aired March 8, 1980.
19. 321. The Whispers / Patrice Rushen; originally aired March 15, 1980.
20. 322. L.T.D. / Cheryl Lynn; originally aired March 22, 1980.
21. 323. Harold Melvin & the Blue Notes / Brass Construction; originally aired March 29, 1980.
22. 324. Sister Sledge / Randy Brown; originally aired April 5, 1980.
23. 325. The Spinners / Con Funk Shun; originally aired April 12, 1980.
24. 326. Captain & Tennille / The Ritchie Family (Introduction by Jacques Morali) / Dance Routine: The Electric Boogaloos; originally aired April 19, 1980
25. 327. Stephanie Mills / Roy Ayers; originally aired April 26, 1980.
26. 328. Village People / Side Effect; originally aired May 3, 1980.
27. 329. Jermaine Jackson / Dramatics; originally aired May 10, 1980.
28. 330. Salute to Gladys Knight & the Pips; originally aired May 17, 1980.
29. 331. Ray, Goodman & Brown / Ray Parker, Jr. & Raydio / Spotlight Dance Routine: Kirk Washington; originally aired May 24, 1980.
30. 332. Salute to the Temptations / Syreeta Wright; originally aired May 31, 1980.
31. 333. Leon Haywood / L.A. Boppers; originally aired June 7, 1980.
32. 334. Salute to Barry White; originally aired June 14, 1980.

Season 10 (1980–1981)

1. 335. Brothers Johnson / Rockie Robbins / Dance Showdown: Bobcat vs. Mr. X; originally aired September 20, 1980.
2. 336. L.T.D. / Seventh Wonder / Kurtis Blow; originally aired September 27, 1980.
3. 337. Larry Graham / Irene Cara; originally aired October 4, 1980.
4. 338. Rick James / The S.O.S. Band; originally aired October 11, 1980.
5. 339. Tyrone Davis / Teena Marie / Comedian: Tom Dreesen; originally aired October 18, 1980.
6. 340. Teddy Pendergrass / The Jones Girls; originally aired October 25, 1980.
7. 341. Cameo / Edmund Sylvers / Special Guest: Kim Fields; originally aired November 1, 1980.
8. 342. Michael Henderson / LaToya Jackson; originally aired November 8, 1980.
9. 343. Shalamar / Mtume; originally aired November 15, 1980.
10. 344. Lakeside / Geraldine Hunt; originally aired November 22, 1980.
11. 345. Lenny Williams / Yellow Magic Orchestra; originally aired November 29, 1980.
12. 346. Ray, Goodman & Brown / Gently; originally aired December 6, 1980.
13. 347. Al Green / The Dells / Soul Train History Book: LaBelle; originally aired January 10, 1981.
14. 348. Dynasty / Tierra / Soul Train History Book: Marvin Gaye; originally aired January 17, 1981.
15. 349. The Stylistics / Spyro Gyra / Soul Train History Book: The Four Tops; originally aired January 24, 1981.
16. 350. The Chi-Lites / Patrice Rushen / Soul Train History Book: Lou Rawls; originally aired January 31, 1981.
17. 351. Deniece Williams / The Gap Band / Soul Train History Book: Curtis Mayfield; originally aired March 7, 1981.
18. 352. The Bar-Kays / Yarbrough & Peoples / Robert Winters; originally aired March 14, 1981.
19. 353. The Pointer Sisters / Con Funk Shun / Soul Train History Book: Billy Paul; originally aired March 21, 1981.
20. 354. The Whispers / Carrie Lucas; originally aired March 28, 1981.
21. 355. Rufus / Dee Dee Sharp; originally aired April 4, 1981.
22. 356. Billy Preston / Lakeside; originally aired April 11, 1981.
23. 357. Shalamar / Teena Marie; originally aired April 18, 1981.

24. 358. A Taste of Honey / Jerry Knight / Soul Train History Book: David Ruffin; originally aired April 25, 1981.
25. 359. Sister Sledge / Atlantic Starr; originally aired May 2, 1981.
26. 360. The Spinners / Skyy / Comedian: Arsenio Hall; originally aired May 9, 1981.
27. 361. Sugarhill Gang / Patrice Rushen / Spotlight Dance Routine: Shabba Doo; originally aired May 16, 1981.
28. 362. Betty Wright / Funkadelic / Soul Train History Book: Joe Tex; originally aired May 23, 1981.
29. 363. Bill Withers / Side Effect / Special Guests: Leon and Jayne Kennedy; originally aired May 30, 1981.
30. 364. Jermaine Jackson / T-Connection / Comedian: Marsha Warfield; originally aired June 6, 1981.
31. 365. Rick James / Brenda Russell; originally aired June 13, 1981.
32. 366. Cameo / Mantra; originally aired June 20, 1981.

Season 11 (1981–1982)

1. 367. Barry White / Glodean White; originally aired September 19, 1981.
2. 368. Phyllis Hyman / Carl Carlton / Mike Weaver; originally aired September 26, 1981.
3. 369. Deniece Williams / Richard "Dimples" Fields; originally aired October 3, 1981.
4. 370. Brothers Johnson / LaToya Jackson; originally aired October 10, 1981.
5. 371. Salute to Rick James / Soul Train History Book: Rick James; originally aired October 17, 1981.
6. 372. The Four Tops / Stacy Lattisaw / Comedian: Arsenio Hall; originally aired October 24, 1981.
7. 373. José Feliciano / Stone City Band; originally aired October 31, 1981.
8. 374. Brick / Frankie Smith / Soul Train History Book: The Supremes; originally aired November 7, 1981.
9. 375. Patti LaBelle / The Time / Comedian: James Wesley Jackson; originally aired November 14, 1981.
10. 376. George Benson / Patti Austin / Soul Train History Book: The Floaters; originally aired November 21, 1981.
11. 377. The Spinners / Bobby Womack / Special Guests: Hal Jackson's Talented Teens; originally aired December 12, 1981.
12. 378. Rockie Robbins / Slave; originally aired December 19, 1981.
13. 379. Skyy / O'Bryan / Comedians: Tim O'Brien and Ken Sevara; originally aired January 9, 1982.

14. 380. L.T.D. / James Ingram; originally aired January 16, 1982.
15. 381. Syreeta / Zoom; originally aired January 23, 1982.
16. 382. Salute to Diana Ross; originally aired January 30, 1982.
17. 383. Irene Cara / Andrae Crouch; originally aired March 27, 1982.
18. 384. Al Jarreau / Aurra; originally aired April 3, 1982.
19. 385. The Whispers / Mary Wells; originally aired April 10, 1982.
20. 386. The Chi-Lites / Bill Summers & Summers Heat; originally aired April 17, 1982.
21. 387. Tribute to Smokey Robinson / Bettye Lavette; originally aired April 24, 1982.
22. 388. Sister Sledge / Ray Parker, Jr. / Soul Train History Book: Smokey Robinson; originally aired May 1, 1982.
23. 389. Lakeside / Sheree Brown; originally aired May 8, 1982.
24. 390. George Duke / D-Train; originally aired May 15, 1982.
25. 391. War / O'Bryan / Soul Train History Book: Chairmen of the Board; originally aired May 22, 1982.
26. 392. Ronnie Dyson / The Dazz Band / *Ebony* Fashion Fair Models; originally aired May 29, 1982.
27. 393. Al Green / Third World; originally aired June 5, 1982.
28. 394. Deniece Williams / Junior / Soul Train History Book: Ben E. King; originally aired June 12, 1982.
29. 395. Cameo / Patrice Rushen / Soul Train History Book: Marvin Gaye; originally aired June 19, 1982.
30. 396. Bobby Womack / The Gap Band; originally aired June 26, 1982.
31. 397. The O'Jays / Gene Chandler; originally aired July 3, 1982.
32. 398. A Taste of Honey / Jeffrey Osborne / Soul Train History Book: Al Green; originally aired July 10, 1982.

Season 12 (1982–1983)

1. 399. A Tribute to Joe Tex; originally aired October 16, 1982.
2. 400. Evelyn "Champagne" King / Glen Edward Thomas / Alice Arthur; originally aired October 23, 1982.
3. 401. A Salute to Jermaine Jackson / DeBarge; originally aired October 30, 1982.
4. 402. Larry Graham / The Busboys; originally aired November 6, 1982.
5. 403. Salute to Lionel Richie / Ozone / Special Guests: Hal Jackson's Talented Teens; originally aired November 13, 1982.
6. 404. Jerry Butler / Daryl Hall & John Oates; originally aired November 20, 1982.
7. 405. Luther Vandross / Cheryl Lynn; originally aired November 27, 1982.

8. 406. Johnnie Taylor / Tavares; originally aired December 4, 1982.
9. 407. Chuck Mangione / Howard Johnson / Soul Train History Book: Aretha Franklin; originally aired December 11, 1982.
10. 408. Michael McDonald / Janet Jackson / Music Video: Stevie Wonder; originally aired December 18, 1982.
11. 409. The Time / Magic Lady / Soul Train History Book: David Bowie; originally aired December 25, 1982.
12. 410. Vanity 6 / Carl Carlton / Soul Train History Book: Frankie Valli; originally aired January 1, 1983.
13. 411. The Bar-Kays / O'Bryan / Special Guests: Los Angeles Lakers featuring Magic Johnson and Norm Nixon; originally aired April 30, 1983.
14. 412. The Gap Band / Yarbrough & Peoples / Robert "Goodie" Whitfield; originally aired May 7, 1983.
15. 413. DeBarge / Champaign / Soul Train History Book: Ramsey Lewis; originally aired May 14, 1983.
16. 414. Evelyn "Champagne" King / Grandmaster Flash & the Furious Five / Soul Train History Book: Sylvia / Special Guest: B.B.D. Banana; originally aired May 21, 1983.
17. 415. Angela Bofill / Con Funk Shun / Soul Train History Book: Herb Alpert; originally aired May 28, 1983.
18. 416. The Temptations / Anita Baker / Music Video: Prince; originally aired June 4, 1983.
19. 417. A Tribute to Marvin Gaye; originally aired June 11, 1983.
20. 418. Deniece Williams / Kiddo / Soul Train History Book: Captain & Tennielle; originally aired June 18, 1983.
21. 419. The Whispers / Nona Hendryx / Soul Train History Book: Gladys Knight & the Pips; originally aired June 25, 1983.
22. 420. Lakeside / High Inergy / Soul Train History Book: The 5th Dimension; originally aired July 2, 1983.
23. 421. Thelma Houston / The System / Soul Train History Book: Blue Magic; originally aired July 9, 1983.
24. 422. O'Bryan / Imagination; originally aired July 16, 1983.

Season 13 (1983–1984)

1. 423. Manhattans / Philip Bailey / Soul Train History Book: Kool & the Gang; originally aired October 15, 1983.
2. 424. Jeffrey Osborne / Midnight Star / Special Guest: T. K. Carter; originally aired October 22, 1983.
3. 425. Al Green / Planet Patrol; originally aired October 29, 1983.
4. 426. The S.O.S. Band / Mary Jane Girls; originally aired November 5, 1983.

5. 427. The Gap Band / Michael Sembello; originally aired November 12, 1983.
6. 428. Sister Sledge / Lillo Thomas; originally aired November 19, 1983.
7. 429. Jennifer Holliday / Klique / Soul Train History Book: Jermaine Jackson; originally aired November 26, 1983.
8. 430. The Manhattan Transfer / Kashif / Music Video: Lionel Richie; originally aired December 3, 1983.
9. 431. Herbie Hancock / DeBarge; originally aired December 10, 1983.
10. 432. Kool & the Gang / Tavares / Special Guests: Hal Jackson and Talented Teen Winner: Delise Jones; originally aired December 17, 1983.
11. 433. The Commodores / Anita Baker; originally aired December 24, 1983.
12. 434. Atlantic Starr / James Ingram / Soul Train History Book: Tower of Power; originally aired December 31, 1983.
13. 435. Cheryl Lynn / Con Funk Shun; originally aired January 14, 1984.
14. 436. Ray Parker, Jr. / New Edition / Music Video: Michael Jackson & Paul McCartney—Say Say Say; originally aired February 11, 1984.
15. 437. Evelyn "Champagne" King / D-Train; originally aired February 18, 1984.
16. 438. Tom Tom Club / Howard Johnson; originally aired February 25, 1984.
17. 439. Teena Marie / Womack & Womack; originally aired March 31, 1984.
18. 440. Patti LaBelle / J. Blackfoot; originally aired April 7, 1984.
19. 441. Bobby Womack / Shannon; originally aired April 14, 1984.
20. 442. The Pointer Sisters / Bobby Nunn; originally aired April 21, 1984.
21. 443. Shalamar / Nona Hendryx / Music Video: Daryl Hall & John Oates; originally aired April 28, 1984.
22. 444. Tribute to Dionne Warwick / NYC Breakers; originally aired May 5, 1984.
23. 445. Dennis Edwards / Newcleus / Music Video: "Weird Al" Yankovic; originally aired May 12, 1984.
24. 446. Yarbrough & Peoples / Stacy Lattisaw & Johnny Gill; originally aired May 19, 1984.
25. 447. O'Bryan / Real to Reel; originally aired May 26, 1984.
26. 448. The O'Jays / The Romantics; originally aired June 9, 1984.

27. 449. The Dazz Band / Run-D.M.C. / Music Video: Huey Lewis and the News / Special Guest: Jesse Peralez; originally aired June 16, 1984.
28. 450. Marilyn McCoo & Billy Davis, Jr. / The Deele / Kim Fields; originally aired June 23, 1984.

Season 14 (1984–1985)

1. 451. O'Bryan / New Edition / Ollie & Jerry; originally aired September 22, 1984.
2. 452. Lakeside / Vanity; originally aired September 29, 1984.
3. 453. Cameo / Billy Ocean / Music Video: Sheila E.; originally aired October 6, 1984.
4. 454. Stephanie Mills / Richard "Dimples" Fields / Special Guest: Michael Winslow; originally aired October 13, 1984.
5. 455. Joyce Kennedy / Randy Hall / Music Video: The Jacksons; originally aired October 20, 1984.
6. 456. Jeffrey Osborne / Alicia Myers / Mr. T; originally aired October 27, 1984.
7. 457. Lillo Thomas / Cherrelle / Music Video: The Fat Boys; originally aired November 3, 1984.
8. 458. Janet Jackson / Beau Williams; originally aired November 10, 1984.
9. 459. Thelma Houston / Krystol; originally aired November 17, 1984.
10. 460. Berlin / The Controllers; originally aired November 24, 1984.
11. 461. Dan Hartman / Champaign / Music Video: Tina Turner; originally aired December 1, 1984.
12. 462. Herb Alpert / Rodney Saulsberry; originally aired December 8, 1984.
13. 463. Donna Summer / The Staple Singers / Hal Jackson's Talented Teen Winner; originally aired December 15, 1984.
14. 464. The Temptations / The Fat Boys / Music Video: Madonna; originally aired January 5, 1985.
15. 465. Teena Marie and Ronnie McNeir / Whodini / Music Video: Daryl Hall & John Oates; originally aired January 12, 1985.
16. 466. New Edition / Rebbie Jackson / Music Video: Kool & the Gang; originally aired January 26, 1985.
17. 467. Rockwell / Redd Foxx; originally aired February 2, 1985.
18. 468. The Commodores / Eugene Wilde; originally aired February 9, 1985.
19. 469. Shalamar / Dreamboy; originally aired February 23, 1985.
20. 470. Bonnie Pointer / Thomas McClary; originally aired March 2, 1985.

21. 471. The Gap Band / Sam Harris; originally aired March 16, 1985.
22. 472. Johnnie Taylor / Klymaxx / Music Video: Sade; originally aired March 23, 1985.
23. 473. Jesse Johnson / LeVert; originally aired March 30, 1985.
24. 474. Ray, Goodman & Brown / Glenn Jones; originally aired April 6, 1985.
25. 475. Sheena Easton / Mary Jane Girls / Music Video: The Commodores; originally aired April 13, 1985.
26. 476. Don Henley / Whitney Houston; originally aired April 20, 1985.
27. 477. Atlantic Starr / Greg Phillinganes; originally aired May 25, 1985.
28. 478. The Four Tops / Spandau Ballet; originally aired June 1, 1985.
29. 479. Shannon / Alexander O'Neal; originally aired June 8, 1985.
30. 480. Natalie Cole / Ready for the World; originally aired June 15, 1985.
31. 481. Womack & Womack / Pennye Ford; originally aired June 22, 1985.
32. 482. Carrie Lucas / Steve Arrington / Music Video: Harold Faltermeyer; originally aired June 29, 1985.

SEASON 15 (1985–1986)

1. 483. Go West / Rosie Gaines / Music Video: Aretha Franklin; originally aired October 5, 1985.
2. 484. Sheila E. / Five Star / Music Video: Dire Straits; originally aired October 12, 1985.
3. 485. Dennis Edwards / 9.9; originally aired October 19, 1985.
4. 486. Cheryl Lynn / a-ha; originally aired October 26, 1985.
5. 487. Ready for the World / Starpoint / Music Video: Paul Young; originally aired November 2, 1985.
6. 488. Rick Dees / U.T.F.O.; originally aired November 9, 1985.
7. 489. New Edition / Lushus Daim and the Pretty Vain; originally aired November 16, 1985.
8. 490. The System / Durrell Coleman; originally aired November 23, 1985.
9. 491. Cameo / Michael McDonald; originally aired November 30, 1985.
10. 492. Sheena Easton / Bernard Wright; originally aired December 7, 1985.
11. 493. The Thompson Twins / The Jets / Doug E. Fresh; originally aired December 14, 1985.
12. 494. Stephanie Mills / Howard Jones; originally aired December 21, 1985.

13. 495. New Edition / Rosie Gaines; originally aired March 8, 1986.
14. 496. Klymaxx / Jack Wagner / Music Video: Wham!; originally aired March 15, 1986.
15. 497. Five Star / LL Cool J; originally aired March 22, 1986.
16. 498. Janet Jackson / Atlantic Starr / Music Video: Billy Ocean; originally aired March 29, 1986.
17. 499. The Gap Band / Force M.D.'s; originally aired April 5, 1986.
18. 500. Zapp / Meli'sa Morgan / Lisa Lisa and Cult Jam; originally aired April 12, 1986.
19. 501. Johnnie Taylor / Yarbrough & Peoples / Full Force; originally aired April 19, 1986.
20. 502. Culture Club / Cherrelle / Alexander O'Neal; originally aired April 26, 1986.
21. 503. Little Richard / Animotion / Colonel Abrams; originally aired May 3, 1986.
22. 504. Morris Day / Tramaine Hawkins / Eddie "E. T." Towns; originally aired May 10, 1986.
23. 505. Al Green / Evelyn "Champagne" King / Music Video: Sly Fox; originally aired May 17, 1986.
24. 506. Roy Ayers / The Pet Shop Boys; originally aired May 24, 1986.
25. 507. Patti Labelle & Michael McDonald / Eugene Wilde; originally aired May 31, 1986.
26. 508. Starpoint / The Dramatics / Ebo; originally aired June 7, 1986.
27. 509. The S.O.S. Band / Jermaine Stewart / Juicy; originally aired June 14, 1986.
28. 510. Philip Bailey / The Controllers; originally aired June 21, 1986.

Season 16 (1986–1987)

1. 511. Midnight Star / Gavin Christopher / Music Video: Michael McDonald; originally aired September 20, 1986.
2. 512. Howard Hewett / Shirley Jones / Music Video: Janet Jackson; originally aired September 27, 1986.
3. 513. Oran "Juice" Jones / The Whitehead Brothers / Special Guests: The Los Angeles Raiders; originally aired October 4, 1986.
4. 514. James Ingram / LeVert / Music Video: Lionel Richie; originally aired October 11, 1986.
5. 515. Jean Carne / Glenn Jones; originally aired October 18, 1986.
6. 516. Run–D.M.C. / Genobia Jeter / Special Guest: Dick Anthony Williams; originally aired October 25, 1986.
7. 517. Melba Moore / Freddie Jackson / Beau Williams; originally aired November 1, 1986.

8. 518. Millie Jackson / Whodini; originally aired November 8, 1986.
9. 519. Anita Baker / Gregory Abbott / Special Guest: Troy Beyers; originally aired November 15, 1986.
10. 520. Luther Vandross; originally aired November 22, 1986.
11. 521. Timex Social Club / Krystol / Music Video: Kool and the Gang; originally aired November 29, 1986.
12. 522. Ready for the World / Rebbie Jackson / Music Video: Cameo (band); originally aired December 6, 1986.
13. 523. Klymaxx / Club Nouveau / Bobby Brown; originally aired December 13, 1986.
14. 524. Al Jarreau / Vesta Williams; originally aired December 20, 1986.
15. 525. Jody Watley / Jeff Lorber featuring Karyn White and Michael Jeffries / Special Guest: Tim Reid; originally aired December 27, 1986.
16. 526. Loose Ends / George Howard; originally aired January 3, 1987.
17. 527. O'Bryan / Beastie Boys / Music Video: Robbie Nevil; originally aired March 7, 1987.
18. 528. James Cleveland / Grace Jones / The Rose Brothers; originally aired March 14, 1987.
19. 529. Rose Royce / Chico DeBarge / Music Video: Jody Watley; originally aired March 21, 1987.
20. 530. Little Richard / Miki Howard; originally aired March 28, 1987.
21. 531. Duran Duran / Stacy Lattisaw; originally aired April 4, 1987.
22. 532. Starpoint / Shirley Murdock; originally aired April 11, 1987.
23. 533. Bunny DeBarge / The System / Georgio; originally aired April 18, 1987.
24. 534. Howard Hewett / Donna Allen / Special Guest: Todd Davis (actor); originally aired April 25, 1987.
25. 535. Nona Hendryx / Robert Brookins / Music Video: Herb Alpert; originally aired May 2, 1987.
26. 536. Stephanie Mills / Surface; originally aired May 9, 1987.
27. 537. Lillo Thomas / Rainy Davis; originally aired May 16, 1987.
28. 538. R. J.'s Latest Arrival / James "D-Train" Williams; originally aired May 23, 1987.
29. 539. Natalie Cole / Robbie Nevil / Millie Scott; originally aired May 30, 1987.
30. 540. Deniece Williams / Lisa Lisa and Cult Jam / Kenny G; originally aired June 6, 1987.
31. 541. The Whispers / 4 By Four / Carrie McDowell; originally aired June 13, 1987.
32. 542. Cheryl Lynn / Lakeside / The Cover Girls; originally aired June 20, 1987.

Season 17 (1987–1988)

1. 543. Jody Watley / LeVert; originally aired September 19, 1987.
2. 544. Shalamar / Alexander O'Neal; originally aired September 26, 1987.
3. 545. Five Star / Babyface / Music Video: Madonna; originally aired October 3, 1987.
4. 546. Atlantic Starr / La La / Giorge Pettus; originally aired October 10, 1987.
5. 547. Anita Pointer / Chico DeBarge / Regina Belle; originally aired October 17, 1987.
6. 548. Barry White / Shanice Wilson; originally aired October 24, 1987.
7. 549. Marlon Jackson / Madame X; originally aired October 31, 1987.
8. 550. DeBarge / Jonathan Butler; originally aired November 7, 1987.
9. 551. Freddie Jackson / Whodini / Lace (U.S. group); originally aired November 14, 1987.
10. 552. LL Cool J / Meli'sa Morgan / Sting; originally aired November 21, 1987.
11. 553. ABC / Colonel Abrams / Eric B. & Rakim; originally aired November 28, 1987.
12. 554. The Jets / Kashif / Public Enemy; originally aired December 5, 1987.
13. 555. Full Force / Angela Winbush / The Controllers; originally aired January 9, 1988.
14. 556. Smokey Robinson / Pretty Poison / Classic Clip: Smokey Robinson (1982); originally aired January 16, 1988.
15. 557. Ray Parker, Jr. / Shanice Wilson / Miles Jaye; originally aired January 23, 1988.
16. 558. The Deele / Georgio / Pebbles / Hal Jackson's Talented Teens Winner; originally aired January 30, 1988.
17. 559. Vanity / Kool Moe Dee / Angela Winbush and Ronald Isley; originally aired March 5, 1988.
18. 560. Lou Rawls / Heavy D and the Boyz / Miki Howard; originally aired March 12, 1988.
19. 561. Peabo Bryson with Regina Belle / Rebbie Jackson / Keith Sweat; originally aired March 19, 1988.
20. 562. Stacy Lattisaw / Salt-N-Pepa / Tony Terry; originally aired March 26, 1988.
21. 563. The Whispers / Miles Jaye / Joyce Sims; originally aired April 2, 1988.

22. 564. Gladys Knight & the Pips / de'Krash; originally aired April 9, 1988.
23. 565. David Ruffin and Eddie Kendricks / Dana Dane / Special Guest: Morris Day; originally aired April 16, 1988.
24. 566. Howard Hewett / Club Nouveau / Michael Cooper; originally aired April 23, 1988.
25. 567. Pebbles / Jermaine Stewart / The Bus Boys; originally aired April 30, 1988.
26. 568. Stephanie Mills / Force MD's; originally aired May 7, 1988.
27. 569. Evelyn "Champagne" King / Brownmark / Sherrick; originally aired May 14, 1988.
28. 570. Hindsight / Mantronix / Pepsi & Shirlie; originally aired May 21, 1988.
29. 571. Teena Marie / Junior / Guy; originally aired May 28, 1988.
30. 572. Gregory Abbott / Siedah Garrett / Al B. Sure; originally aired June 4, 1988.
31. 573. Melba Moore / Narada Michael Walden; originally aired June 18, 1988.
32. 574. New Edition / Johnny Kemp / Bobby Brown; originally aired June 25, 1988.

Season 18 (1988–1989)

1. 575. Thomas Dolby / Vanessa L. Williams / Tony Terry; originally aired September 24, 1988.
2. 576. The O'Jays / New Kids on the Block; originally aired October 1, 1988.
3. 577. Johnny Mathis / Nia Peeples / Tracie Spencer; originally aired October 8, 1988.
4. 578. New Edition / Paula Abdul; originally aired October 15, 1988.
5. 579. The Commodores / Brenda Russell / The Boys; originally aired October 22, 1988.
6. 580. Deniece Williams / Midnight Star / Kiara; originally aired October 29, 1988.
7. 581. Jeffrey Osborne / The Mac Band / Giant Steps (band); originally aired November 5, 1988.
8. 582. Ziggy Marley / Karyn White with Freddie Jackson; originally aired November 12, 1988.
9. 583. Ready for the World / Cheryl Pepsii Riley / Billy Always; originally aired November 19, 1988.
10. 584. Sheena Easton / Howard Huntsberry / Sweet Obsession; originally aired November 26, 1988.

11. 585. Keith Sweat / Surface / EPMD; originally aired December 3, 1988.
12. 586. LeVert / James "D-Train" Williams / Special Guest: Gregory Hines; originally aired December 10, 1988.
13. 587. The Boys / Breathe / Desiree Coleman; originally aired January 14, 1989.
14. 588. Chaka Khan Tribute / Fishbone / Cameo: Arsenio Hall; originally aired January 21, 1989.
15. 589. George Benson / Guy / Cameo: Keenan Ivory Wayans; originally aired January 28, 1989.
16. 590. Starpoint / Cherrelle / Robert Brookins & Stephanie Mills; originally aired February 4, 1989.
17. 591. El DeBarge / Vesta Williams / Troop; originally aired March 11, 1989.
18. 592. Midnight Star / Gerald Alston / Kiara & Shanice Wilson; originally aired March 18, 1989.
19. 593. Betty Wright / K-9 Posse / Today; originally aired March 25, 1989.
20. 594. George Duke / Tony! Toni! Tone! / Marcus Lewis; originally aired April 1, 1989.
21. 595. Milli Vanilli / Was (Not Was) / Z-Looke; originally aired April 8, 1989.
22. 596. Skyy / Desiree Coleman / Apollonia; originally aired April 15, 1989.
23. 597. Ashford & Simpson / Rob Base & DJ E-Z Rock / Johnny Kemp; originally aired April 22, 1989.
24. 598. Georgio / The Bar-Kays / Tone Loc; originally aired April 29, 1989.
25. 599. E.U. / Grady Harrell / Joyce "Fenderella" Irby with Doug E. Fresh; originally aired May 6, 1989.
26. 600. Third World / Donna Allen; originally aired May 13, 1989.
27. 601. The Manhattan Transfer / René Moore / Lateasha; originally aired May 20, 1989.
28. 602. Wendy & Lisa / Charlie Singleton; originally aired May 27, 1989.
29. 603. Robert Palmer / Atlantic Starr / Stephanie Mills; originally aired June 3, 1989.
30. 604. Eugene Wilde / Tribute to Patti LaBelle; originally aired June 10, 1989.
31. 605. M. C. Hammer / Hiroshima / James Ingram; originally aired June 17, 1989.
32. 606. Lisa Lisa & Cult Jam / June Pointer / Christopher Max; originally aired June 24, 1989.

Season 19 (1989–1990)

1. 607. Debbie Allen / Heavy D & the Boyz / Music Video: Eddie Murphy; originally aired September 23, 1989.
2. 608. Full Force / Chuckii Booker / Music Video: Jonathan Butler; originally aired September 30, 1989.
3. 609. James Ingram / Exposé / Music Video: Paula Abdul; originally aired October 7, 1989.
4. 610. Regina Belle / Alyson Williams / After 7; originally aired October 14, 1989.
5. 611. Sharon Bryant / Michael Bolton / Young M.C.; originally aired October 21, 1989.
6. 612. Kool & the Gang / David Peaston / Music Video: Prince; originally aired October 28, 1989.
7. 613. Stephanie Mills / Michael Cooper / The Good Girls; originally aired November 4, 1989.
8. 614. BeBe & CeCe Winans / Christopher Williams / Music Video: James Ingram; originally aired November 11, 1989.
9. 615. Barry White / Sybil; originally aired November 18, 1989.
10. 616. Billy Ocean / Kashif / Stacy Lattisaw; originally aired November 25, 1989.
11. 617. Cheryl Lynn / Entouch / Wreckx-N-Effect; originally aired December 2, 1989.
12. 618. Jermaine Jackson / Finest Hour / D'Atra Hicks; originally aired December 9, 1989.
13. 619. Soul II Soul / The Main Ingredient / Foster and McElroy; originally aired January 13, 1990.
14. 620. The O'Jays / Troop / Tyler Collins; originally aired January 20, 1990.
15. 621. The Temptations / Beastie Boys / Michael Jeffries / Karyn White; originally aired January 27, 1990.
16. 622. Calloway / Pieces of a Dream / Eric Gable; originally aired March 3, 1990.
17. 623. Maze featuring Frankie Beverly / Big Daddy Kane / Body; originally aired March 10, 1990.
18. 624. The Winans / Miki Howard / Jeff Redd; originally aired March 17, 1990.
19. 625. The Jets / George Howard / Michel'le; originally aired March 24, 1990.
20. 626. Angela Winbush / David Peaston / Seduction; originally aired March 31, 1990.
21. 627. Jody Watley / The Newtrons / Music Video: Janet Jackson; originally aired April 7, 1990.

22. 628. Randy Crawford / Bell Biv Devoe / Music Video: Bobby Brown; originally aired April 14, 1990.
23. 629. Regina Belle / Timmy Gatling / Music Video: Jody Watley; originally aired April 21, 1990.
24. 630. Stacy Lattisaw / Sherman Hemsley / KYZE; originally aired April 28, 1990.
25. 631. Johnny Gill / Stacey & Kimiko / The Jamaica Boys; originally aired May 5, 1990.
26. 632. Jeffrey Daniel / The Brat Pack / Music Video: Maze featuring Frankie Beverly; originally aired May 12, 1990.
27. 633. Tyler Collins / En Vogue / Music Video: Luther Vandross; originally aired May 19, 1990.
28. 634. Klymaxx / Def Con 4 / Misa; originally aired May 26, 1990.
29. 635. Kid 'n Play / Perfect Gentlemen / Music Video: Madonna; originally aired June 2, 1990.
30. 636. The Gap Band / The Superiors / Domino Theory; originally aired June 9, 1990.
31. 637. The Pointer Sisters / Mantronix / Music Video: MC Hammer; originally aired June 16, 1990.
32. 638. The Good Girls / Today / The U Krew; originally aired June 23, 1990.

SEASON 20 (1990–1991)

1. 639. The Time / J. T. Taylor / Kwamé; originally aired September 22, 1990.
2. 640. Lalah Hathaway / Tevin Campbell / Tony! Toni! Tone!; originally aired September 29, 1990.
3. 641. Force MD's / Lakeside / Mellow Man Ace; originally aired October 6, 1990.
4. 642. Body / The Afros / Midnight Star; originally aired October 13, 1990.
5. 643. Quincy Jones Tribute featuring Tevin Campbell, Siedah Garrett, Al B. Sure, The Winans, El DeBarge, Valerie Mayo, Big Daddy Kane, Melle Mel, Kool Moe Dee, and Quincy Jones; originally aired October 20, 1990.
6. 644. D-Nice / Al B. Sure / Black Box / Music Video: Johnny Gill; originally aired October 27, 1990.
7. 645. The Whispers / The Boys / Terry Steele; originally aired November 3, 1990.
8. 646. Salt-N-Pepa / The Mac Band / Brenda Russell; originally aired November 10, 1990.
9. 647. Snap! / E.U. / Jasmine Guy; originally aired November 17, 1990.

10. 648. Guy / Thelma Houston; originally aired November 24, 1990.
11. 649. Father MC / LeVert / Music Video: Jasmine Guy; originally aired December 1, 1990.
12. 650. Z-Looke / Maxi Priest / Music Video: Whitney Houston; originally aired December 8, 1990.
13. 651. Ralph Tresvant / Samuelle; originally aired January 12, 1991.
14. 652. Teena Marie / LL Cool J / The Rude Boys; originally aired January 19, 1991.
15. 653. Loose Ends / Jeffrey Osborne / Music Video: Vanilla Ice; originally aired January 26, 1991.
16. 654. EPMD / Tracie Spencer / Freddie Jackson; originally aired February 2, 1991.
17. 655. Bernadette Cooper / Big Daddy Kane / Music Video: Al B. Sure; originally aired February 9, 1991.
18. 656. Pebbles / Hi-Five / Music Video: Bell Biv DeVoe; originally aired February 16, 1991.
19. 657. Howard Hewett / Monie Love / Another Bad Creation; originally aired February 23, 1991.
20. 658. Today / Joey B. Ellis & Tynetta Hare / Music Video: Big Daddy Kane with Barry White; originally aired March 2, 1991.
21. 659. Johnny Gill / Gerald Alston / M. C. Trouble; originally aired March 9, 1991.
22. 660. Run-D.M.C. / Ice-T / Oleta Adams; originally aired March 16, 1991.
23. 661. The O'Jays / Chubb Rock / Music Video: Jasmine Guy; originally aired March 23, 1991.
24. 662. Keith Sweat / Shawn Christopher / Brand Nubian; originally aired March 30, 1991.
25. 663. Sheena Easton / Altitude / Nikki D; originally aired May 4, 1991.
26. 664. Al B. Sure / K-9 Posse / Color Me Badd; originally aired May 11, 1991.
27. 665. Christopher Williams / Five Star / Tara Kemp; originally aired May 18, 1991.
28. 666. Surface / Keith Washington / Victoria Wilson-James; originally aired May 25, 1991.
29. 667. Boyz II Men / Ex-Girlfriend / Omar Chandler; originally aired June 1, 1991.
30. 668. Junior / Cheryl Pepsii Riley / Ed O. G. & Da Bulldogs; originally aired June 8, 1991.
31. 669. Damian Dame / Jodeci / Lisa Fischer; originally aired June 15, 1991.
32. 670. B Angie B / Tony Terry / Small Change; originally aired June 22, 1991.

Season 21 (1991–1992)

1. 671. Tribute to Stevie Wonder; originally aired September 21, 1991.
2. 672. C + C Music Factory / James "J. T." Taylor; originally aired September 28, 1991.
3. 673. Tribute to Gladys Knight / Riff; originally aired October 5, 1991.
4. 674. Color Me Badd / Ready for the World; originally aired October 12, 1991.
5. 675. DJ Jazzy Jeff & the Fresh Prince / Brand New Heavies; originally aired October 19, 1991.
6. 676. BeBe & CeCe Winans / Young MC / Chris Pittman; originally aired October 26, 1991.
7. 677. Lenny Kravitz / Oaktown's 3-5-7; originally aired November 2, 1991.
8. 678. Lisa Lisa & Cult Jam / Pretty in Pink / Chris Walker; originally aired November 9, 1991.
9. 679. Kid n' Play / Tony! Toni! Tone! / Ralph Tresvant; originally aired November 16, 1991.
10. 680. Keith Washington / The S.O.S. Band / F.S. Effect; originally aired November 23, 1991.
11. 681. Big Daddy Kane / Atlantic Starr; originally aired November 30, 1991.
12. 682. Ziggy Marley & the Melody Makers / Tevin Campbell / Public Enemy; originally aired December 7, 1991.
13. 683. Patti LaBelle / Chubb Rock; originally aired January 11, 1992.
14. 684. Vanessa L. Williams / Shanice Wilson / Jodeci; originally aired January 18, 1992.
15. 685. Jody Watley / Vesta Williams; originally aired January 25, 1992.
16. 686. Karyn White / Eric Gable / Nice & Smooth; originally aired February 1, 1992.
17. 687. Barry White with Isaac Hayes / Vickie Winans with Marvin Winans; originally aired February 8, 1992.
18. 688. Mariah Carey / Sounds of Blackness; originally aired February 15, 1992.
19. 689. Peabo Bryson / MC Lyte; originally aired February 22, 1992.
20. 690. Gerald Levert with Eddie Levert / Phyllis Hyman; originally aired February 29, 1992.
21. 691. Naughty by Nature / Glenn Jones / Hen G & Gen E; originally aired March 7, 1992.
22. 692. Atlantic Starr / UMC's / Aaron Hall; originally aired March 14, 1992.

23. 693. Nia Peeples / Eric B. & Rakim; originally aired March 21, 1992.
24. 694. Tony Terry / Patti Austin / D-Nice; originally aired March 28, 1992.
25. 695. Chaka Khan / Joe Public; originally aired May 2, 1992.
26. 696. El DeBarge with Chanté Moore / Kris Kross / Lisa Taylor; originally aired May 9, 1992.
27. 697. Meli'sa Morgan / Chris Walker / Little Shawn; originally aired May 16, 1992.
28. 698. Kathy Sledge / Mint Condition / KCM; originally aired May 23, 1992.
29. 699. TLC / Eugene Wilde / Doug E. Fresh; originally aired May 30, 1992.
30. 700. Good 2 Go / Brotherhood Creed; originally aired June 6, 1992.
31. 701. The Boys / Sue Ann Carwell / Das EFX; originally aired June 13, 1992.
32. 702. Cherrelle / Men at Large; originally aired June 20, 1992.

Season 22 (1992–1993)

Season 22 was Don Cornelius's last season as host of *Soul Train*. A revolving-guest format started with season 23 and lasted through season 26.

1. 703. Al B. Sure / Tyler Collins / Father MC; originally aired September 26, 1992.
2. 704. Al Jarreau / Mary J. Blige / Pete Rock & C. L. Smooth; originally aired October 3, 1992.
3. 705. CeCe Peniston / After 7 / Gary Brown / Everette Harp; originally aired October 10, 1992.
4. 706. Charlie Wilson / Rachelle Ferrell / Me Phi Me; originally aired October 17, 1992.
5. 707. Freddie Jackson / Miki Howard / Da Youngsta's; originally aired October 24, 1992.
6. 708. Morris Day / Third World / The Cover Girls; originally aired October 31, 1992.
7. 709. George Duke / Hi-Five / Yo-Yo; originally aired November 7, 1992.
8. 710. Big Bub / EPMD / The Voices; originally aired November 14, 1992.
9. 711. Bobby Brown / Wreckx-N-Effect; originally aired November 21, 1992.
10. 712. Christopher Williams / Chanté Moore / Prince Markee Dee & the Soul Convention; originally aired November 28, 1992.

11. 713. Chuckii Booker / Nona Gaye / Arrested Development; originally aired December 5, 1992.
12. 714. Howard Hewett / Jade / Tamrock / Trey Lorenz; originally aired December 12, 1992.
13. 715. Keith Sweat with Jacci McGhee / Lo-Key / Aries Spears; originally aired January 16, 1993.
14. 716. Shanice Wilson / Simple Pleasure / TNT; originally aired January 23, 1993.
15. 717. Full Force / Jacci McGhee; originally aired January 30, 1993.
16. 718. Silk / Toni Braxton / Portrait; originally aired February 6, 1993.
17. 719. Monie Love / R. Kelly & Public Announcement; originally aired February 13, 1993.
18. 720. Kris Kross / Brian McKnight / Stacey McClain; originally aired February 20, 1993.
19. 721. Mad Cobra / Immature / SWV; originally aired February 27, 1993.
20. 722. Tisha Campbell / Lorenzo Smith / Young Black Teenagers; originally aired March 6, 1993.
21. 723. Heavy D / Force One Network / P.O.V. / Positive K; originally aired March 13, 1993.
22. 724. Naughty by Nature / Miki Howard; originally aired March 20, 1993.
23. 725. Regina Belle / Lords of the Underground; originally aired March 27, 1993.
24. 726. Troop / The Good Girls / Prince Markie Dee & the Soul Convention; originally aired April 3, 1993.
25. 727. LL Cool J / Shai (band) / Mystro Clark; originally aired May 8, 1993.
26. 728. Run-D.M.C. / Richard Osborne; originally aired May 15, 1993.
27. 729. LeVert / Michael Cooper / T.C.F.; originally aired May 22, 1993.
28. 730. AZ-1 / Tene Williams / Redman; originally aired May 29, 1993.
29. 731. Walter Scott & Scotty Scott / Paperboy / Kirk Whalum; originally aired June 5, 1993.
30. 732. Chanté Moore / Intro / Gumbo; originally aired June 12, 1993.
31. 733. PM Dawn / Blackstreet / U.N.V.; originally aired June 19, 1993.
32. 734. The Commodores / II D Extreme / Mahogany Blue; originally aired June 26, 1993.

SEASON 23 (1993–1994)

1. 735. Host: Kim Wayans / Guests: H-Town / Keith Washington / Xscape; originally aired October 23, 1993.
2. 736. Host: T. K. Carter / Guests: MC Lyte / Maze featuring Frankie Beverly / Mica Paris; originally aired October 30, 1993.
3. 737. Host: Aries Spears / Guests: Bell Biv Devoe / Zhane / Freedom Williams; originally aired November 6, 1993.
4. 738. Host: Ajai Sanders / Guesst: Raven-Symoné / Aaron Hall / Tag Team; originally aired November 13, 1993.
5. 739. Host: Steve White / Guests: Teddy Pendergrass / II D Extreme; originally aired November 20, 1993.
6. 740. Host: Tyra Banks / Guests: Me'Shell Ndegeocello / James "J. T." Taylor / Usher; originally aired November 27, 1993.
7. 741. Host: Mystro Clark / Guests: Das EFX / Tevin Campbell / Angie & Debbie; originally aired December 4, 1993.
8. 742. Host: T'Keyah Crystal Keymáh / Guests: Onyx / Jody Watley / Erick Sermon; originally aired December 11, 1993.
9. 743. Host: Melanie Comarcho / Guests: Snoop Doggy Dogg / Color Me Badd / Domino; originally aired December 18, 1993.
10. 744. Host: John Henton / Guests: LL Cool J / Kris Kross; originally aired December 25, 1993.
11. 745. Host: Daniel Heath / Guests: D.R.S. / Queen Latifah / Souls of Mischief; originally aired January 1, 1994.
12. 746. Host: Tisha Campbell / Guests: Coming of Age / De La Soul / Riff; originally aired January 8, 1994.
13. 747. Host: Mario Van Peebles / Guests: Mavis Staples / Funky Poets; originally aired January 15, 1994.
14. 748. Host: Lewis Dix / Guests: Mint Condition / K-7 / UMC's; originally aired January 22, 1994.
15. 749. Host: Karyn Parsons / Guests: Zhane / Another Bad Creation; originally aired January 29, 1994.
16. 750. Host: A. J. Jamal / Guests: Chris Walker / 7669 / Me 2 U; originally aired February 5, 1994.
17. 751. Host: Tichina Arnold / Guests: Xscape / Gerald Albright; originally aired February 12, 1994.
18. 752. Host: John Witherspoon / Guests: Michael McDonald / Jeru the Damaja / Main Source; originally aired February 19, 1994.
19. 753. Host: Sheryl Lee Ralph / Guests: Joe / Chantay Savage; originally aired February 26, 1994.
20. 754. Host: Lester Barrie / Guests: Lisette Melendez / Intro / Gangstarr; originally aired March 5, 1994.

21. 755. Host: Alfonso Ribeiro / Guests: R. Kelly / Gabrielle; originally aired March 12, 1994.
22. 756. Host: Paula Jai Parker / Guests: Outkast / CeCe Peniston / Tashan; originally aired March 19, 1994.
23. 757. Host: Adam Jeffries / Guests: Kid 'n Play / Damion Hall; originally aired March 26, 1994.
24. 758. Host: George Wallace / Guests: Ralph Tresvant / Eric Gable / Justin Warfield; originally aired April 2, 1994.
25. 759. Host: Holly Robinson / Guests: Prince / For Lovers Only; originally aired May 7, 1994.
26. 760. Host: Alex Thomas / Guests: Angela Winbush / Glenn Jones; originally aired May 14, 1994.
27. 761. Host: Byron Allen / Guests: Atlantic Starr / Patra / The DBGz; originally aired May 21, 1994.
28. 762. Host: Thea Vidale / Guests: Blackgirl / Company / Sudden Change; originally aired May 28, 1994.
29. 763. Host: Morris Chestnut / Guests: Patti LaBelle / Sounds of Blackness / Simple E; originally aired June 4, 1994.
30. 764. Host: Jackee Harry / Guests: Lalah Hathaway / Melvin Riley / Immature; originally aired June 11, 1994.
31. 765. Host: Kristoff St. John / Guests: Philip Bailey / For Real; originally aired June 18, 1994.
32. 766. Host: Ella Joyce / Guests: Lisa Lisa / Masta Ace / Smooth Sylk; originally aired June 25, 1994.

Season 24 (1994–1995)

1. 767. Host: Robert Townsend / Guests: Blackstreet / Take 6 / The Conscious Daughters; originally aired September 24, 1994.
2. 768. Host: Telma Hopkins / Guests: Tony! Toni! Tone! / Jonathan Butler / Lady of Rage; originally aired October 1, 1994.
3. 769. Host: Tyra Banks / Guests: Public Enemy / El DeBarge / Brownstone; originally aired October 8, 1994.
4. 770. Host: Garcelle Beauvais / Guests: Teena Marie / Warren G / N II U; originally aired October 15, 1994.
5. 771. Host: George Wallace / Guests: Karyn White / BeBe & CeCe Winans / London Jones; originally aired October 22, 1994.
6. 772. Host: Karen Alexander / Guests: Gerald Levert / Zhane / Brandy; originally aired October 29, 1994.
7. 773. Host: Jonelle Allen / Guests: Barry White / Shanice Wilson / The Boogiemonsters; originally aired November 5, 1994.
8. 774. Host: Thyme Lewis / Guests: Aaron Hall / Ex-Girlfriend; originally aired November 12, 1994.

9. 775. Host: Joseph Marcell / Guests: Boyz II Men / Casserine; originally aired November 19, 1994.
10. 776. Host: Roshumba Williams / Guests: Angela Winbush / The Whitehead Brothers / Pete Rock & C. L. Smooth; originally aired November 26, 1994.
11. 777. Host: Melonee Rodgers / Guests: Tony Terry / Blackgirl / Craig Mack; originally aired December 3, 1994.
12. 778. Host: T. C. Carson / Guests: Rachelle Ferrell / A Few Good Men / Ill Al Skratch with Brian McKnight; originally aired December 10, 1994.
13. 779. Host: Sinbad / Guests: Cameo / Men at Large / Method Man; originally aired January 14, 1995.
14. 780. Host: Lana Ogilvie / Guests: Mary J. Blige / Lords of the Underground / Ebony Vibe Everlasting; originally aired January 21, 1995.
15. 781. Host: Veronica Webb / Guests: Chanté Moore / Immature / Subway; originally aired January 28, 1995.
16. 782. Host: Beverly Peele / Guests: Howard Hewett / H-Town / Da Brat; originally aired February 4, 1995.
17. 783. Host: Gail O'Neill / Guests: 69 Boyz / Tanya Blount / Y. N. Vee; originally aired February 11, 1995.
18. 784. Host: Dorien Wilson / Guests: All-4-One / Hiroshima (band) / Redman; originally aired February 18, 1995.
19. 785. Host: Cynthia Bailey / Guests: BeBe & CeCe Winans / RajaNee / Usher; originally aired February 25, 1995.
20. 786. Host: Michelle Griffin / Guests: Digable Planets / Soul 4 Real / Trisha Covington; originally aired March 4, 1995.
21. 787. Host: Victoria Rowell / Guests: George Duke / Mint Condition / Fu-Schnickens; originally aired March 11, 1995.
22. 788. Host: T. K. Carter / Guests: The Whispers / Lo-Key / Coolio; originally aired March 18, 1995.
23. 789. Host: Leah Gregory / Guests: Blackstreet / Miss Jones / Vicious; originally aired March 25, 1995.
24. 790. Host: Anna Getaneth / Guests: Jade / Des'ree / Quo; originally aired April 1, 1995.
25. 791. Host: Amy Hunter / Guests: Freddie Jackson / Rottin Razkals / Kut Klose; originally aired May 6, 1995.
26. 792. Host: Steve Harvey / Guests: Da Brat / Brownstone / Diana King; originally aired May 13, 1995.
27. 793. Host: Kellie Shanygne Williams / Guests: Portrait / Jesse Powell; originally aired May 20, 1995.
28. 794. Host: Regina Monte / Guests: Branford Marsalis / Fabu / Changing Faces / Keith Murray; originally aired May 27, 1995.

29. 795. Host: Waris Dirie / Guests: Donna Summer / Shabba Ranks / Monica; originally aired June 3, 1995.
30. 796. Host: Michael Michele / Guests: Naughty by Nature / Brian McKnight / E-40; originally aired June 10, 1995.
31. 797. Host: Georgianna Robertson / Guests: Stevie Wonder / Jody Watley / Vertical Hold; originally aired June 17, 1995.
32. 798. Host: Karla Otis / Guests: Brandy / Sean Levert / Heather B; originally aired June 24, 1995.

Season 25 (1995–1996)

1. 799. Host: Mark Curry / Guests: CeCe Winans / Ini Kamoze / Mokenstef; originally aired September 23, 1995.
2. 800. Host: Tatyana Ali / Guests: KRS-One / Deborah Cox / Shaggy; originally aired September 30, 1995.
3. 801. Host: Kenya Moore / Guests: Jon B / Soultry / Faith Evans; originally aired October 7, 1995.
4. 802. Host: Senait Ashenafi / Guests: Aaron Hall / D'Angelo / Solo; originally aired October 14, 1995.
5. 803. Host: Tisha Campbell / Guests: All-4-One / Vybe / The Twinz; originally aired October 21, 1995.
6. 804. Host: Mari Marrow / Guests: Michael Bolton / Anointed / AZ featuring Miss Jones; originally aired October 28, 1995.
7. 805. Host: Stacey Dash / Guests: Shai / Maysa Leak / Mystikal; originally aired November 4, 1995.
8. 806. Host: Shemar Moore / Guests: Brandy Norwood / A Few Good Men / Groove Theory; originally aired November 11, 1995.
9. 807. Host: Darnell Williams / Guests: After 7 / Intro / 3T; originally aired December 16, 1995.
10. 808. Host: Reagan Gomez-Preston / Guests: Immature / Terry Ellis / Asante; originally aired December 23, 1995.
11. 809. Host: Renée Jones / Guests: Aaron Neville / Silk / Jason Weaver; originally aired December 30, 1995.
12. 810. Host: Vivica A. Fox / Guests: MC Hammer / Skillz; originally aired January 6, 1996.
13. 811. Host: Joseph C. Phillips / Guests: Brian McKnight / Goodie Mobb / Barrio Boyzz; originally aired January 13, 1996.
14. 812. Host: Lark Voorhies / Guests: LL Cool J / Pure Soul / Monifah; originally aired January 20, 1996.
15. 813. Host: Jeffrey Anderson Gunther / Guests: Gerald Levert & Eddie Levert / Monica / Tamia; originally aired January 27, 1996.
16. 814. Host: Stephanie Roberts / Guests: Jodeci / Faith Evans / Jesse Powell & Trina; originally aired February 3, 1996.

17. 815. Host: James Reynolds / Guests: Tha Dogg Pound with Snoop Doggy Dogg & Michel'le / J'Son / Total; originally aired February 10, 1996.
18. 816. Host: Carl Anthony Payne II / Guests: Deborah Cox / Speech / Somethin' for the People; originally aired February 17, 1996.
19. 817. Host: Dorien Wilson / Guests: PM Dawn / Erick Sermon with Aaron Hall / Keith Murray & Redman / LBC Crew; originally aired February 24, 1996.
20. 818. Host: Sheryl Lee Ralph / Guests: Tony Rich / Boyz of Paradise / Suga; originally aired March 2, 1996.
21. 819. Host: Thomas Mikal Ford / Guests: H-Town with Shirley Murdock / Solo / Jesse Powell; originally aired March 9, 1996.
22. 820. Host: Arthel Neville / Guests: Kris Kross with Da Brat / Jermaine Dupri & Mr. Black / Chantay Savage / Earth Gyrlz; originally aired March 16, 1996.
23. 821. Host: Brian Austin Green / Guests: The Winans / 3T / Yvette Michelle; originally aired March 23, 1996.
24. 822. Host: Tia Mowry and Tamera Mowry / Guests: D'Angelo / Patra with Aaron Hall / NonChalant; originally aired March 30, 1996.
25. 823. Host: Michelle Thomas / Guests: Ladae! featuring Al B. Sure / II D Extreme / Puff Johnson; originally aired May 4, 1996.
26. 824. Host: Clarence Gilyard Jr. / Guests: Busta Rhymes featuring Zhane / Horace Brown / Art N'Soul; originally aired May 11, 1996.
27. 825. Host: Anne-Marie Johnson / Guests: Men of Vizion / Monifah featuring AZ / Mr. X; originally aired May 18, 1996.
28. 826. Host: Lisa Canning / Guests: Brian Austin Green / Silk; originally aired May 25, 1996.
29. 827. Host: Khandi Alexander / Guests: Shai / Kenny Lattimore / Sa-Deuce; originally aired June 1, 1996.
30. 828. Host: Lanai Chapman / Guests: The Whitehead Brothers / Jon B / Mista; originally aired June 8, 1996.
31. 829. Host: Kristoff St. John / Guests: SWV / Donell Jones / MC Lyte; originally aired June 15, 1996.
32. 830. Host: Shemar Moore / Guests: Kirk Franklin & the Family / Mona Lisa (singer) / Quindon Tarver; originally aired June 22, 1996.

SEASON 26 (1996–1997)

1. 831. Host: Darius McCray / Guests: Mint Condition / For Real / Case featuring Foxy Brown / Southside B.O.I.Z.; originally aired October 26, 1996.

2. 832. Host: Aisha Henderson / Guests: Montell Jordan / Dru Hill / 702; originally aired November 2, 1996.
3. 833. Host: Fawn Reed / Guests: The Isley Brothers / Tevin Campbell; originally aired November 9, 1996.
4. 834. Host: Jamie Foxx / Guests: Blackstreet / Aaliyah / The Braxtons; originally aired November 16, 1996.
5. 835. Host: Christopher B. Duncan / Guests: Keith Sweat / Tony! Toni! Tone! / Ginuwine; originally aired November 23, 1996.
6. 836. Host: Nefta Perry / Guests: Take 6 / Alfonso Hunter / 112; originally aired November 30, 1996.
7. 837. Host: Tasha Smith / Guests: Immature / Az Yet / Shades; originally aired December 7, 1996.
8. 838. Host: Tracy Vilar / Guests: Da Brat featuring Jermaine Dupri / Mona Lisa (singer) / Quindon Tarver; originally aired December 14, 1996.
9. 839. Host: Dorian Gregory / Guests: CeCe Peniston / Soul for Real / A+; originally aired December 21, 1996.
10. 840. Host: Maria Costa / Guests: Eric Benet / Dru Hill / Wild Orchid; originally aired December 28, 1996.
11. 841. Host: Shaun Baker / Guests: Donell Jones / Yo-Yo / Gina Thompson; originally aired January 4, 1997.
12. 842. Host: Shawn Michael Howard / Guests: Deborah Cox / Westside Connection / Day Ta Day; originally aired January 11, 1997.
13. 843. Host: Dorien Wilson / Guests: Maxwell / II D Extreme / Goodfellas; originally aired January 18, 1997.
14. 844. Host: Maia Campbell / Guests: Johnny Gill / Monica / Premiere; originally aired January 25, 1997.
15. 845. Host: Donald Faison / Guests: Chaka Khan / Kenny Lattimore; originally aired February 1, 1997.
16. 846. Host: Lamont Bentley / Guests: Roger Troutman & Zapp (band) / Rashaan Patterson / Outkast; originally aired February 8, 1997.
17. 847. Host: Vivica A. Foxx / Guests: Zhane / Horace Brown / Jeru the Damaja; originally aired February 15, 1997.
18. 848. Host: Shari Headley / Guests: Mint Condition / Erykah Badu / Quad City D.J.'s; originally aired February 22, 1997.
19. 849. Host: Terrence Dashon Howard / Guests: LeVert / Ray J / Lil' Kim; originally aired March 1, 1997.
20. 850. Host: John Salley / Guests: Tony! Toni! Tone! / Montell Jordan / Music Video: Heavy D / "Ms. Soul Train" & "Mr. Soul Train" Ford/AT&T Viewer Sweepstakes—preliminary; originally aired March 8, 1997.

21. 851. Host: David Michael / Guests: MC Lyte featuring Missy Elliott / Hiroshima (band) / Twice / Lil' Bud and Tizone; originally aired March 15, 1997.
22. 852. Host: Michelle Thomas / Guests: Heavy D / Monifah / Tha Truth; originally aired March 22, 1997.
23. 853. Host: Tamala Jones / Guests: Snoop Doggy Dogg / Nate Dogg / Ginuwine / Dean Phil! and Al B. Sure; originally aired March 29, 1997.
24. 854. Host: Traci Bingham / Guests: Brownstone / Yvette Michelle / Next Levels / "Ms. Soul Train" & "Mr. Soul Train" Ford/AT&T Viewer Sweepstakes—Finals; originally aired April 5, 1997.
25. 855. Host: Thomas Mikal Ford / Guests: Day Ta Day / Goodfellas / Music Video: Mary J. Blige; originally aired April 12, 1997.
26. 856. Host: T'Keyah Keymáh / Guests: Dru Hill / Zakiya / Gyrl; originally aired April 19, 1997.
27. 857. Host: Cedric the Entertainer / Guests: Warren G / 702 / Nu Flavor; originally aired April 26, 1997.
28. 858. Host: Malik Yoba / Guests: Maxwell / Tasha Holiday / Melky & Day / "Ms. Soul Train" & "Mr. Soul Train" Ford/AT&T Viewer Sweepstakes Grand Prize Presentation; originally aired May 3, 1997.
29. 859. Countess Vaughn / Guests: Sounds of Blackness / Joose / Dionne Farris; originally aired May 10, 1997.
30. 860. Host: Aaron Neville / Guests: Joe / Billy Lawrence / Phajja; originally aired May 17, 1997.
31. 861. Host: Rona Bennett / Guests: Brand New Heavies / Allure / Rome; originally aired May 24, 1997.

Season 27 (1997–1998)

The revolving-guest format ended with season 26. Starting with season 27, Mystro Clark became the first of several full-time hosts of *Soul Train*.

1. 862. Immature / K-Ball / ST Library: Whitney Houston; originally aired September 20, 1997.
2. 863. SWV / Az Yet (live performance) / Next; originally aired September 27, 1997.
3. 864. Rome / Robyn / Sam Salter; originally aired October 4, 1997.
4. 865. Brian McKnight / Davina / ST Library: Bobby Brown; originally aired October 11, 1997.
5. 866. Wyclef / Destiny's Child / Chico DeBarge; originally aired October 18, 1997.
6. 867. Jon B / Somethin' for the People / Nadanuf featuring Kurtis Blow; originally aired October 25, 1997.

7. 868. Brownstone / Usher Raymond / Queen Pen featuring Teddy Riley; originally aired November 1, 1997.
8. 869. K-Ci & JoJo / 98 Degrees / Myron; originally aired November 8, 1997.
9. 870. Aaron Neville / Busta Rhymes / MQ3; originally aired November 15, 1997.
10. 871. Immature with Bizzy Bone / Sounds of Blackness with Roger Troutman / Mase; originally aired November 22, 1997.
11. 872. Backstreet Boys / Simone Hines / Uncle Sam; originally aired November 29, 1997.
12. 873. Eric Benet / Ol' Skool; originally aired December 6, 1997.
13. 874. Missy Elliott / Jagged Edge / Big Bub; originally aired January 10, 1998.
14. 875. Jody Watley / Mack 10 / Ice Cube & Snoop Doggy Dogg / Sam Salter; originally aired January 17, 1998.
15. 876. H-Town / Kimberly Scott / Mic Geronimo; originally aired January 24, 1998.
16. 877. Joe / Born Jamericans / Veronica; originally aired January 31, 1998.
17. 878. LL Cool J / Dru Hill / Billy Porter; originally aired February 7, 1998.
18. 879. The Whispers / Ginuwine / Public Announcement; originally aired February 14, 1998.
19. 880. Bebe Winans / Ol' Skool with Xscape / Ice Cube; originally aired February 21, 1998.
20. 881. Rome / God's Property / K. P. & Envyi; originally aired February 28, 1998.
21. 882. Playa / Mýa featuring Sisqó / CeCe Winans; originally aired April 4, 1998.
22. 883. Tamia / Elusion / Luke; originally aired April 11, 1998.
23. 884. Keith Washington / Destiny's Child / Outta Order; originally aired April 18, 1998.
24. 885. Robyn / Next / Rufus Blaq; originally aired April 25, 1998.
25. 886. Jon B / Militia / Tami Hert; originally aired May 2, 1998.
26. 887. Rebbie Jackson / Ali / Kurupt; originally aired May 9, 1998.
27. 888. Big Daddy Kane / Xscape / Sylke-E Fyne; originally aired May 16, 1998.
28. 889. Daz Dillinger / David Miller / Angel Grant; originally aired May 23, 1998.
29. 890. Color Me Badd / Davina / Charli Baltimore with Cam'ron; originally aired May 30, 1998.
30. 891. Will Downing / Kelly Price / Christión / Imajin; originally aired June 6, 1998.

31. 892. Chico DeBarge / Silk 130 / Joe (singer); originally aired June 13, 1998.
32. 893. Gerald Levert / Yo-Yo (rapper) / Mo Thugs Family / Tami Davis; originally aired June 20, 1998.

SEASON 28 (1998–1999)

1. 894. Nate Dogg featuring Warren G / Montell Jordan / Terrance Quaites; originally aired September 19, 1998.
2. 895. Kenny Lattimore / Monifah / Nicole Wray; originally aired September 26, 1998.
3. 896. Regina Belle / Jesse Powell / Tatyana Ali; originally aired October 3, 1998.
4. 897. Deborah Cox / Tyrese / Voices of Theory; originally aired October 10, 1998.
5. 898. Shaquille O'Neal featuring Peter Gunz / Kelly Price with Ronald Isley & R. Kelly / Levi Little; originally aired October 17, 1998.
6. 899. Temptations / 69 Boyz / The Black Eyed Peas / Andrea Martin (singer); originally aired October 24, 1998
7. 900. Tamia / Link / Pee Wee's Mag 7; originally aired October 31, 1998.
8. 901. Next / MC Lyte featuring Gina Thompson / Sparkle (singer); originally aired November 7, 1998.
9. 902. Jermaine Dupri featuring Slick Rick / Lord Tariq & Peter Gunz / Nicole Renee; originally aired November 14, 1998.
10. 903. 112 / Willie Max featuring Raphael Saadiq / Jerome; originally aired November 21, 1998.
11. 904. Kurupt / Divine / A+ (rapper); originally aired November 28, 1998.
12. 905. Bizzy Bone / Tyrese / 4Kast; originally aired December 5, 1998.
13. 906. Terrance Quaites / Uncle Sam; originally aired January 9, 1999.
14. 907. Jon B / Before Dark; originally aired January 16, 1999.
15. 908. Kenny Lattimore / Public Announcement / Shae Jones; originally aired January 23, 1999.
16. 909. Total (band) / Reel Tight; originally aired January 30, 1999.
17. 910. Tevin Campbell / Kelly Price / 3rd Storee; originally aired February 6, 1999.
18. 911. Faith Evans / Shanice; originally aired February 13, 1999.
19. 912. Dru Hill / Deborah Cox; originally aired February 20, 1999.
20. 913. Monica / Outkast / Marc Dorsey; originally aired February 27, 1999.

21. 914. Mýa / Silk / Cool Breeze featuring Goodie Mobb & Outkast; originally aired March 6, 1999.
22. 915. Krayzie Bone / Men of Vizion / Cherokee; originally aired March 13, 1999.
23. 916. DJ Quik featuring El DeBarge, 2nd II None, and Suga Free / Sparkle / Dave Hollister; originally aired March 20, 1999.
24. 917. Ginuwine / Imajin / Baby DC featuring Imajin; originally aired March 27, 1999.
25. 918. Chanté Moore / Blaque / MC Eiht; originally aired May 1, 1999.
26. 919. Nas / Chantay Savage / Donell Jones; originally aired May 8, 1999.
27. 920. Divine / Shae Jones / Harlem World; originally aired May 15, 1999.
28. 921. Tyrese / Trina & Tamera / JT Money; originally aired May 22, 1999.
29. 922. Naughty by Nature / Jesse Powell / Les Nubians; originally aired May 29, 1999.
30. 923. C-Note / Before Dark / Juvenile (rapper); originally aired June 5, 1999.
31. 924. Case (singer) / Liberty City; originally aired June 12, 1999.
32. 925. Eric Benet / Marc Dorsey / TWDY; originally aired June 19, 1999.

Season 29 (1999–2000)

Shemar Moore becomes the second (of several) full-time hosts of *Soul Train* starting with season 29.

1. 926. Kevon Edmonds / Grenique / Cha Cha; originally aired September 18, 1999.
2. 927. Tracie Spencer / Mark Nelson / C. J. Mack / Mack 10 featuring Terrance Quaites; originally aired September 25, 1999.
3. 928. Ginuwine / 702 / Profyle; originally aired October 2, 1999.
4. 929. Destiny's Child / Christina Aguilera / Coko; originally aired October 9, 1999.
5. 930. Silk / Eve / Lost Boyz; originally aired October 16, 1999.
6. 931. Brian McKnight / IMx / Youngbloodz; originally aired October 23, 1999.
7. 932. Chico DeBarge / 112 / Trin-I-Tee 5:7; originally aired October 30, 1999.
8. 933. DMX / Mint Condition / Keesha; originally aired November 6, 1999.
9. 934. Jagged Edge / Donell Jones / Children of the Ghetto; originally aired November 13, 1999.

10. 935. Yolanda Adams / Kurupt / Ideal (band); originally aired November 20, 1999.
11. 936. Goodie Mob / ShanDozia / Sole (rapper) featuring J. T. Money; originally aired November 27, 1999.
12. 937. Olu / Angie Stone / Humanwreck; originally aired December 4, 1999.
13. 938. Q-Tip / Catero / 2nd II None; originally aired January 8, 2000.
14. 939. Blaque / Rome / Eve; originally aired January 15, 2000.
15. 940. Dave Hollister / Before Dark / Vega; originally aired January 22, 2000.
16. 941. Eric Benet / Sounds of Blackness / Amyth; originally aired January 29, 2000.
17. 942. Kevon Edmonds / Ideal (band) / B.G.; originally aired February 5, 2000.
18. 943. Snoop Doggy Dogg / Sisqó / Sammie; originally aired February 12, 2000.
19. 944. Goodie Mob / Beverly / Lil' Wayne; originally aired February 19, 2000.
20. 945. Ginuwine / Juvenile / Amel Larrieux; originally aired February 26, 2000.
21. 946. Montell Jordan / The Roots / Lil' Zane; originally aired March 4, 2000.
22. 947. Bone Thugs N Harmony / Jaze / F.A.T.E.; originally aired March 11, 2000.
23. 948. Gerald Levert / N-Toon / Blaxuede; originally aired March 18, 2000.
24. 949. IMx / BB Jay / Rah Digga; originally aired March 25, 2000.
25. 950. Product G & B / Lucy Pearl / The Temptations; originally aired April 29, 2000.
26. 951. Dwayne Wiggins / Mary Mary / Strings; originally aired May 6, 2000.
27. 952. Tracie Spencer / Avant / Erick Onasis featuring DJ Quik & Xzibit; originally aired May 13, 2000.
28. 953. 504 Boyz / Erica Foxx / Tamar Braxton; originally aired May 20, 2000.
29. 954. Ideal (band) / Carl Thomas / Miracle; originally aired May 27, 2000.
30. 955. 69 Boyz / Something for the People / Ruff Endz; originally aired June 3, 2000.
31. 956. Next / Kelis / Nelly; originally aired June 10, 2000.
32. 957. Kelly Price / Jagged Edge / J-Shin; originally aired June 17, 2000.

Season 30 (2000–2001)

1. 958. L.V. / So Plush / Big Tymers; originally aired September 16, 2000.
2. 959. Lil' Kim / No Question / Major Figgas; originally aired September 23, 2000.
3. 960. Rachelle Farrell / Changing Faces / Lil' Bow Wow / Jermaine Dupri; originally aired September 30, 2000.
4. 961. Joe / Trina / Yolanda Adams; originally aired October 7, 2000.
5. 962. Tamia / Avant / Ced featuring C. Black; originally aired October 14, 2000.
6. 963. Stephen Simmonds / Public Announcement / Cole; originally aired October 21, 2000.
7. 964. Ricky Bell / Toni Estes / Tank; originally aired October 28, 2000.
8. 965. Kandi Burruss / 3LW / Mack 10; originally aired November 4, 2000.
9. 966. Mýa / Lil' Zane / Jill Scott; originally aired November 11, 2000.
10. 967. Mystikal / Pru / Sunday; originally aired November 18, 2000.
11. 968. Charlie Wilson / Snoop Dogg / Monifah / Shaggy; originally aired November 25, 2000.
12. 969. Macy Gray / Profyle / Doggy's Angels; originally aired December 2, 2000.
13. 970. Chanté Moore / Ja Rule / Bilal; originally aired January 6, 2001.
14. 971. Ruff Endz / Sparkle / Bad Azz; originally aired January 13, 2001.
15. 972. Outkast / Dave Hollister / Slimm Calhoun; originally aired January 20, 2001.
16. 973. Carl Thomas / Crystal Sierra / Shyne; originally aired January 27, 2001.
17. 974. K-Ci & JoJo / Musiq / Xzibit; originally aired February 3, 2001.
18. 975. Common & Macy Gray / The Transitions / Olivia; originally aired February 10, 2001.
19. 976. Nelly / Jamie Hawkins / Case; originally aired February 17, 2001.
20. 977. 112 / Jaheim; originally aired February 24, 2001.
21. 978. Lil' Bow Wow / Alicia Keys / Silkk the Shocker / Trina; originally aired March 31, 2001.
22. 979. Jesse Powell / Koffee Brown / India.Arie; originally aired April 7, 2001.
23. 980. Jon B / JT Money / R.L.; originally aired April 14, 2001.

24. 981. Eric Benet / Master P & Lil' Romeo; originally aired April 21, 2001.
25. 982. Chanté Moore / Da Brat / Dark Blu / P.Y.T.; originally aired April 28, 2001.
26. 983. The Product G&B / The Iconz / Craig David; originally aired May 5, 2001.
27. 984. L-Burna / Tank / Canela; originally aired May 12, 2001.
28. 985. Tyrese / City High / Trick Daddy; originally aired May 19, 2001.
29. 986. IMx / Dante / Lil' Mo; originally aired June 9, 2001.
30. 987. Nelly & the St. Lunatics / Spooks / B2K; originally aired June 16, 2001.
31. 988. Silk / Angie Martinez / Syleena Johnson; originally aired June 23, 2001.
32. 989. Full Force featuring Bambue / Sunshine Anderson / Toya / LOL; originally aired June 30, 2001.

Season 31 (2001–2002)

1. 990. Tyrese / Keke Wyatt; originally aired October 13, 2001.
2. 991. Kenny Lattimore / India.Arie / Mr. Cheeks; originally aired October 20, 2001.
3. 992. Ray J / Angie Stone / Coo Coo Cal; originally aired October 27, 2001.
4. 993. P. Diddy / Lil' J / Allure; originally aired November 3, 2001.
5. 994. Ruff Endz / Dena Cali / Jimmy Cozier; originally aired November 10, 2001.
6. 995. Bell Biv DeVoe / Jesse Powell / Won G; originally aired November 17, 2001.
7. 996. Ludacris & Jermaine Dupri / Pru / Lil' Romeo; originally aired November 24, 2001.
8. 997. Montell Jordan / Master P / Christina Milian / Prophet Jones; originally aired December 1, 2001.
9. 998. Fabolous featuring Nate Dogg / IMx / Glenn Lewis; originally aired December 22, 2001.
10. 999. Warren G / Mpress / Nate Dogg featuring Fabolous; originally aired December 29, 2001.
11. 1000. Faith Evans / Rayvon / Mack 10; originally aired January 5, 2002.
12. 1001. Regina Belle / B2K / G. Dep; originally aired January 12, 2002.
13. 1002. Busta Rhymes / R. L. featuring Erick Sermon / Corey; originally aired January 26, 2002.

14. 1003. Isley Brothers featuring Ronald Isley / Method Man / Redman / Ali; originally aired February 2, 2002.
15. 1004. Ja Rule featuring Case and Ashanti / Jaguar Wright featuring Bilal / Pretty Willie; originally aired February 9, 2002.
16. 1005. Nelly / Jagged Edge / Jaheim; originally aired February 16, 2002.
17. 1006. Avant / Ashanti / Code 5; originally aired March 23, 2002.
18. 1007. Donell Jones / Sharissa / Horace Brown; originally aired March 30, 2002.
19. 1008. Fat Joe featuring Ashanti / Joi / Mr. Cheeks featuring Horace Brown; originally aired April 6, 2002.
20. 1009. Kirk Franklin / Lindsay Pagano / Cee Lo Green; originally aired April 13, 2002.
21. 1010. B2K / Baha Men / Truth Hurts featuring Rakim; originally aired May 18, 2002.
22. 1011. Musiq Soulchild / Tweet / Ying Yang Twins; originally aired May 25, 2002.
23. 1012. Keke Wyatt / Nappy Roots / Jerzee Monet; originally aired June 1, 2002.
24. 1013. Naughty by Nature / 3LW / DJ Quik / Mario; originally aired June 8, 2002.
25. 1014. Winans Phase 2 / Soluna / Ms. Jade; originally aired June 15, 2002.
26. 1015. IMx / Yasmeen; originally aired June 22, 2002.
27. 1016. Mary Mary / LovHer / Cee Lo Green; originally aired June 29, 2002.
28. 1017. Bow Wow / Raphael Saadiq / Lady May featuring Blu Cantrell; originally aired July 6, 2002.

SEASON 32 (2002–2003)

1. 1018. Nelly / Ali / Prymary Colors and Rah Digga / Isyss; originally aired September 14, 2002.
2. 1019. Avant / Beenie Man featuring Calibe / 3rd Storee featuring Joe Budden; originally aired September 21, 2002.
3. 1020. Glenn Lewis featuring Amel Larrieux / Cam'ron / Exhale; originally aired September 28, 2002.
4. 1021. Ruff Endz / Tg4 / Jade Anderson; originally aired October 5, 2002.
5. 1022. India.Arie / Heather Headley / Robin Thicke; originally aired October 12, 2002.
6. 1023. Deborah Cox / Dave Hollister / Pastor Troy; originally aired October 19, 2002.

7. 1024. Angie Martinez / Tank / Black Coffey; originally aired October 26, 2002.
8. 1025. Kelly Rowland / Trinitee 5:7 / Clipse; originally aired November 2, 2002.
9. 1026. Amerie / Fabolous / Big Tymers; originally aired November 9, 2002.
10. 1027. Shaggy / Brian and Tony Gold / Lil' Wayne / 3LW; originally aired November 16, 2002.
11. 1028. Jaheim / Floetry / W.C. from Nate Dogg; originally aired November 23, 2002.
12. 1029. The Unit featuring Queen Latifah / Michelle Williams / Baby from Big Tymers; originally aired November 30, 2002.
13. 1030. Marques Houston / Solange Knowles / Benzino; originally aired January 4, 2003.
14. 1031. Ashanti / Sounds of Blackness / Smilez & Southstar; originally aired January 11, 2003.
15. 1032. Busta Rhymes / Syleena Johnson / B2K; originally aired January 18, 2003.
16. 1033. Darius Rucker / Slum Village / Talib Kweli; originally aired January 25, 2003.
17. 1034. K-Ci & JoJo / Cam'ron / Field Mob; originally aired February 1, 2003.
18. 1035. Next / Howard Hewett / Nappy Roots; originally aired February 8, 2003.
19. 1036. Dru Hill / Lil' Romeo / Needa S.; originally aired February 15, 2003.
20. 1037. Deborah Cox / Tyrese; originally aired February 22, 2003.
21. 1038. Ginuwine / MC Lyte / Nivea; originally aired March 1, 2003.
22. 1039. Bone Thugs-N-Harmony / 702 / Amanda Perez; originally aired March 8, 2003.
23. 1040. Floetry / Mr. Cheeks / Choppa featuring Master P; originally aired March 15, 2003.
24. 1041. Chico DeBarge / Nick Cannon / Sean Paul; originally aired March 22, 2003.
25. 1042. Jody Watley / Roscoe featuring Kurupt / Wayne Wonder; originally aired May 3, 2003.
26. 1043. Vivian Green / Impromp2 featuring Kim Fields / Chingy; originally aired May 10, 2003.
27. 1044. Brian McKnight / Deep Side / Deitrick Haddon; originally aired May 17, 2003.
28. 1045. 3LW / B.G. / Donnie; originally aired May 24, 2003.
29. 1046. Lil' Kim / Latif; originally aired May 31, 2003.

30. 1047. Tamia / Loon / Novel; originally aired June 7, 2003.
31. 1048. Blu Cantrell / Smokie Norful / Allen Anthony; originally aired June 14, 2003.
32. 1049. Tyrese / Da Brat / Cherish / Question; originally aired June 21, 2003.

Season 33 (2003–2004)

Dorian Gregory becomes the third (of several) full-time hosts of *Soul Train* starting with season 33.

1. 1050. Jeffrey Osborne / Anthony Hamilton / Jacki-O; originally aired October 11, 2003.
2. 1051. Big Gipp featuring Sleepy Brown / JS / Lumidee; originally aired October 18, 2003.
3. 1052. Avant / Ramiyah / Da Band; originally aired October 25, 2003.
4. 1053. Chanté Moore / Kenny Lattimore / Lil' Zane featuring Tank; originally aired November 1, 2003.
5. 1054. Montell Jordan / Tarralyn Ramsey / Justin Guarini; originally aired November 8, 2003.
6. 1055. Nick Cannon / Javier / Music Video: P. Diddy featuring Lenny Kravitz and Pharrell Williams; originally aired November 15, 2003.
7. 1056. The Isley Brothers featuring Ronald Isley; originally aired November 22, 2003.
8. 1057. Rhian Benson / Marques Houston / ATL; originally aired November 29, 2003.
9. 1058. Dwele / Baby Bash & Frankie J / Joe; originally aired December 6, 2003.
10. 1059. Brian McKnight / Kindred the Family Soul / Kem; originally aired December 13, 2003.
11. 1060. Loon / Glenn Lewis / Jhene; originally aired December 20, 2003.
12. 1061. Dave Hollister / Jagged Edge; originally aired December 27, 2003.
13. 1062. En Vogue / C. L. Ryderz (Nine Up & Nobody); originally aired January 31, 2004.
14. 1063. Michelle Williams / Teedra Moses; originally aired February 7, 2004.
15. 1064. Goapele / YahZarah; originally aired February 14, 2004.
16. 1065. Master P / Freddie Jackson; originally aired February 21, 2004.
17. 1066. Tamia / Van Hunt / Crea; originally aired March 13, 2004.
18. 1067. Musiq / Knoc-Turn'al; originally aired March 20, 2004.

19. 1068. Murphy Lee / Tiffany Villarreal / Young Rome featuring Omarion; originally aired March 27, 2004.
20. 1069. Carl Thomas / ATL / Lil' Scrappy; originally aired April 3, 2004.
21. 1070. Mr. Cheeks / Del / Tawny; originally aired May 8, 2004.
22. 1071. Lorenzo Owens / JoJo; originally aired May 15, 2004.
23. 1072. Teena Marie / Ricky Fanté; originally aired May 22, 2004.
24. 1073. Rhian Benson / Tonx / Tino Brown; originally aired May 29, 2004.
25. 1074. Lil' Wayne / Trina Broussard / LaShell Griffin; originally aired June 5, 2004.
26. 1075. Freddie Jackson / Houston; originally aired June 12, 2004.
27. 1076. Truth Hurts / Akon; originally aired June 19, 2004.
28. 1077. Nina Sky / Mishon / Keyshia Cole; originally aired June 26, 2004.

Season 34 (2004–2005)

1. 1078. Ying Yang Twins / Billy Miles; originally aired October 9, 2004.
2. 1079. Tiffany Evans / Deitrick Haddon / Won-G; originally aired October 16, 2004.
3. 1080. Regina Belle / 4Mula1; originally aired October 23, 2004.
4. 1081. Boyz II Men / O'Ryan / Silkk the Shocker; originally aired October 30, 2004.
5. 1082. New Edition / Lina; originally aired November 6, 2004.
6. 1083. Guerilla Black / Toshi / Urban Mystic; originally aired November 13, 2004.
7. 1084. K. Young / Generation J / Lil' Eddie; originally aired November 20, 2004.
8. 1085. Allure / Terrance Quaites; originally aired November 27, 2004.
9. 1086. Fantasia Barrino / Ray / Razah; originally aired February 12, 2005.
10. 1087. John Legend / Nina Shaw / Lil' iROCC; originally aired February 19, 2005.
11. 1088. Brian McKnight / B5; originally aired February 26, 2005.
12. 1089. Mario / Lyfe Jennings; originally aired March 5, 2005.
13. 1090. Smokie Norful / N2U / Frankie J; originally aired April 9, 2005.
14. 1091. Trillville / J'Adore / Ee-De; originally aired April 16, 2005.
15. 1092. Omarion / Kierra "Kiki" Sheard; originally aired April 23, 2005.

16. 1093. Lalah Hathaway / Tye Tribbett; originally aired April 30, 2005.
17. 1094. Vivian Green / Cuban Link featuring Mýa / Pretty Ricky; originally aired May 7, 2005.
18. 1095. Mint Condition / Nicole C. Mullen; originally aired May 14, 2005.
19. 1096. The Avila Brothers / Emelee; originally aired May 21, 2005.
20. 1097. Leela James / J. Moss / Anisha Nicole; originally aired May 28, 2005.
21. 1098. Mike Jones / Corey Clark; originally aired June 4, 2005.
22. 1099. LaToya London / Michael Spencer / Dame; originally aired June 11, 2005.
23. 1100. Ciara / T.I. / P$C; originally aired June 18, 2005.
24. 1101. Marques Houston / Fatty Koo / Slim Thug; originally aired June 25, 2005.

SEASON 35 (2005–2006)

1. 1102. Chris Brown / The Pussycat Dolls / Na'sha; originally aired November 5, 2005.
2. 1103. Mary Mary / Ginuwine / Nivea; originally aired November 12, 2005.
3. 1104. Ray J / Ebony Eyez; originally aired November 19, 2005.
4. 1105. Trey Songz / Dwele / Keke Wyatt; originally aired November 26, 2005.
5. 1106. Floetry / Pretty Ricky; originally aired January 7, 2006.
6. 1107. Eric Benet / Dem Franchize Boyz; originally aired January 14, 2006.
7. 1108. Jazze Pha and Cee-Lo Green / Kindred the Family Soul / Taurus; originally aired January 21, 2006.
8. 1109. Heather Headley / Chamillionaire; originally aired January 28, 2006.
9. 1110. Kirk Franklin / T-Pain / Music Video: Beyoncé featuring Slim Thug and Bun-B "Check On It"; originally aired February 4, 2006.
10. 1111. Donell Jones / LeToya Luckett; originally aired February 11, 2006.
11. 1112. Charlie Wilson / Youngbloodz; originally aired February 18, 2006.
12. 1113. Karen Clark-Sheard / Urban Mystic / Marcos Hernandez; originally aired February 25, 2006.
13. 1114. Final Draft / Flipsyde / Cruna; originally aired March 4, 2006.
14. 1115. T.I. / Sammie; originally aired March 11, 2006.
15. 1116. Javier / D4L; originally aired March 18, 2006.
16. 1117. Goapele / Lorenzo Owens; originally aired March 25, 2006.

Season 36 (2006–2007): The Best of Soul Train

The last two seasons of *Soul Train*, seasons 36 and 37, were no longer live shows, but were reruns of randomly selected archived episodes from between 1973 and 1988.

1. 76. Barry White / Love Unlimited / The Temprees; rerun aired December 9, 2006; originally aired October 27, 1973.
2. 158. War / The Main Ingredient; rerun aired December 16, 2006; originally aired November 15, 1975.
3. 375. Patti LaBelle / The Time; rerun aired December 23, 2006; originally aired November 14, 1981.
4. 514. James Ingram / Levert; rerun aired December 30, 2006; originally aired October 11, 1986.
5. 93. Al Green / The Impressions; rerun aired January 6, 2007; originally aired April 6, 1974.
6. 136. Blue Magic / Sister Sledge / Major Harris; rerun aired January 13, 2007; originally aired April 12, 1975.
7. 361. The Sugarhill Gang / Patrice Rushen; rerun aired January 20, 2007; originally aired May 16, 1981.
8. 567. Pebbles / Jermaine Stewart / The Bus Boys; rerun aired January 27, 2007; originally aired April 30, 1988.
9. 161. Average White Band / The Undisputed Truth; rerun aired February 3, 2007; originally aired November 29, 1975.
10. 338. Rick James / The S.O.S. Band; rerun aired February 10, 2007; originally aired October 11, 1980.
11. 414. Evelyn "Champagne" King / Grandmaster Flash & the Furious Five; rerun aired February 17, 2007; originally aired May 21, 1983.
12. 463. Donna Summer / The Staple Singers; rerun aired February 24, 2007; originally aired December 15, 1984.
13. 164. Billy Preston / The Sylvers; rerun aired March 3, 2007; originally aired December 27, 1975.
14. 410. Carl Carlton / Vanity 6; rerun aired March 10, 2007; originally aired January 1, 1983.
15. 449. The Dazz Band / Run-D.M.C.; rerun aired March 17, 2007; originally aired June 16, 1984.
16. 551. Freddie Jackson / Whodini / Lace; rerun aired March 24, 2007; originally aired November 14, 1987.
17. 107. Billy Preston / Rufus / George McCrae; rerun aired March 31, 2007; originally aired September 7, 1974.
18. 137. The Dramatics / Barbara Mason / Ben E. King; rerun aired April 7, 2007; originally aired April 19, 1975.
19. 174. Wilson Pickett / Betty Wright / The Modulations; rerun aired April 14, 2007; originally aired March 6, 1976.

20. 227. Johnny "Guitar" Watson / The Whispers; rerun aired April 21, 2007; originally aired September 10, 1977.
21. 242. Brick / Sister Sledge; rerun aired April 28, 2007; originally aired December 24, 1977.
22. 269. Peabo Bryson / Stargard; rerun aired May 5, 2007; originally aired September 30, 1978.
23. 273. Freda Payne / Atlantic Starr; rerun aired May 12, 2007; originally aired October 28, 1978.
24. 283. Marilyn McCoo and Billy Davis, Jr. / Lakeside; rerun aired May 19, 2007; originally aired January 6, 1979.
25. 292. Gino Vanelli / Gloria Gaynor; rerun aired May 26, 2007; originally aired March 10, 1979.
26. 303. A Tribute to Minnie Riperton (featuring Stevie Wonder, Wintley Phipps, Lorraine Fields, and Larry Vickers); rerun aired June 2, 2007; originally aired September 15, 1979.
27. 318. Chic / High Inergy; rerun aired June 9, 2007; originally aired February 9, 1980.
28. 325. The Spinners / Con Funk Shun; rerun aired June 16, 2007; originally aired April 12, 1980.
29. 326. Captain and Tennille / The Ritchie Family; rerun aired June 23, 2007; originally aired April 19, 1980.
30. 329. Jermaine Jackson / The Dramatics; rerun aired June 30, 2007; originally aired May 10, 1980.
31. 339. Tyrone Davis / Teena Marie; rerun aired July 7, 2007; originally aired October 18, 1980.
32. 345. Lenny Williams / Yellow Magic Orchestra; rerun aired July 14, 2007; originally aired November 29, 1980.
33. 362. Betty Wright / Funkadelic; rerun aired July 21, 2007; originally aired May 23, 1981.
34. 388. Sister Sledge / Ray Parker Jr.; rerun aired July 28, 2007; originally aired May 1, 1982.
35. 398. A Taste of Honey / Jeffrey Osborne; rerun aired August 4, 2007; originally aired July 10, 1982.
36. 415. Angela Bofill / Con Funk Shun; rerun aired August 11, 2007; originally aired May 28, 1983.
37. 429. Jennifer Holiday / Klique; rerun aired August 18, 2007; originally aired November 26, 1983.
38. 465. Teena Marie / Whodini; rerun aired August 25, 2007; originally aired January 12, 1985.
39. 475. Sheena Easton / The Mary Jane Girls; rerun aired September 1, 2007; originally aired April 13, 1985.
40. 484. Sheila E. / Five Star; rerun aired September 8, 2007; originally aired October 12, 1985.

41. 509. The S.O.S. Band / Juicy / Jermaine Stewart; rerun aired September 15, 2007; originally aired June 14, 1986.
42. 516. Run-D.M.C. / Genobia Jeter; rerun aired September 22, 2007; originally aired October 25, 1986.
43. 529. Rose Royce / Chico DeBarge; rerun aired September 29, 2007; originally aired March 21, 1987.
44. 559. Vanity / Kool Moe Dee / Angela Winbush and Ronald Isley; rerun aired October 6, 2007; originally aired March 5, 1988.
45. 98. Sylvia / The Moments / Ecstasy, Passion & Pain; rerun aired October 13, 2007; originally aired May 11, 1974.
46. 102. The Staple Singers / Bunny Sigler; rerun aired October 20, 2007; originally aired June 8, 1974.
47. 103. Kool & the Gang / Al Wilson / Natural Four; rerun aired October 27, 2007; originally aired June 15, 1974.
48. 115. The Fifth Dimension / Al Wilson / Formula IV; rerun aired November 3, 2007; originally aired November 2, 1974.
49. 123. Graham Central Station / Zulema / Leon Haywood; rerun aired November 10, 2007; originally aired January 11, 1975.
50. 152. The Pointer Sisters / B.T. Express / Ralph Carter; rerun aired November 17, 2007; originally aired October 4, 1975.
51. 169. The Dells / Bloodstone; rerun aired November 24, 2007; originally aired January 31, 1976.
52. 194. Marilyn McCoo and Billy Davis Jr. / Deniece Williams; rerun aired December 1, 2007; originally aired October 23, 1976.
53. 218. B.T. Express / Letta Mbulu / Enchantment; rerun aired December 8, 2007; originally aired April 9, 1977.
54. 264. The Brothers Johnson / The Dells; rerun aired December 15, 2007; originally aired August 26, 1978.
55. 286. Brass Construction / Peaches and Herb / Captain Sky; rerun aired December 22, 2007; originally aired January 27, 1979.
56. 289. Joe Simon / Cheryl Lynn; rerun aired December 29, 2007; originally aired February 17, 1979.

SEASON 37 (2008): THE BEST OF SOUL TRAIN

1. 292. Gino Vanelli / Gloria Gaynor; rerun aired January 5, 2008; originally aired March 10, 1979.
2. 283. Marilyn McCoo and Billy Davis, Jr. / Lakeside; rerun aired January 12, 2008; originally aired January 6, 1979.
3. 303. A Tribute to Minnie Riperton; rerun aired January 19, 2008; originally aired September 15, 1979.
4. 318. Chic / High Inergy; rerun aired January 26, 2008; originally aired February 9, 1980.

5. 273. Freda Payne / Atlantic Starr; rerun aired February 2, 2008; originally aired October 28, 1978.
6. 325. The Spinners / Con Funk Shun; rerun aired February 9, 2008; originally aired April 12, 1980.
7. 269. Peabo Bryson / Stargard; rerun aired February 16, 2008; originally aired September 30, 1978.
8. 326. Captain and Tennille / The Ritchie Family; rerun aired February 23, 2008; originally aired April 19, 1980.
9. 242. Brick / Sister Sledge; rerun aired March 1, 2008; originally aired December 24, 1977.
10. 174. Wilson Pickett / Betty Wright / The Modulations; rerun aired March 8, 2008; originally aired March 6, 1976.
11. 329. Jermaine Jackson / The Dramatics; rerun aired March 15, 2008; originally aired May 10, 1980.
12. 339. Tyrone Davis / Teena Marie; rerun aired March 22, 2008; originally aired October 18, 1980.
13. 227. Johnny "Guitar" Watson / The Whispers; rerun aired March 29, 2008; originally aired September 10, 1977.
14. 429. Jennifer Holliday / Klique; rerun aired April 5, 2008; originally aired November 26, 1983.
15. 137. The Dramatics / Barbara Mason / Ben E. King; rerun aired April 12, 2008; originally aired April 19, 1975.
16. 415. Con Funk Shun / Angela Bofill; rerun aired April 19, 2008; originally aired May 28, 1983.
17. 107. Billy Preston / Rufus / George McCrae; rerun aired April 26, 2008; originally aired September 7, 1974.
18. 398. A Taste of Honey / Jeffrey Osborne; rerun aired May 3, 2008; originally aired July 10, 1982.
19. 551. Freddie Jackson / Whodini / Lace; rerun aired May 10, 2008; originally aired November 14, 1987.
20. 388. Sister Sledge / Ray Parker, Jr.; rerun aired May 17, 2008; originally aired May 1, 1982.
21. 449. The Dazz Band / Run-D.M.C.; rerun aired May 24, 2008; originally aired June 16, 1984.
22. 362. Betty Wright / Funkadelic; rerun aired May 31, 2008; originally aired May 23, 1981.
23. 410. Carl Carlton / Vanity 6; rerun aired June 7, 2008; originally aired January 1, 1983.
24. 345. Lenny Williams / Yellow Magic Orchestram; rerun aired June 14, 2008; originally aired November 29, 1980.
25. 289. Joe Simon / Cheryl Lynn; rerun aired June 21, 2008; originally aired February 17, 1979.

26. 76. Barry White / Love Unlimited / The Temprees; rerun aired June 28, 2008; originally aired October 27, 1973.
27. 567. Pebbles / Jermaine Stewart / The Bus Boys; rerun aired July 5, 2008; originally aired April 30, 1988.
28. 218. B.T. Express / Letta Mbulu / Enchantment; rerun aired July 12, 2008; originally aired April 9, 1977.
29. 93. Al Green / The Impressions; rerun aired July 19, 2008; originally aired April 6, 1974.
30. 559. Vanity / Kool Moe Dee / Angela Winbush and Ronald Isley; rerun aired July 26, 2008; originally aired March 5, 1988.
31. 286. Brass Construction / Peaches and Herb / Captain Sky; rerun aired August 2, 2008; originally aired January 27, 1979.
32. 98. Sylvia / The Moments / Ecstasy, Passion & Pain; rerun aired August 9, 2008; originally aired May 11, 1974.
33. 529. Rose Royce / Chico DeBarge; rerun aired August 16, 2008; originally aired March 21, 1987.
34. 264. The Brothers Johnson / The Dells; rerun aired August 23, 2008; originally aired August 26, 1978.
35. 102. The Staple Singers / Bunny Sigler; rerun aired August 30, 2008; originally aired June 8, 1974.
36. 516. Run-D.M.C. / Genobia Jeter; rerun aired September 6, 2008; originally aired October 25, 1986.
37. 514. James Ingram / Levert; rerun aired September 13, 2008; originally aired October 11, 1986.
38. 463. Donna Summer / The Staple Singers; rerun aired September 20, 2008; originally aired December 15, 1984.

SELECTED BIBLIOGRAPHY

In my research for this work, I came across many sources that helped inspire and inform my writing. Those cited below have proved to be key in the process.

ARTICLES

"All Aboard for the Soul Train Dance Contest." *Los Angeles Times*. August 27, 1975.

"Anthony Sabatino." *Variety*. April 1993.

"Black Music Pioneer Saluted: Don Cornelius, Legendary Host of *Soul Train* to Be Honored by Legislature." *Sacramento Observer*. June 4, 1997.

Black, Stu. "She Took the Soul Train to Stardom." *Los Angeles Times*. December 13, 1987.

Bolden, James. "Soul Train Still on Track After 23 Years." *Los Angeles Sentinel*. March 4, 1993.

Browne, David. "The Diva and Her Dark Side: Whitney Houston." *Rolling Stone*. March 15, 2012.

Chapman-Ayala, Aida. "Soul Train." *Billboard*. September 28, 1974.

"Cornelius Still on Track." *Advertising Age*. March 2005.

"Couples Dance for Scholarships." *Chicago Defender*. May 13, 1972.

"Damita Jo, Resident Dance Diva." *Los Angeles Sentinel*. November 1999.

"E. Rodney Jones, 75, Disc Jockey." *Chicago Sun-Times*. January 7, 2004.

English, Priscilla. "Don Cornelius: Man Who Engineers Soul Train." *Los Angeles Times Calendar*. November 18, 1973.

Fong-Torres, Ben. "Soul Train vs. Dick Clark: Battle of the Bandstands." *Rolling Stone*. June 7, 1973.

Holden, Stephen. "Solar Could Be the Motown of the '80s." *New York Times*. March 23, 1980.

"Jerry Butler Kicks Off WCIU's Soul Train." *Chicago Defender*. August 17, 1970.

"Johnson Products Trading on AMEX." *New York Times*. January 15, 1971.

Johnson, Allan. "Don Cornelius Is Still Rolling Along." *Chicago Tribune*. September 26, 1995.

Leah, Davis. "Soul Train: We've Got Our Own." *Soul*. February 14, 1972.

"Making Black Beautiful." *Time*. December 7, 1970.

Medina, Jennifer. "When the Music Stopped for Don Cornelius." *New York Times*. March 9, 2012.

Meisler, Andy. "The Beat Goes On for Soul Train Conductor." *New York Times*. August 7, 1995.

Millner, Denene. "Love, Peace and Soul . . . Don Cornelius." *Jet*. February 20, 2012.

Mitchell, Gail. "Don Cornelius 1936–2012." *Billboard*. February 11, 2012.

"Photos Send Visitors Back to Soul Train Time." *Chicago Tribune*. September 1, 2011.

Reeves, Charles. "The Soul Train." *Philadelphia Tribune*. June 1996.

Riley, Clayton. "A Train on the Soul Track." *New York Times*. February 4, 1973.

Peterson, Clarence. "Soul Train Is a Hit in Spite of Itself." *Chicago Tribune*. June 3, 1971.

"Soul Awards Honors Artists Often Ignored." *St. Petersburg Times*. March 29, 1996.

"Soul Rides the Party Train." *Soul*. July 3, 1978.

"Soul Train Goes National CBS." *Chicago Defender*. October 23, 1971.

"Soul Train Hits the Big 4-0." *Jet*. October 10–17, 2011.

"Soul Train Puts Black Comics on Track." *Chicago Tribune*. August 1993.

"Soul Train Rolls Into Its 20th Season." *Michigan Chronicle*. October 1989.

"Soul Train 30 Years Strong." *Los Angeles Sentinel*. February 14, 2001.

Strauss, Neil. "You Say Soul Train Is How Old?" *New York Times*. December 31, 1995.

"Super Tall, Super Cool and Here." *Washington Post*. December 13, 1972.

"The Sound of Soul, Aretha Franklin." *Time*. 1968.

Thompson, Cordell M. "New York Beat." *Jet*. February 5, 1976.

"Ups and Downs of Hip-Hop Pioneers." *The New York Times*. March 16, 2012.

Weaver, Maurice. "Soul Train Awards Are a 1st for Black Music." *Chicago Tribune*. March 23, 1987.

BOOKS

Acham, Christine. *Revolution Televised*. University of Minnesota Press, 2004.

Austen, Jake. *TV-a-Go-Go*. Chicago Review Press, 2005.

Barlow, William. *Voiceover, the Making of Black Radio*. Temple University Press, 1999.

Bogle, Donald. *Primetime Blues: African Americans on Network Television*. Farrar, Straus and Giroux, 2001.

Charnas, Dan. *The Big Payback*. New American Library, December 2010.

Clark, Dick, and Fred Bronson. *Dick Clark's American Bandstand*. Collins Publishers, 1997.

Delmont, Matthew F. *The Nicest Kids in Town: American Bandstand, Rock 'n' Roll, and the Struggle for Civil Rights in 1950s Philadelphia*. University of California Press, 2012.

Echols, Alice. *Hot Stuff*. W.W. Norton & Company, 2010.

Frady, Marshall. *Jesse: The Life and Pilgrimage of Jesse Jackson*. Random House, 1996.

George, Nelson. *The Death of Rhythm and Blues*. Pantheon Books, 1988.

George, Nelson. *Where Did Our Love Go? The Rise and Fall of the Motown Sound*. St. Martin's Press, 1985.

Gordy, Berry. *Berry Gordy: To Be Loved—The Music, the Magic, the Memories of Motown*. Time Warner, 1994.

Hunt, Darnell, and Ana-Christina Ramon. *Black Los Angeles: American Dreams and Racial Realities*. New York University Press, 2010.

Lehman, Christopher P. *A Critical History of Soul Train on Television*. McFarland, 2008.

Posner, Gerald. *Motown, Music, Money, Sex, and Power*. Random House, 2005.

Reeves, Marcus. *Somebody Scream! Rap Music's Rise to Prominence in the Aftershock of Black Power*. Faber and Faber, Inc., 2008.

Rolling Stone: The '70s. Little Brown and Company. Rolling Stone Press, 1998.

Vincent, Ricky. *Funk: The Music, The People, and The Rhythm of The One*. St. Martin's Griffin, 1996.

DOCUMENTS

Los Angeles court records and police reports

DVDS

Graffiti Rock pilot
Soul Train episodes
VH-1 documentary: *The Hippest Trip in America*

Interviews

Aida Chapman-Ayala
Al Bell
Al Sharpton
Alyson Williams
Andrew Kitchen
Anthony Maddox
Audrey Mumpower
The Barry White Family:
    Glodean White, Shaherah
    White
Ben Jealous
Beth Yenni-Soloway
Beverly Paige
Big Daddy Kane
Bill Adler
Bobby Hutton
Bobby Womack
Bootsy Collins
Bowlegged Lou
Brooke Payne
Carl Davis
Cedric the Entertainer
Cheryl Song
Chuck D
Chuck Johnson
Clint Ghent
Damita Jo Freeman
Dan Myers
Darnell Hunt
David Lombard
Dennis Coffey
Derek Fleming
Diesel
Dina Andrews
Don Campbell
Don Jackson
Edna Wright
Fantasy
Fawn Quinones
Flo Jenkins
Frank Chambers

Fred Alexander
Gary Harris
George O'Hare
Gerald Alston
Gerald Brown
Greg Williams
Herb Kent
The History Makers
Howard Hewett
J. Kevin Swain
Jake Austen
Janis Gaye
Jay King
Jody Watley
Joe Walker
Jon Leiberman
Kangol, Mixmaster Ice
Karen Sundell
Karyn White
Keedah Gianetti
Keith Washington
Keith Wilder
Kenard Gibbs
LaDonna Tittle
Lee Bailey
Lenny Williams
Leo Sullivan
Liane Mori
LJ Reynolds
Louie "Ski" Carr
Marshall Thompson
Mary Anne Campbell
Master Gee
Melissa Haizlip
Miki Howard
Milton Allen
Monica Alexander
Mo' Nique Chambers
Nick Puzo
Nieci Payne
O'Bryan Burnette II

Oran "Juice" Jones
Perry Jones
Peter Allen
Philip Ghent
Phyllis Kelly
Questlove
Reggie Calloway
Reggie Rutherford
Reginald Brass
Rhonda Cowan
Russell Simmons
Scot Brown
Shabba Doo
Sharon Hill
Stephen McMillian
Stephen Shockley
Dr. Todd Boyd

Tom Tom Washington
Toni Basil
Tony Cornelius
Tony Maiden
Tyrone Proctor
Vickie Jones
Vicky Ghoulson
Vincent Calloway
Virgil Roberts
Wanda Hutchinson
Ward Crescendo
The Whispers: Walter Scott,
    Wallace Scott, Leaveil
    Degree, Nicholas Caldwell
Willie Davis
Wonder Mike
Zoro

Websites

"Don Cornelius Is a Businessman with Soul," March 8, 2006, http://www.msnbc.msn.com

"Legendary 'Soul Train' Creator Don Cornelius Battled Demons in Final Years," *The Daily Beast*: http://www.thedailybeast.com/articles/2012/02/02/legendary-soul-train-creator-don-cornelius-battled-demons-in-final-years.html

"Soul Train Laid the Rails of a Cultural Revolution," *Life*: http://usatoday30.usatoday.com/life/people/obit/story/2012-02-01/don-cornelius-soul-train-dies/52913978/1

"Soul Train Local": http://www.chicagoreader.com/chicago/soul-train-local/Content?oid = 1106014

Soultrain.com

"Steven Ivory: Don Cornelius": http://www.eurweb.com/2012/02/steven-ivory-don-cornelius/

"When Walter Payton Danced on Soul Train": http://www.beachwoodreporter.com/books/when_walter_payton_danced_on_s.php

INDEX